# Heaven and Hell

## Make My Day – Book 25
## Larry M. Henares, Jr.

**Dr. Hilarion M. Henares Jr.,** *known as* **Larry Henares,** *is a graduate of Ateneo de Manila, University of the Philippines, and the Massachusetts Institute of Technology, an engineer, economist, educator, big businessman, writer, civic leader, public servant, and hobbyist (guns, books, amateur radio and electronics).*

*He is a writer known for his essays on economics, history, art and culture, a front page columnist in the pre-martial law Manila Times and the most widely read column in the Philippines, according to all surveys, the daily "Make my Day" in the Philippine Daily Inquirer, after the EDSA revolt.*

ooooo

# Tatay Jobo Elizes. Self-Publisher

*This book is published under permission of*

## DR. HILARION M. HENARES, JR.

*This permission is subject to withdrawal any time so desired, in which case,* **Tatay Jobo Elizes,** *as self-publisher will cease publishing this book. LARRY HENARES is free to republish with other publishers. Tatay Jobo disclaims any responsibility for writings of the Author. Printing of this book is using the present day method of Print-on-Demand (POD) system, where prints will never run out of copies.*

*ISBN – 13: 978 - 1985727878*
*and ISBN – 10: 1985727870*

*No part of this book may be reproduced or copied in any form without written permission from Larry Henares, and Tatay Jobo Elizes. Contact; job_elizes@yahoo.com Websites: http:www.tinyurl.com/mj76ccq*

ooooo

# About the book, "HEAVEN AND HELL"

Almost one half of this Book 25 of the Make My Day series, is devoted to "The Saga of Breastfeeding" an epic battle between the Unholy Trinity of Breastfeeding Advocates – Larry the Father, Elvira the Daughter, and Nona the Holy Skeleton – against the entire cabal of Milk Companies.  It details the second part, The Milk Wars II, continued from a previous Milk Wars I in Book 24, "Salvation and Damnation."  It reprints the special and rare White Paper of President Gloria Macapagal about how the Breastfeeding Movement triumphed during her administration.  And it ends with the Nomination by the Secretary of Health Francisco T. Duque III. of Elvira L. Henares-Esguerra, MD, FPDS, FABM, IBCLC, RPh for the prestigious Prince Mahidol Award of Thailand (the award as usual went to clinical scientists instead of public health advocates).

"Stage and Shadows" is the usual fare of Larry's writings – scripts of unfilmed home movies from earlier years: *Big Brother*, a fantasy about a bully who became a dictator; *Mang Serapio,* a special tribute to an author who might have been one of the nation's best if he did not surrender his mind and will to the Opus Dei, the Spanish Inquisition; a play staged for Larry's grandmother when she was chosen Mother of the Year; an oratorical piece by Atom Henares when he won second prize in the Voice of Democracy; an enchanting vignette from one of Jennifer Lopez's movies; and the many faces of Jesus Christ and Judas Iscariot.

"The Human Condition" is a potpourri of stories, of the miracle of two daughters; of remembrances of Edsa; of the musical resurrection of Enrico Caruso; of two rich men quarreling in a hotel lobby; of exploding novas and steady suns in our society; of carpetbaggers and their Filipino satraps; and above all, an epic speech by Nick Joaquin.

But the piece de resistance are the personalities of Larry's world, whom you will discover in a new light:  lawyer Tom del Castillo and his sweet dance with death; Baby Arenas, the Madame Pompadour/Madame Du Barry of our times; Earl Hornbostel, the American who became a Filipino; Jaime *Cardinal* Sin, the super-heroic Pinoy; Gloria Macapagal-Arroyo on her way to her destiny; the irrepressible "insider" who is neither a pastor nor a boy nor a psycho. Read and enjoy.

ooooo

# BOOK 25: HEAVEN AND HELL
## Table of Contents

THE SAGA OF BREASTMILK – *p9*

CHAPTER ONE: THE MILK WARS II – *p9*
- I.    The Birthday, the Vision of Dr. Elvira L. Henares – Esguerra – *p9*
- II.   SUPREME COURT CASE, VICTORY !! – *p11*
- III..  Lawyer Ipat Luna on the Supreme Court Decision: - *p12*
- IV..  Elvira Esguerra on the SC decision, giving us more than we asked for!.. – *p14*
- V..   EXPOSURE OF THE WYETH MILK CONTAMINATION – *p16*
- VI..  IN CHARGE OF THE YEARLY WORLD BREASTFEEDING WEEK – *p16*
- VII.. ONE OF 50 GREATEST ALUMNI OF HER MEDICAL SCHOOL – *p17*
- VIII.. PHOTO EXHIBITS OF BREASTFEEDING ROLE MODELS – *p17*
- IX..  BREASTFEEDING STATIONS IN THE SM SUPERMALLS – *p18*
- X..  BREAKING THREE GUINNESS WORLD RECORDS, AND INSTITUTING SYNCHRONIZED BREASTFEEDING WORLDWIDE – *p18*
- XI..  FUNDING FROM FOUNDATIONS – *p19*
- XII.  ORGANIZING THE BROAD FRONT – *p20*
- XIII.. PHILIPPINE LACTATION RESOURCE AND TRAINING CENTER – *p21*
- XIV.  PHILIPPINE ACADEMY OF LACTATION CONSULTANTS, INC – *p21*
- XV.  A PERMANENT OFFICE – *p22*
- XVI.  THE GRAND COALITION AGAINST CORPORATE GREED – *p23*
- XVII.  EDUCATION FOR A PERMANENT COMMITMENT – *p24*

XVIII.  PETITION ON US INTERVENTION AGAINST BREASTFEEDING – *p24*

XIX.  DSWD COMMITMENT TO PROMOTE INDIGENOUS FOOD INSTEAD OF IMPORTED MILK – *p26*

XX.  CHANGING THE ATTITUDE AGAINST EXPOSURE OF BREASTS – *p27*

XXI.  INTERNATIONAL ETHICS AGAINST INVOLVEMENT WITH MILK COMPANIES – *p28*

XXII.  INTERNATIONAL CONFERENCES – *p29*

XXIII.  BREASTFEEDING AS A UNIVERSAL ISSUE – *p30*

XXIV.  Environmentalist LEE ANN FORD JOINS THE TEAM – *p31*

XXV.  SUMMARY AND EPILOGUE – *p31*


CHAPTER TWO: THE WHITE PAPER ON BREAST-FEEDING – *p33*

Executive  Summary – *p34*

I.  From the National Anti-Poverty Hearings to the Presidential Cabinet Meeting  - *p35*

II. Presidential Proclamation and first World Breastfeeding Week in Malacañang- *p37*

III.Revised Implementing Rules and Regulations of EO 51  - *p45*

IV.      Guinness World Records, Synchronized Breastfeeding Worldwide – *p48*

V. Ripple Effect: Breastfeeding Stations in SM Supermalls,  Bare-Breasted Virgin  - *p50*

VI. Virgin Mother's 12 Apostles, & other Exhibits – *p52*

VII. Mobilizing Government Agencies and non-Government Organizations – *p54*

VIII.      Presidential Awards for Pioneering Breastfeeding Advocates – *p56*

IX.      Urgent Legislative Measures, and other Public Health Initiatives – *p60*

X. CONCLUSION: Tribute to the President – *p61*

XI. The Non-Government Organizations' Profiles – *p64*


CHAPTER THREE:
NOMINATION FOR MAHIDOL AWARD – *p67*

I.  Nominee – *p67*
II.  Mailing Address – *p67*
III. Statement Of The Nature Of The Work And Its Relevance To The Objectives Of The Award – *p67*
IV. JUSTIFICATION FOR NOMINATION – *p70*
V. AWARDS AND HONOURS RECEIVED – *p85*
VI. EDUCATIONAL BACKGROUND – *p88*
VII. POSITIONS OCCUPIED – *p89*
VIII. PUBLICATIONS – *p91*
IX. NOMINATED BY – *p94*
X.  LETTER OF REFERENCE # 1 – *p94*
XI.  LETTER OF REFERENCE # 2 – *p95*

STAGE AND SHADOWS – *p97*
I.  BIG BROTHER – *p97*
II.  MANG SERAPIO – *p106*
III.  MOMENT OF DECISION – *p112*
IV.  The Most Perfect Form from Gigli w/ *Jennifer Lopez*, Ben Affleck – *p119*
V.  NOT IN VAIN by Atom L. Henares, 1969, Voice of Democracy – *p121*
VI.  The Many Faces of Christ – *p124*
  Part 1. Ben Hur: A Tale of the Christ – *p124*
  Part 2.  The Four Versions of Judas Iscariot – *p126*
  Part 3. The Many Faces of Christ – *p127*

THE HUMAN CONDITION – *p129*
I.  The joys of parenthood – *p129*
II.  The Story of Two Miracles – *p130*
III.  I Was There, I Was There! – *p132*
IV. From Caruso to Carreras, from shellac to CD – *p133*
V.  Blow by blow account of the Tokyo Incident between Manny and Zobel – *p136*
VI.  Rah Rah Boys and Magnificent Loners – *p138*
VII.  Caltex strike ended racial discrimination – *p140*
VIII.  A HERITAGE OF SMALLNESS, - Nick Joaquin – *p142*

PERSONALITIES – *p153*

CHAPTER ONE: Tom del Castillo – *p153*
  Part 1: To die of cancer is to have an orgasm – *p153*
  Part 2: What is normal sex?  Cancer, a stigma or stigmata? – *p155*
  Part 3: My own sweet dance with death, the chance to write my dying scene – *p156*

CHAPTER TWO: Rosemary "Baby" Arenas – *p158*
  Part 1.  Baby Takes a Bow, Bringing Up Baby – *p158*
  Part 2.  Baby Arenas, Present Tense, Subjunctive Mood – *p160*
  Part 3. Baby Arenas, past tense, indicative mood – *p161*
  Part 4.  Baby in pluperfect tense, imperative mood – *p162*
  Part 5. Baby in the future tense, transitive and copulative – *p162*

CHAPTER THREE: Earl Hornbostel – *p163*
  Part 1. Filipinos helped liberate Indonesians from the Dutch – *p163*
  Part 2. Why an American helped the Indonesians in their war – *p164*
  Part 3.  Philippines, Puerto Rico were not the only US colonies – *p166*

CHAPTER FOUR: Jaime Cardinal Sin – *p168*
  Part 1. Jaime Cardinal Sin, the greatest Filipino of this century! – *p168*
  Part 2. Cardinal Sin prefers to die first before giving up the fight – *p170*

CHAPTER FIVE:  Gloria Macapagal Arroyo – *p171*
  Part 1.  Now it can be told: how Gloria became veep candidate – *p171*
  Part 2.  Beset by Lakas, Third Force and Kampi, Gloria consults God – *p173*
  Part 3.  Clinton is Gloria's classmate and pen-pal – *p173*
  Part 4.  An evil spirit rules our lives – *p174*
  Part 5.  Edsa Forces at first refused to support Gloria against Erap – *p176*

Part 6.  Gloria earns the right to lead the fight – *p179*
Part 7.  At last the Edsa Forces coalesce around Gloria – *p181*

CHAPTER SIX:  Jose Mari Gonzalez – *p183*
Part 1. Jose Mari: ham actor, radio ham, smoked ham – *p183*
Part 2.  Jose Mari shows off his *je ne se qua* – p184
Part 3.   Not embalmed or cremated but stuffed by a taxidermist – *p186*

CHAPTER SEVEN: Pastor "Boy" Saycon – *p188*
Part 1. Happy Birthday, Boy! – *p188*
Part 2. Making a Difference by Boy Saycon as told to Larry Henares – *p190*
The loose ball situation – *p194*
Who is Bravo Alpha? – *p194*
Part 3.  A Requiem for Becky Saycon – *p198*

END OF BOOK – *p200*

ooooo

# THE SAGA OF BREASTMILK
## CHAPTER ONE:
## THE MILK WARS II
*(continued from Book 24, Salvation and Damnation,
Page 110, THE MILK WARS I )*

**I. The Birthday, the Vision of Dr. Elvira L. Henares - Esguerra**

My daughter Elvira was born on June 6, 1956.  On June 6, 2006 she celebrated her 50th birthday.  She was now middle-aged, halfway through her life, with a husband and three children.  She was a bit apprehensive that both her birthdate and her birthday bore the devil's number 666.  So she went to her parish church, Sanctuario de San Antonio in Forbes Park, to meditate.  And she was there for 6 straight hours! -- What for? She explained later.

She said, "...to take stock of my life, my past, present and future."  Ever since she was a child, Elvira has always been close to God; the only times she displayed tantrums was when we failed to bring her to Sunday mass. Since childhood, she stayed long in church, carefully planning what to do with her life, and viewing it in her mind like a moving picture or a PowerPoint presentation, and in most instances made it come true.  In every family, there is always one who is a little different from the other siblings.  Elvira was such a one. While her brothers and sisters were all comparatively tall and fair-skinned due to their Spanish and German heritage, Elvira was short at five feet and one half inch, and was comparatively *morena* in complexion like a Filipino.  While the others stood out in school activities and garnered gold medals by the gross, Elvira was less accomplished, tried harder and was always in second place – second to Presidential daughter Imee Marcos in Assumption Convent, and second place in the nation-wide Voice of Democracy contest in the United States.  While the others painted their thoughts in broad bright strokes like a master painter, Elvira thought in intricate black-and-white patterns and microscopic relief like a woodcut or a high resolution photograph – she demands full attention while telling stories in intricate detail, just like my own late mother.  While the others pursued high profile activities on the stage and in society, reveling in public recognition, Elvira spent her time just helping people on the quiet, organizing Christmas programs to entertain charity patients in the wards, picking up an accident victim on Edsa, rescuing someone being shot amidst a hail of bullets, leaving the comfort of her home and her Mercedes Benz to ride in buses and live in cramped apartments as a bed-spacer among rats and cockroaches.  While the others went on short tours in style, Elvira would spend six months on a paltry $2,000.00, backpacking all over Europe by herself.  While the others breezed through easy college courses in management and mass communication, Elvira would challenge herself to take up the hardest courses where half the students drop out: a five-year course in Pharmacy (UP Diliman), another four year course in Medicine, a diplomate and fellowship in Dermatology, passing an exam to be an International Board Certified Lactation Consultant – with more degrees than her siblings.

And as she stood at the threshold of her fiftieth birthday, she thanked God for giving her a third child at the age of 45.  She had spent the past eleven years of her life, taking care of her family and is now poised on resuming her practice as a dermatologist.  She got involved in the Breastfeeding Movement with her father and partner Nona D. Andaya-Castillo, and achieved unbelievable success (see The Milk Wars, Part I), despite a singular lack of resources.  Now Elvira asked God what to do with the rest of her life.  Scoff you unbelievers, but Elvira swears God commanded her to continue to the end, her fight against the corporate greed and crass commercialism of the Milk Companies, and depicted for her in those six hours in church, in full Technicolor, Cinemascope and Stereophonic Sound the grand adventure that she will devote her life to, that will come to light in the following pages of the account of The Milk Wars II.

**The story so far in Milk Wars I:  The Presidential Proclamation on World Breastfeeding Week was declared.  The nationwide campaign for Infant and Young Child Feeding launched.  The Guinness World Record for the Most Number of Mothers Breastfeeding in a single site, broken.  The Implementing Rules for the**

National Milk Code approved but stymied by a Supreme Court Temporary Restraining Order.  Now the stage is set for the Second Part of the Milk Wars.

## II.  SUPREME COURT CASE, VICTORY !!

The biggest news during the Malacañang Affair of 2006 was the signing and launching of the Revised Implementing Rules of the National Milk Code by the Secretary of Health, against the opposition of the Milk companies, a feat that was accomplished by Elvira and her group, Children for Breastfeeding Inc. with the help of the Department of Health and the UNICEF, in the short span of 6½ months, after 20 years of frustration since the law was passed in 1986.  It was signed into effect on May 15, 2006, published on June 22, to take effect on July 7.  Suddenly, on June 28, 2006, the Milk Companies filed a case before the Supreme Court (SC) against the Department of Health, requesting a Temporary Restraining Order against the implementation of the IRR, which was denied on July 11.  Then on August 16, 2006, two days after the launching of the IRR in Malacañang, the Supreme Court, on the eve of the retirement of Chief Justice Artemio Panganiban, suddenly, inexplicably and without hearing the side of the breastfeeding advocates, issued a Temporary Restraining Order, until the issues are finally resolved.  Not only that, the Supreme Court under Chief Justice Reynato Puno, refused to accept the Intervention of Breastfeeding Advocates; and refused as well to accept the offer of the Unicef and the WHO to act as friends of the Court, as *amicus curiae*.  For a time we were worried that the Milk Companies had influenced the Supreme Court of Chief Justice Reynato Puno, as it did the Supreme Court of retiring Chief Justice Artemio Panganiban.

On June 19, 2007, during the first hearing of the case before the Supreme Court, a glimmer of hope appeared.  The Supreme Court Chief Justice challenged the contention of the Milk Companies that the Department of Health may derive its powers only from national laws passed by the legislature.  Two other sources of power were cited: (1) International Treaties and Covenants upon Senate Ratification, and (2) the police power mandated by the Constitution and the Administrative Code.  This was bolstered by the discovery that Wyeth Philippines had secretly violated the procedure for the recall of contaminated formula milk a year before, duly exposed by Nurturers of the Earth and Children for Breastfeeding Inc. with the help of principled whistle-blowers within Wyeth.

On October 9, 2007, the Court rendered its final judgment. The TRO is lifted, and the IRR is now in effect. Only two provisions were stricken off: (1) the total ban on advertising (but approval is still necessary and effective), and (2) the administrative sanctions (fines) on violators of the Code (but the ultimate weapon of canceling the permit for repeated violations is still in force). The rest is VICTORY. The Milk Companies' claim of "Legal Parameters," long accepted by the BFAD, were struck down one after another.

The result is one of the most stringent regulations ever imposed on the Milk Companies. The SC ruled that the DOH's power to regulate embraces ALL breastmilk substitutes, even those sold to children beyond two years of age. That power may be exercised through the Inter-Agency Committee, to effect a total ban on all advertisements that undermine Breastfeeding; to impose labeling requirements that warn of the hazards of formula milk; to forbid the Milk Companies from ever contacting mothers, pregnant women and health workers with their propaganda or "gifts of any sort"; to forbid all kinds of nutritional claims, deceptive brand names and use of baby pictures in their advertisements, on the basis of their "total effect"; to forbid milk donations even to the Red Cross, especially those with pending expiry dates, and those that need energy for boiling and clean water for mixing, usually unavailable during disasters; to forbid milk company representation in policy making bodies. The real victory lies in the difficulty of official bribery under the public scrutiny and awareness generated by Elvira's NGO.

### III. Lawyer Ipat Luna on the Supreme Court Decision:
Initially, news reports claimed that the SC decision was a blow to breastfeeding. Nothing could be farther than the truth. In fact, the Supreme Court decision was in favor of the

respondent, the Department of Health. The Supreme Court lifted the temporary restraining order on the Revised IRR -- with a few exceptions -- which means that the IRR is now in effect. The Supreme Court ruled largely in favor of the Health Department: "Except Sections 4(f), 11 and 46, the rest of the provisions of the IRR are in consonance with the objective, purpose and intent of the MIlk Code, constituting reasonable regulation of an industry which affects public health and welfare and, as such, the rest of the IRR do not constitute illegal restraint of trade nor are they violative of the due process clause of the Constitution."

Sections 4(f) and 11 call for the prohibition of the advertising, promotion or sponsorships of infant formula, breastmilk substitutes and other related products. Section 46 imposes administrative sanctions for the violation of the Milk Code, including fines higher than what the Milk Code originally specified. Other than these, the rest of the IRR can now be implemented! And the rest of the IRR calls for significantly tighter regulation on the marketing of breastmilk substitutes and related products, most notably:

+ The Milk Code's coverage is not limited to children 0-12 months old. Rather, the Supreme Court upholds that the Milk Code's scope covers all breastmilk substitutes including those to be used by children aged over 12 months. (The Milk Code defines "breastmilk substitutes" as "any food being marketed or otherwise represented as partial or total replacement of breastmilk whether or not suitable for that purpose.")

+ Advertising, promotion or other marketing materials for breastmilk substitutes need to be approved by the Inter-Agency Committee and should not contain, among others, terms like "close to mother's milk," pictures or texts that idealize infant and milk formula. Any health and nutrition claims, false or misleading information or claims of products are prohibited.

+ Breastmilk substitutes have to follow labeling requirements, in both English and Filipino, which include a message on the "health hazards of [the use] unnecessary or improper use of infant formula and other related products including information that powdered infant formula may contain pathogenic microorganisms and must be prepared and used appropriately."

+ Milk companies are prohibited from giving financial or material inducements or gifts of any sort to promote products to health workers and to any member of the general public. They cannot give donations to the general public, hospitals, health facilities, their personnel and members of their families.

+ Milk companies are prohibited from conducting or being involved in any activity on breastfeeding promotion, education and production of materials on breastfeeding, or to act as speakers in classes or seminars for women and children's activities, and to use these venues to market their brands or company names. Neither can milk companies have point-of-sale advertising, give away samples and other promotional items, etc. directly to consumers at retail level.

+Milk companies shall not form part of any policymaking body involved in the advancement of breastfeeding.

+ Section 56, Extending Prohibition for Brandnames and Company Logo Identification, says, "The Department (of Health) shall periodically review whether or not to allow or prohibit the use of brandnames or company logos of products within the scope of this Code which are similar to the brandnames or logos utilized for products not covered by this Code, including the physical appearance of the container...." This is the best of all provisions, ignored by the press.


**IV.  Dr. Elvira Esguerra on the SC decision, giving us more than we asked for!**

In the original Revised IRR adjudicated by the Supreme Court, there are 59 Sections.  Only 2 of the 59 were struck down by the Supreme Court.  Likewise, there are 55 Subsections.  Only 6 of the 55 were struck down by the Supreme Court.  A majority of 57 out of 59 sections of the revised IRR, and a majority of 49 out of 55 subsections were positively affirmed by the Supreme Court.  Also the Temporary Restraining Order (TRO) was lifted.

+Everything considered, the Supreme Court decision was a DECISIVE AND OVERWHELMING VICTORY for the Department of Health and the breastfeeding advocates. **It gave the Breastfeeding movement MORE than it asked for.   for the Department of Health to regulate all advertisements for formula milk intended for babies at least up to two years of** age.    What it got was an OPEN-ENDED, ALMOST LIMITLESS, AND ALMOST ABSOLUTE POWER of the Department to regulate ALL milk advertisements and flow of information, irregardless of age classification, in pursuit of its policy to discourage the undermining of Breastfeeding.

+Milk Companies may no longer sponsor maternity classes in hospitals and health facilities among pregnant and nursing mothers – may no longer sponsor conferences, seminars, travel grants and even scientific studies among health workers and doctors -- without the request and approval of the DOH and its Inter-Agency Committee.

+Milk Companies may no longer give "gifts of any sort" to pregnant and nursing mothers, to doctors and health workers, without the approval of the DOH.  No donation of formula milk, especially those with very near expiry dates, may be given to the Red Cross or any charity agency without the approval of the DOH which will determine whether emergency conditions allow the use of clean water and fuel to boil the water for the adequate preparation of formula milk.

+All advertisements of Milk Companies are **subject to the approval of the DOH and the Inter-Agency Committee** – and the AdBoard (a private organization of Advertising Agencies) and the Movie Television and Radio Classification Board (MTRCB) may be asked to pass upon such advertisements.  No advertisement may use deceptive brandnames, pictures of babies and/or make any nutritional claims whatsoever. All scientific studies by Milk companies are subject to review by the Ethics Committee of the DOH, and made available only to doctors and the academe. We anticipate that the Milk Companies may undermine Breastfeeding through so-called scientific magazines (Medical Observer) made available to the public in the anterooms of doctors, and through movie scenes showing bottlefeeding; and we suggest that such magazines are forbidden to carry unauthorized ads and articles, and such movies should carry disclaimers saying, "Scenes of bottle-feeding undermine breastfeeding and are against the national policy of the Philippine government.  Breastfeeding is still the best for babies.  Formula milk is the least option and last resort, and only under certain medical indications."

+Section 46 on administrative sanctions, was struck down by the SC.  However, Section 13(b) of EO 51, the basic law, remains:  *Any license, permit or authority issued by any government agency to any health worker, distributor, manufacturer, or marketing firm or personnel for the practice of their profession or occupation, or for the pursuit of their business, may, upon recommendation of the Ministry of Health, be suspended or revoked in the event of **repeated violations** of this Code, or of the rules and regulations issued pursuant to this Code.*  All the DOH needs to do is to define "repeated violations" to give teeth to the power of the DOH.  We suggest that "Each violation is counted for the entire company, not for each product.  A total of five violations will initiate proceedings for the cancellation of license."

## V.    EXPOSURE    OF    THE    WYETH    MILK CONTAMINATION

Inspired by Elvira's group's ethical behavior, some persons within the organization of Wyeth Philippines were moved to blow the whistle and expose the scandal of Wyeth's management's silent and illegal attempt last year to recall 4 million cans of Wyeth formula milk contaminated by typhoon *Milenyo* without the knowledge of the Bureau of Food and Drugs and the consuming public..  The exposure of this shameful scandal, Elvira believes, has turned the tables on the Milk Companies in their case before the Supreme Court.

## VI.    IN CHARGE OF THE YEARLY WORLD BREASTFEEDING WEEK

President Gloria Macapagal Arroyo's experience with breastfeeding her own babies was less than ideal, but after Elvira talked to her about breastfeeding, she was moved to say publicly, "I have a PhD, but I never knew or appreciated all these important things.  I wish I had a support group like you have now."

The President acceded to Elvira's request for a Presidential Proclamation to celebrate World Breastfeeding Week, and put her in charge over the yearly affair in the Palace.  To date the World Breastfeeding Week was celebrated in Malacañang for the THIRD straight year.

## VII.   ONE OF THE 50 GREATEST ALUMNI OF HER MEDICAL SCHOOL.

Dr. Elvira L. Henares-Esguerra of Children for Breastfeeding Inc. enrolled in the UERM to take up medicine, and graduated in 1986.  In 2007, on the 50th anniversary of the founding of UERM, the school chose Elvira Lichauco Henares-Esguerra (doctor, dermatologist, pharmacist, IBCLC) as one of the 50 greatest alumni among the 15,000 graduates of the school, for her advocacy of Breastfeeding, "transcending the narrow confines of her specialty to embrace the concerns of all humanity."

Elvira was recently nominated for The Outstanding Filipino Physician (TOFP) Award being sponsored by the Jaycee Senate and the Department of Health.

Her partner Nona D. Andaya - Castillo was also recently nominated as one of the Ten Outstanding Women in the Nation's Service (TOWNS).

## VIII.   PHOTO EXHIBITS OF BREASTFEEDING ROLE MODELS

On the second WBW celebration in Malacañang on August 14, 2006, Elvira's Children for Breastfeeding,Inc. launched two Photo Exhibits: "Beauty, Brains and Breastfeeding" by Elvira's cousin, Pancho Escaler; and "Apostles of the Virgin Mary," by Blow-Up Babies Photo Studio of Elvira's nephew, Quark Henares, as conceptualized by Elvira and her partner Nona..   Both depict role models for breastfeeding mothers, which were publicly displayed in Malacañang, in all SM Supermalls, and in Congress during hearings on Breastfeeding.

Elvira's Photo Exhibits of Role Models in the Breastfeeding Movement, who are rich, beautiful, glamorous working mothers, serve to convince the hoi-poloi (the common masses) that breastfeeding is a privilege, more than an obligation, that bottle-feeding is NOT acceptable even to those who are educated and who could afford the expense of formula milk, and that working outside the home is not an obstacle to Breastfeeding.   Above all, they give a positive image of a breastfeeding mother, with full and erect breasts that elicit envy and admiration.

For this Unicef Philippines issued a heartfelt Commendation to Elvira's Children for Breastfeeding,Inc..

### IX.    BREASTFEEDING STATIONS IN THE SM SUPERMALLS

On March 14, 2006, SM Supermalls partnered with Elvira's Children for Breastfeeding, Inc. and Unicef Philippines to set up Breastfeeding Stations in all the 32 SM malls nationwide.

Most gratifying of all is the regular inauguration of Breastfeeding Stations in each and every one of the 18 so far of the scheduled 32 SM Supermalls in the country.  It is a whole day affair that starts from 7:00 AM up to 10:00 AM, when Elvira and her Group speak to some 100 to 300 SM employees that includes (1) the Maintenance Crew and janitors, (2) the Security Force, (3) Mall tenants, and (4) Administrative staff.  Then the Supermall opens up to the public, and Elvira's Group is entertained and given a tour.  After lunch at 1:00 PM to 3:00 PM, Elvira's Group gives Breastfeeding lectures to pregnant and nursing mothers from communities around the SM Supermall and those invited by non-government organizations and SM clients. Then at 3:00 PM to 5:00 PM, the formal program and launching of the Breastfeeding Station occurs.

Convincing SM Supermalls to build Breastfeeding Stations was a wonderful way to get businessmen to realize that they have a Social Responsibility to the family and the people. This led Ramon Jacinto to offer the use of his radio and TV for the movement free of charge, and Washington Sycip to lend the facilities of Sycip Gorres Velayo to audit, pro-bono, her four Guinness Record attempts.

### X. BREAKING THREE GUINNESS WORLD RECORDS, AND INSTITUTING SYNCHRONIZED BREASTFEEDING WORLDWIDE

On May 4, 2006, in partnership with the City of Manila, the Department of Health, Unicef Philippines and Nurturers of the Earth Inc. -- Elvira's Children for Breastfeeding Inc. was accorded recognition by the Guinness World Record Ltd., for having broken the world record for the **Most Number of Mothers Simultaneously Breastfeeding in a Single Site** with 3,541 mothers in the City of Manila.

On August 25, 2006, in partnership with the Department of Environment and Natural Resources, and the Nurturers of the Earth Inc. and the participation of Green Army Philippines and Green Philippine Highways, Elvira's Children for Breastfeeding,Inc. was accorded recognition by the Guinness World Record Ltd. for having broken the world record for the **Most Trees Simultaneously Planted in Multiple Sites**, 653,143 trees by 516, 317 citizen-volunteers along 3,917.83 kilometers of National Highways. By telling Angelo Reyes of the Department of Environment and Natural Resources that "a woman's breast is the nation's greatest natural resource and is worth your support,." he responded by promising to plant food-bearing trees to support her movement.

On May 2, 2007, in partnership with the Department of Social Welfare and Development, and the Technical Education and Skills Development Authority (TESDA) and the Nurturers of the Earth Inc., Elvira's Children for Breastfeeding Inc. established the world record for **Most Number of Mothers Simultaneously Breastfeeding in Multiple Sites** with 15,128 mothers in 295 sites nationwide, although the results, recently audited by Sycip Gorres Velayo, is being submitted to the Guinness World Record Ltd.

On August 8, 2007, Elvira's Children for Breastfeeding,Inc. in partnership with the World Alliance for Breastfeeding Action (WABA), conducted for the first time in the history of the world, the **Synchronized Breastfeeding Worldwide** with the participation of 25 countries, in 24 time zones, at 10 AM local time, over a period of 24 hours, like the celebration of New Year on the same day. **Yesterday, Manila. Today, the Philippines. And Forever, the entire World, for Elvira's Breastfeeding Advocacy.**

### XI. FUNDING FROM FOUNDATIONS

In 2006 she was awarded a partnership with funding from Unicef Philippines. In the same year 2006, she was also given funding by the Ramon Aboitiz Foundation Inc. and by the Gregorio Araneta Foundation Inc., and in 2007 was shown interest by the Canadian Fund foundation (CIDA). She is also being considered for continued funding by Unicef Philippines.

### XII.  ORGANIZING THE BROAD FRONT

As a Breastfeeding Advocate, Elvira finds herself inextricably linked in partnership with Secretary Francisco T. Duque III's Department of Health and Dr. Nicholas Alipui's Unicef Philippines.  Yet she dares to think "out of the box," and broaden her team to include others seemingly remote from her advocacy:

1.  **Local government** organizations like Mayor Atienza's City of Manila and James Marty Lim's Liga ng mga Barangay sa Pilipinas.

2.  **National agencies** like Secretary Esperanza Cabral's Department of Social Welfare and Development, Secretary Angelo Reyes' Department of Environment and Natural Resources, Secretary Boboy Syjuco's Technical Education and Skills Development Authority (TESDA), Secretary Carlito Puno's Commission on Higher Education and Development (CHED), the National Anti-Poverty Commission, Lorna Fajardo's PhilHealth Insurance, Cecile B. Gutierrez's TESDA Women's Center, Office of President Gloria Arroyo in Malacañang -- dealing directly with their highest officials.

3.  **Legislative** bodies like the Senate Committee on Health and Demography, the House Committee on Health, the House Committee on Trade and Investment, all the senators and many Congressmen and women – appearing in most of their public hearings.

4.  **Church organizations** like the Catholic Bishops Conference, the Protestant United Churches of Christ, the Buddhist Universal Wisdom Foundation, and others.

5.  **Professional Associations** with whom Elvira has signed Memorandums of Agreement, or is affliliated with -- such as Philippine Pharmaceutical Association, La Salle University Medical Association, Philippine Medical Association.

6.  **Non Government Organizations** with whom Elvira signed Memorandums of Agreement or have Joint Projects with -- like Environmental Studies Institute, *Bantay Kalikasan*, Father James B. Reuter of the Catholic Media, Sister Pilar Verzosa of Pro-Life Movement, Our Lady of La Leche Movement, four Rotary Clubs, SM Supermalls, DZRJ and RJTV, NU-107, among many others.

7.  **International Organizations** with whom Elvira

signed Memorandums of Agreement, such as UNICEF Philippines, Guinness World Record Ltd.; World Alliance for Breastfeeding Action (WABA, Malaysia); Framework Convention Alliance (Mary Assunta, Geneva); Public Health Advocacy (Richard Daynard, Boston); Global Alliance for Incinerator Alternatives (GAIA), Baby Action Network.

8.      **Individuals** who supported the IRR with their signatures, gathered by Elvira's Group, more than 600 of them, including President Fidel V. Ramos, 20 out of 23 senators, 76 Congressman, Bro. Mike Velarde of El Shaddai, all of the bishops of the Catholic Bishops Conference, the Buddhist Foundation including two Tibetan monks, ex-Solicitor General Francisco Chavez.

Also, Elvira and her Group make themselves available to any organization that wants to hear from them, from the Philippine Air Force, the Association of Pathologists, Miriam and Assumption Colleges, St. Luke's and the World City Medical Center; ZOTO and PRRM.

## XIII.  THE PHILIPPINE LACTATION RESOURCE AND TRAINING CENTER

Dr. Elvira L. Henares-Esguerra of the Children for Breastfeeding, Inc. also established the Philippine Lactation Resource and Training Center, and with the cooperation of the Technical Education and Skills Development Authority (TESDA), embarked on the training of nurses, midwives and health workers as Lactation Consultants and Breastfeeding Counselors who will be of service to the nation in the implementation of the Breastfeeding and Rooming In Act (RA 7600) and in the 5 year National Plan for Infant and Young Child Feeding, thus motivating them to stay in the Philippines instead of migrating abroad in search of greener pastures. The Philippine Lactation Resource and Training Center funded with scholarships, runs regular live-in workshops for NGOs, GOs and individuals on (1) Breastfeeding Counseling, and (2) the promotion and protection of Breastfeeding, with a special treat of vegetarian menus that has proven to be very popular among the audience.

## XIV.    THE PHILIPPINE ACADEMY OF LACTATION CONSULTANTS, INC.

Dr. Elvira L. Henares - Esguerra of Children for Breastfeeding, Inc. is a member of good standing in the Philippine Medical Association, where there are doctors sympathetic to drug and milk companies, and antagonistic to the Breastfeeding Movement, arguing that the doctor and mother must be given the absolute right to choose between breastfeeding and bottle-feeding, in the face of laws designed to level the playing field between the $100 million used to promote formula milk and expensive drugs, and the Zero budget of Breastfeeding advocates.

Elvira is also a member of the US based Academy of Breastfeeding Medicine, and established the local Philippine Academy of Lactation Consultants, Inc., as an affiliate of the Philippine Medical Association.

**She was able to convince the Philippine Medical Association (PMA), during its 100th anniversary convention, to support Breastfeeding as an essential part of the Continuing Medical Education (CME) of doctors, and through the Philippine Academy of Lactation Consultants, getting them to be informed of the latest developments in the fields of Lactation and Breastfeeding, and their contribution to the health, well-being, intellectual development and emotional stability of the child, now and in the future. It was the first CME on Breastfeeding in a PMA Convention, and it won't be the last.**

### XV. A PERMANENT OFFICE

When told that TESDA Women's Center is concerned only with the empowerment of women in their productive role in society (livelihood projects), Elvira countered that "women cannot be fully empowered in their productive role in the workplace, if they are not also empowered in their REproductive role as a mother in the home." For this Elvira and her Group were given an office and a home in the TESDA Women's Center.

The Technical Skills and Education Development Authority (TESDA) under Secretary Director General Augusto "Boboy" Syjuco, gave Children for Breastfeeding,Inc. an office 12 x 6 meters free of charge, complete with air-conditioning, lights, telephone and Internet access, plus use of their entire facilities for training classes.  It became the office of Children for Breastfeeding,Inc., Nurturers of the Earth, Inc. and the Philippine Lactation Resource and Training Center.  It also became the world headquarters for the Synchronized Breastfeeding Worldwide.

## XVI.  THE GRAND COALITION AGAINST CORPORATE GREED

The multiplicity of the manifestations of corporate greed, so manifest in the violations of tobacco laws, the proliferation of genetically modified organisms in our farm products, and resistance against the Clean Air Act, as well as violations of the National Milk Code, resulted in 38 Consumer and Health Advocacy groups here and abroad, led by Children for Breastfeeding, Inc., and Nurturers of the Earth, Inc. announcing the formation of a Grand Coalition against Corporate Greed and Predatory Commercial Interests (1) in defense of the health and well-being of our Fellowmen; (2) for the protection of the environment and Mother Earth and (3) for the prevention of corporate exploitation of the economy of this world.

The Framework Convention Alliance (FCA) of Geneva, Switzerland, led by Mary Assunta and the Public Health Advocacy Institute of Boston, Massachusetts, led by Professor Richard Daynard, the most successful health lobby in the history of advocacy, joined the alliance, promising to lend their expertise in instituting class suits against milk companies for the death of 16,000 babies every year.  Baby Milk Action of UK, represented by Patti Rundall, and INFACT of Canada, represented by Elizabeth Sterken, as well as *Liga ng mga Barangay sa Pilipinas*, the Philippine Pharmaceutical Association, the Global Alliance for Incinerator Alternatives (GAIA), *Bantay Kalikasan, Tanggol Kalikasan,* Pro-Life Philippines and many others are making each other's concerns the concern of all -- a "one-for-all and all-for-one" Grand Alliance against Corporate Greed, abuse and corruption.

Of the few advocates for breastfeeding in the Philippines, Maurice Maeterlink once wrote: "At every crossing on the road that leads to the future, every progressive spirit is opposed by a thousand men appointed to guard the past."  They were once described by a high UNICEF official thus: "Each has the strength of ten because her heart is pure. Without funds, against all odds, against government bureaucracies and multinational corporations, but with the help of the Almighty, each has contributed mightily to the ultimate good of mankind"

## XVII. EDUCATION FOR A PERMANENT COMMITMENT

It is amazing how far Elvira has gone to promote and protect breastfeeding. The roles she played in the finalization of the new IRR to enforce the National Milk Code, and in the National Plan of Action on Infant and Young Child Feeding, her breaking the Guinness world breastfeeding records (in one site, in multiple sites and in world-wide synchronization), Breastfeeding stations in all SM Supermalls – all define the scope, magnitude and **BREADTH** of her advocacy. But it is not enough.

She knows that she must INSTITUTIONALIZE Breastfeeding, give it relevance in the lives of all the people and define the **DEPTH** of her commitment so that the movement will continue to grow in the years to come, long after she is gone. What is needed is **EDUCATION** at all levels -- to crank in the culture of breastfeeding **(1)** into all Nursing and Medicine courses, **(2)** into Health related Courses in the NSTP program in the first year of College, **(3)** into other Health related college courses, like Physical Therapy, **(4)** together with all Extension classes and *Practicums*; **(5)** also in Health related subjects at the vocational level; **(6)** also in the Continuing Medical Education (CME) of doctors already practicing. These will definitely be done together with the **Philippine Medical Association, the TESDA and the Commission on Higher Education (CHED)**, with two of whom Elvira has already a Memorandum of Agreement. All that remains to be done is an agreement with the **Department of Education** to introduce Breastfeeding in as many subjects as possible in the **(7)** elementary and **(8)** high school level, which Elvira already tried to do, but she just got bogged down in the bureaucracy.


## XVIII. PETITION ON US INTERVENTION AGAINST BREASTFEEDING

During the La Leche League International Convention on July 22, 2007, Elvira and Nona were able to convince 62 top leaders and breastfeeding advocates in the League to sign a petition addressed "TO THE PEOPLE AND LEADERS OF THE UNITED STATES OF AMERICA" from the mothers and breastfeeding advocates of the world. This is in protest against the intervention of US officials (Economic Attache Robert Ludan and David Katch of President Bush's White House Office) to the new IRR issued by the Department of Health.

This petition was also posted in the Internet and to date, after only three days got a response with the signing of 468 persons, in addition to the 62 from La Leche League, and increasing exponentially, with the realization that in addition to the disaster of the Iraq War and the repudiation of the Kyoto Initiatives, Bush is also spending against Breastfeeding.

This petition is also being readied for distribution during the coming Convention of the U.S. Academy of Breastfeeding Medicine in October 11-14, 2007.

The Preamble

"*Whereas*, the people of the United States is facing a presidential election year in 2008 that may bring to the fore, a leadership dedicated to the betterment of mankind, a role reserved by destiny for them as a democratic nation and as the greatest military and economic power the world has ever known; and as such are in a position to help the underdeveloped nations resolve many of their concerns in their struggle to survive;

"*Whereas*, Formula Milk Manufacturers, mainly based in the United States, for the most part violate international treaties and covenants, in letter and in spirit, legally or illegally, especially in Third World underdeveloped countries, where their tremendous financial power with the help of the American Chamber of Commerce and certain agencies of the US Embassy, have allowed them to unduly influence government officials, health workers, doctors, medical societies, media (print, radio, TV), to subvert the breastfeeding culture with massive advertising campaigns and preposterous nutritional claims they would not even claim in their own countries."

"Now therefore, the undersigned mothers and breastfeeding advocates, representing themselves, their organizations and their respective nations, as well as American citizens who believe in the cause of breastfeeding, do humbly and respectfully petition the people and leaders of the United States,

"(1) to enjoin the multinational milk companies as well as the United States government to respect the 2001 Doha Declaration on TRIPS and Public Health that Public Health is far more important than issues involving intellectual property rights (WTO on 14 November 2001 declared, "The TRIPS Agreement does not and should not prevent members from taking measures to protect public health"; a joint WTO-WHO study in 2002 reaffirmed that statement);

"(2) to enjoin US embassies to observe international protocol in presenting their demands to other countries, that is, to course its demands in writing through the Foreign Ministry of the country involved, instead of utilizing back channels and verbal intervention to impose its will on government officials, especially when it involves issues of Breastfeeding;

"(3) to make sure that the breastfeeding issue is taken up in every political platform in the coming US presidential elections for the consideration of the entire electorate; and finally

"(4) to make it understood among all nations on earth that America's main business is NOT "business itself" or corporate profits, but more importantly, international amity and the betterment of all humankind, as befits a nation with the might and power to lead the world."

### XIX.     DSWD COMMITMENT TO PROMOTE INDIGENOUS FOOD INSTEAD OF IMPORTED MILK

When Department of Social Welfare and Development (DSWD) asked what it has to do with breastfeeding since its mandate concerns children from 3 to 5 years old, Elvira answered, "**First,** our purpose is to introduce breastfeeding up to 2 years old and beyond, I am still breastfeeding my 6-year old son up to now because he wants it. **Second,** we want to invite breastfeeding mothers to your day care centers for *Sabay-Sabay Sumuso*, so that your children will learn that it is normal and desirable to breastfeed, and in time, they may become the support group for their own mothers breastfeeding their siblings. **Third**, we want you to replace the cow's milk in your school hot lunch program with indigenous foods full of proteins, calcium and nutrients, more nutritious than imported milk. **Fourth**, we want you to have a livelihood program for mothers under your care to make slings for babies, and to learn to massage breastfeeding mothers to help them lactate. **Fifth**, you may join our tree-planting project with the DENR, by making available your Day Care sites for your children to plant fruit and food-bearing trees, which they will care for and in the future, enjoy the fruits of their labor."

The most important and far-reaching result of the collaboration with DSWD is the change of policy for the feeding of young children of school age, with indigenous foods like *malunggay*, *gabi* and root crops and others far more nutritious than cow's milk in calcium and other nutrients, instead of imported cow's milk which costs the nation $400 million a year to import.

## XX.  CHANGING THE ATTITUDE AGAINST EXPOSURE OF BREASTS

After an incident in a mall wherein a courageous, empowered, single mother named Elizabeth Cariño quarreled with a guard who insisted she breastfeed her baby in the comfort room, Elvira's reaction was: "It is about time that breasts are considered, not as sex objects to stimulate men's libido, but as the provider of food and nourishment for the future citizens of the land that God meant them to be.  My father says that in the 80 years that he has been a movie addict he has yet to see a Hollywood movie showing mothers breastfeeding their infants, because the Catholic League of Decency and the Hays Office objected to them.  Instead, bottle-feeding with cow's milk has been the norm, even in Walt Disney movies.  One of the most tender and moving scenes in literature, the climax of the novel *Grapes of Wrath* by John Steinbeck, wherein the heroine after losing her own baby, fed a starving old man from her breasts – was excised from the movie version because of the public outcry.  Barbara Walters, the famous journalist, was outraged that a mother seated beside her in an airplane, breastfed her baby without hiding her breast.  The head of Makati Med, confronted with a statue of the Virgin Mary suckling Baby Jesus, kept putting a napkin over her breast.  The Catholic Bishops and

Mayor Atienza asked that breastfeeding babies be hidden from public view." "It is about time we react," Elvira said.

Convincing (a) *Catholic Cardinal* Ricardo Vidal to approve the layout of Mama Mary breastfeeding Jesus, (b) SM Supermalls to allow any nursing mother to breastfeed anywhere and at any time in all their malls (the Breastfeeding Stations are for those who want privacy) and (c) the City of Manila to break the Guinness World Record, resulting in publicity of a plethora of women baring their breasts everywhere in the Internet, on television and print media all over the world -- have the greatest effect of all. Suddenly we see pictures of bare breasts of nursing mothers being shown everywhere without the usual protests by religious leaders and self-appointed moral guardians. The Breast should not be a sex object to stimulate libido. As the source of nutrition for babies, it is not only natural, it is desirable and ennobling. A US senator even introduced amendments to the Nudity Law allowing the baring of breasts for breastfeeding.

## XXI. INTERNATIONAL ETHICS AGAINST INVOLVEMENT WITH MILK COMPANIES.

The place was the Japanese Restaurant of Hotel Shangri-la Makati. Around the luncheon table were two top executives of the Milk Companies, their designated negotiator and his wife, and Elvira's Group. The negotiator spoke, "Elvira, we realize that the Breastfeeding Movement has no money to promote breastfeeding. We are prepared to help in a big way. We offer P200 million to be used in any way you feel is for the good of the Breastfeeding Movement. Would you like to think this over?"

Elvira's answer was immediately forthcoming, "I do not think we will accept any help from the Milk Companies, no matter how well-intentioned. We belong to organizations that promote breastfeeding around the world, and we swore to adhere to an international standard of ethics that forbids us from having any dealings with Milk Companies. You offer P200 million for the promotion of breastfeeding, that is hardly on par with the P3 billion Milk Companies spend every year to market their formula milk. Please do not misunderstand. If you offered P200 BILLION, the answer is still NO."

There is a perfectly logical reason for this. Every

year Milk and Drug Companies spend billions of dollars in travel grants, research funds, honorariums and outright gifts, sponsorships of conferences, conventions and junkets for legislators, government officials, doctors, health workers, nurses and consumers. And these charitable efforts never ever did any public health initiative any good.

## XXII.  INTERNATIONAL CONFERENCES

Elvira and Nona in partnership with of Ines Fernandez of *Arugaan*, since 2001 attended WABA's Breastfeeding Conferences in Kuala Lumpur, Malaysia, in Tanzania in Africa, in India and the United States.

In 2007, they continued on their own to take an active part in two conferences, with some funding from Pagcor: (1) as speakers, in the Conference of the World Alliance for Breastfeeding Action (WABA) on July 17-19, and (2) as presentors and speakers in the 50th Anniversary Conference of the La Leche League International on July 20-23, both in Chicago Hilton.  On the same occasion they paid a call in the offices of Senator Edward Kennedy, Senator Barack Obama, and Senators Barbara Boxer and Charles Shumer, to ask them for support against the US Embassy's active opposition to breastfeeding in the Philippines.  They were able to get the leaders of the La Leche League and the WABA to sign a petition in their personal capacity in opposition to US Intervention against Breastfeeding.

Elvira .attended her third international conference this year, the 12th annual convention in Fort Worth, Texas, on October 11-14, 2007, of the Academy of Breastfeeding Medicine (ABM), based in the USA, an international organization of doctors of different specialties concerned with the promotion, protection and support of Breastfeeding, of which she is a member.  It was a huge success.  The reputation of Elvira preceded her as the Academy of Breastfeeding Medicine informed her that the officials of ABM have already signed en banc the same petition protesting US Intervention, for which the ABM International Committee created a Task Force on the Philippine Situation.  In addition, Elvira got appointed as the ABM Coordinator for the Philippines and became a member of the International Committee, and her Philippine Academy of

Lactation Consultants, Inc. applied for an affiliation with ABM International. Elvira attended the workshop for Basic Research, and was told that her advocacy of Breastfeeding in the Philippines itself was a worthy subject for Basic Research for ABM members.

### XXIII.  BREASTFEEDING AS A UNIVERSAL ISSUE

Faced with the lack of interest of the nation's leaders and world leaders in breastfeeding as a **gender** issue, Elvira was able to convince them in the most dramatic way that breastfeeding is even more so a **public health** issue, an **economic** issue, an **ecology** issue, a **political** issue, and above all, a **human rights** issue.

It is a **public health** issue because breastfeeding is the gold standard that provides immunity from childhood diseases, and nutrients that guarantee emotional stability and intellectual development no breastmilk substitutes could ever hope to provide.

It is an **economic issue** because breastfeeding is the most far-reaching and cheapest strategy for the alleviation of poverty, and while breastmilk is free, massive importation of cow's milk and milk products divert resources that might have been used to encourage agricultural production of indigenous foods more nutritious than cow's milk, and build more educational and housing facilities.

It is an **ecology** issue because breastfeeding does not require clean water, fuel, disposable containers as breastmilk substitutes do.

It is a **political** issue because it pits powerful multinational corporations, sometimes with the help of the US government, against weak governments and unfunded breastfeeding advocates.

Above all, it is a **human rights issue** because it addresses the issue of the right of women to equality and empowerment, and the right of children, as defined in the Convention on the Rights of the Child, to the best nutrition and care available, and finally because it concerns the SOCIAL CAPITAL by which the future citizens of the world may survive, prosper, and contribute to the betterment of all humankind.

## XXIV. Environmentalist LEE ANN FORD JOINS THE TEAM

The core team of Children for Breastfeeding Inc. consists of the father Hilarion. M. Henares Jr. who is an economist, former cabinet member, and civic leader; Elvira herself, and Ms. Nona D. Andaya Castillo, a thin and dedicated vegetarian, an International Board Certified Lactation Consultant and a mass communication expert. This team is facetiously referred to as the Unholy Trinity: God the Father, God the Daughter, and God the Holy Skeleton. The next circle is that of Fund Raiser Sylvia Coe Lichauco, Elvira's aunt; Flora T. Suaverdez (secretary of the family's corporations) for finance and bookkeeping, and lawyer Ipat Luna, a TOYM Awardee in Environmental Law.

To the team is added Canadian Environmentalist Ms. Lee-Ann Ford, now the team's strategist and new Board member. Ms. Lee-Ann Ford is the President and Founder of Linking Individuals for Nature Conservation (LINC), a Hong Kong based non-profit environmental organization dedicated to conservation, education, employment and restoration. She has contributed to the US Marine Mammal Report to Congress, participated in the US Marine Mammals Commission meeting in London 2004, the UN Commission on Sustainable Development (UNCSD) in 2007 and plans to hold a panel at the UN Commission meeting on the Status of Women in 2008. Ms. Ford has led environmental movements in Taiwan to preserve habitat, raise awareness and has contributed to policy making strategies around SE Asia. Ms. Lee-Ann Ford fully supports the work of Children for Breastfeeding Inc and is eager to demonstrate the benefits of breastfeeding related to the environment. Ms. Lee-Ann Ford's organization (LINC) has various projects in the Philippines, Sri Lanka, Hong Kong and China.

## XXV. SUMMARY AND EPILOGUE

The 12 chapters of Milk Wars Part 1 covers the breastfeeding advocacy of Elvira L. Henares-Esguerra from its inception in 2001 to May 4, 2006 when Elvira and her Group were about to break the Guinness World Record for Simultaneous Breastfeeding in a Single Site. It consists for the most part the efforts exerted to formulate the new Revised

Implementing Rules and Regulations for the National Milk Code which was proclaimed a law 20 years before and was never really implemented, because of the opposition of the Milk Companies and the US government, the Association of Broadcasters and the media itself. A TRO was issued against its implementation by the Supreme Court in a court case initiated by the Milk Companies.

The 25 chapters of Milk Wars Part 2 covers a period of one and a half years between May 4, 2006 to October 18, 2007 – the continuing story of the Breastfeeding Movement in the Philippines, and the role of Children for Breastfeeding, Inc. in it. It recounts (1) the ultimate triumph of the Breastfeeding Movement in the Supreme Court decision ruling on the revised IRR; (2) the four successful involvements of Children for Breastfeeding, Inc. with the Guinness World Records Ltd. to secure world-wide attention; (3) the partnership with SM Supermalls to set up a breastfeeding-friendly atmosphere including Breastfeeding Stations in all its 32 supermalls; (4) the multiplicity of Memoranda of Agreements signed with Local Governments, National Agencies, Church Organizations, Professional Associations, Non-Governmental Organizations, and International Organizations; (5) the organization of the Philippine Academy of Lactation Consultants, Inc. to promote Continuing Medical Education (CME) within the Philippine Medical Association; (6) the organization of the Philippine Lactation Resource and Training Center to train lactation consultants and breastfeeding monitors; (7) the organization of the Grand Coalition Against Corporate Greed to counter the financial muscle of Milk and Tobacco companies; (8) the acquisition of a home and office in the TESDA Women's Center; (9) moving into the International Scene under partnership with World Alliance for Breastfeeding Action (WABA) and the US based Academy of Breastfeeding Medicine, (10) protesting and posting a petition against US official intervention against Breastfeeding in Third World countries; (11) issuing two successful Photo Exhibits of Breastfeeding Role Models; (12) moving into the entire field of Education from Grade School to Vocational to University education, (13) promoting the International Standard of Ethics rejecting any involvement with Milk Companies; (14) changing the universal attitude against exposure of breasts for breastfeeding; (15) promoting the use of more nutritious indigenous foods and the planting of food bearing trees, in place of imported milk; (16) promoting breastfeeding world-wide as a universal issue (public health, economic, ecology, political and human rights) rather than merely a gender issue; and (17) the continued responsibility for the official celebration of World Breastfeeding Week in the Presidential Palace.  Quite an accomplishment in a mere one and a half years.

The epilogue is short and sweet.  The Holy Skeleton, Nona D. Andaya-Castillo left for Malaysia to work with WABA, and to the USA to pursue advance studies in childbirth education and contact Mayor Bloomberg to promote the Synchronized Breastfeeding Worldwide with New York as central site.  She is being considered for a position as a consultant under the US AID funded Health Policy and Health Promotion Fellowship Program being administered by the UP School of Economics, upon the recommendation of Under-Secretary Alexander Padilla of the Department of Health, in order to help formulate the criteria and guidelines for the implementation of the Revised Rules and Regulations of the National Milk Code, recently upheld by the Supreme Court, while Elvira is planning to set up Monitoring facilities to ensure implementation.  In the meantime, Elvira just back from abroad, says, was she quoting the Greek warrior Xenophon?  *Now. lay me down to rest awhile before I rise to fight again!*

ooooo

# CHAPTER TWO:
# THE WHITE PAPER ON
# BREASTFEEDING:

**Beating the Odds, Achieving Greater Heights**
**The National Movement to Promote, Protect and Support**
**Breastfeeding and Optimal Young Child Feeding:**
**A GO-NGO Partnership**

**Children for Breastfeeding, Inc.   !   HEAL the Philippines Foundation   !**
**Nurturers of the Earth, Inc.**
**Under the Administration of President Gloria Macapagal-Arroyo (2005-2010)**

**Executive Summary:**

President Gloria Macapagal-Arroyo's policies and programs increased the exclusive breastfeeding duration to almost four times and ushered in a new direction establishing breastfeeding as an important part of public healthcare and national development.

The President's compassion and political will saved breastfeeding from the brink of extinction, reversing 20 years of frustration from among its advocates. Under President Arroyo's administration the importance of breastfeeding and optimal young child feeding practices and its crucial role in national development as a means to reach the country's Millennium Development Goal (MDG) of significantly reducing maternal mortality and deaths among children under the age of five was given the attention it deserves.

Among others, the President issued Presidential Proclamation No. 1113 promulgating the yearly celebration of World Breastfeeding Week every August 1-7. The President also launched the National Plan of Action on Infant and Young Child Feeding 2005-2010; and made available a bigger budget for the hunger mitigation program which provided funds for advertisements during prime time on breastfeeding as well as information, education and communication materials. Her program and policies have averted the rapid decline of breastfeeding rates among mothers.

The result: the higher public awareness and social support for breastfeeding mothers and the duration of exclusive breastfeeding increasing to almost four times from 24 days to 84 days and a recognition from Save the Children for these efforts.

The DOH issued guidelines that forbid exemptions to the national policy of regulating advertisements for milk intended for children up to three years of age and likewise forbid the use of false nutritional and health claims that undermine breastfeeding.

As part of a global public health recommendation to achieve optimal growth and development, infants should be exclusively breastfed for the first six months of life and sustain breastfeeding beyond two years with the addition of indigenous foods.

### I. The National Anti-Poverty Hearings to the Presidential Cabinet Meeting

In May 2005, two International Board Certified Lactation Consultants (IBCLC), Dr. Elvira L. Henares-Esguerra and Nona D. Andaya-Castillo initiated a Senate hearing where Hilarion M. Henares Jr., a Presidential Adviser on National Affairs made a testimony on the "Economic Consequences of the Loss of the Breastfeeding Culture."

Henares explained that: (a) US$ 400 million worth of milk and milk products are being imported by the Philippine economy which imperils the use of available indigenous agricultural products of greater nutritional value; (b) Of these, US$ 57 million accounts for formula milk and according to the World Health Organization (WHO), are sold to the public at seven times their cost (30% of the income of the poor family is spent on buying the product), while breastmilk of superior quality is available practically free; (c) Because many infants are not breastfed, they are deprived of the excellent immunological properties of breastfeeding. WHO estimates that 16,000 infants die annually and P536 million a year is spent on medical expenses, labor time lost, and funerals.

Upon hearing about this, the President instructed Secretary Imelda Nicolas of the National Anti-Poverty Commission (NAPC) to investigate the testimony of Henares in preparation for a presidential cabinet meeting. The NAPC hearings on May 30 and June 6, 2005 not only revealed the unnecessary importation of milk products but also the sponsorship of these milk companies to government agencies like the National Nutrition Council (NNC), Department of Social Welfare and Development (DSWD) and the Department of Health (DOH). The breastfeeding advocates pointed out that this practice is unethical while the donation of milk products especially during disaster could be detrimental to the children's health and could disrupt breastfeeding."

# Heaven and Hell

The following week, on June 14, Hilarion M. Henares Jr., Henares- Esguerra and Andaya- Castillo appeared before the Presidential Cabinet to expound on their views, supported by the newly- appointed Health Secretary Francisco T. Duque III.

The Cabinet Meeting proceeded without a hitch, Henares and Duque spoke in tandem, perfectly synchronized. The President was impressed, and the three-pronged request for a World Breastfeeding Week, a program for Infant and Young Child Feeding, and the finalization of the new IRR were approved in principle. Henares objected to the importation of milk and instead proposed the encouragement of the consumption of indigenous calcium-rich foods for the nutrition program of the DSWD. This moved the President to remark, "it does no good to encourage consumption of milk, since our milk industry can only supply one percent of the demand." It helped that Director Sally Bulatao of the National Dairy Authority, a niece of Henares, supported the position of the Breastfeeding advocates not to rely on imported milk.

Unequivocally, the President decided to support the Breastfeeding Movement and directed the Department of Social Welfare and Development to change its Food for School Program of distributing cow's milk to that of distributing iron-fortified rice.

This was better expressed by the President's Speech (in part) during a Luncheon with the Filipino Olympians and the Filipino Community in Beijing, Saturday, August 09, 2008 at the Grand Ballroom, Asia Hotel, Beijing, China:

*Nagtuturo rin tayo ng Nutrition Education o wastong pagkaing hindi masyadong magastos. Kasama na nga dito ang pagpapa-iral ng breastfeeding para hindi tayo kailangan umangkat masyado ng gatas mula sa ibang bansa. At kaya naman tinanggap natin na ilunsad dito sa harap ninyo ang 2008 Breastfeeding Olympics o Worldwide Synchronized Breastfeeding. Kaya, congratulations!*

(We are also teaching Nutrition Education or the right way of eating that will not be expensive. This includes the promotion of breastfeeding so that we do not need to import milk from other countries. That is the reason why we accepted to launch the 2008 Breastfeeding Olympics or Worldwide Synchronized Breastfeeding. So Congratulations!)

**II. Presidential Proclamation and first World Breastfeeding Week.**

In a private dinner hosted by the President for the Henares family in Malacanang on July 18, 2005, the President agreed to issue a Presidential roclamation on the national celebration of World Breastfeeding Week following the international standards of ethics of not partnering with ompanies manufacturing or distributing milk, babyfoods, bottles, teats and pacifiers.

Both Henares–Esguerra and Castillo presented their credentials to the President as International Board Certified Lactation Consultants introducing a new profession to help mothers perform their nurturing roles and pledging their commitment to help the country.

The Presidential Proclamation No. 884 was launched on July 29, 2005, which was amended with Presidential Proclamation No. 1113 on August 1, 2006, as follows:

PRESIDENTIAL PROCLAMATION NO. 1113 DECLARING

AUGUST 1 TO 7 OF EVERY YEAR AS WORLD BREASTFEEDING WEEK

WHEREAS, the World Breastfeeding Week from August 1 to 7 is being celebrated every year in 120 countries consistent with the Innocenti Declaration on the Protection, Promotion and Support of Breastfeeding, the Baby-Friendly Hospital Initiative, the International Code on the Marketing of Breastmilk Substitutes and Related Products and subsequent resolutions of the World Health Assembly, to which the Philippines is a signatory;

WHEREAS, the "Global Strategy on Infant and Young Child Feeding" jointly developed by the World Health Organization and the UNICEF pursues to revitalize world attention to the impact of feeding practices on the nutritional status, growth and development and thus the very survival of infants and young children;

WHEREAS, the Republic of the Philippines has two laws, Executive Order No. 51, 1986, known as the National Code on the Marketing of Breastmilk Substitutes and Related Products and Republic Act No. 7600, known as the Rooming-In and Breastfeeding Act of 1992, to protect breastfeeding in accordance with its international commitments;

WHEREAS, latest scientific evidence have shown that breastfeeding provides protection against major illnesses in infants and children such as respiratory infections, diarrhea and malnutrition and reduces risk of degenerative diseases well into adulthood; and ensures maternal health by protecting against hemorrhages, uterine prolapse, anemia, certain cancers, osteoporosis, diabetes and other illnesses as well as by facilitating the recovery of mothers from the rigors of pregnancy and birthing, and by helping prevent closely-spaced pregnancies;

WHEREAS, breastfeeding is the most far-reaching and least costly Poverty Alleviation Strategy of developing countries, especially in the Philippines where the breastfeeding culture is being diminished beyond all reason. It addresses the issue of national health aside from the issues of food security, economy, ecology, empowerment of women, bonding between mother and child, love and faith;

WHEREAS, the World Alliance for Breastfeeding Action (WABA), which initiated the World Breastfeeding Week with the support of WHO and UNICEF, has urged that "no funding, donation or sponsorship from industries promoting breastmilk substitutes and related products" shall be accepted for the celebration of World Breastfeeding Week, in accordance with its international standard of ethics;

WHEREAS, the Department of Health is mandated to promote, protect and defend the health of infants and children through provision of sound policies and programs for breastfeeding and young child feeding with the end goal of reducing infant and under five mortality and morbidity.

NOW, THEREFORE, I, GLORIA MACAPAGAL-ARROYO, President of the Republic of the Philippines, by virtue of the powers vested in me by law, do hereby declare the week of August 1 to 7 of every year as World Breastfeeding Week, in accordance with international practice, and in consonance with the international standard of ethics, to be celebrated nationwide, directs the following:

With the Department of Health as lead, all government agencies and in particular the Department of

Education, the Department of Social Welfare and Development, the Department of Interior and Local Government, Local Government Units, the Philippine Information Agency and the Council for the Welfare of the Children, are hereby enjoined to participate and mobilize their networks to sustain a high level of awareness, support and protection of breastfeeding;

All non-government organizations, professional and civic organizations, the religious sector, private sector to work together and promote this endeavor;

All international agencies and organizations, within their respective mandate and programs give high priority and support to this undertaking.

IN WITNESS WHEREOF, I have hereunto set my hand and caused the seal of the Republic of the Philippines to be affixed.

Done in the City of Manila, this 1st day of August, in the year of Our Lord, Two Thousand and Six.

(Sgd.) H.E. GLORIA MACAPAGAL-ARROYO
By the President:
(Sgd.) EDUARDO R. ERMITA
Executive Secretary

With the first celebration of World Breastfeeding Week on August 1, 2005, and the launching of the National Plan of Action for Infant and Young Child Feeding 2005-2010, comes this description of the occasion by Henares in a memo to the President:

"There are times, Madam President when you have that know-it-all look of a schoolmarm that makes people look stupid and feel resentful.  But then there are times when you look positively radiant with an inner glow that clutches at the hearts of those with you.  Such a time it was during the August 1, 2005, affair in the Ceremonial Hall when you declared August 1 to 7 as World Breastfeeding Week.  You were really at your best and loveliest.

"We had only 10 days to accomplish the task, planning only a simple affair with 300 guests.  The Bright Child Affair of the DSWD, with busloads of schoolchildren and totaling 500 guests, impressed UNICEF head Dr. Alipui and DOH Secretary Duque so much that they texted me to try hard to surpass it.  We had three days to gather 700 guests but we did it.  Duque brought the doctors who were hospital heads, Senator Gordon a 20- man delegation of Japanese Red Cross, Father Reuter a whole community of indigenous tribes.  And of course everyone brought as many nursing mothers as possible.  We filled the Ceremonial Hall to the rafters with extra chairs from end to end, a record, the Protocol told me."

"Asked to compare the Bright Child with the Breastfeeding Affair, Protocol rated ours 10 and the Bright Child 7.5; and for the first time in 300 years, Malacañang Protocol was breached.  Down at Gate One, a long line of newly born babies with their fathers and mothers from Fabella Hospital waited, while my breastfeeding daughter Elvira pleaded, 'I know their names are not posted and they are wearing sandals, blue jeans and dusters, but this affair is for them.  They simply cannot afford shoes and good clothes.  They are fresh from the delivery room and we did not have time to post their names.'  They were let in, after a fervent prayer of the group to the Virgin Mother."

"The Henares technique for winning Oratorical Contests (we won Voice of Democracy three times) worked like a charm: 'First make them laugh, to open their minds.  Then plant the seeds of thought and water them with tears.'  With my introduction of La Nuestra Señora de la Leche y Buen Parto, our bare-breasted Virgin Mother, I made the audience laugh.  The speeches and the PowerPoint presentations planted the seeds of thought, and you, Madam President, you watered them with the tears of the audience.

"It was most moving, the way you left the stage to approach Dr. Clavano, to congratulate her for making history as the first Breastfeeding advocate in the world.  It moved the audience to ears to hear the mother and daughter Andaya-Castillo and Sierra Isabelle Castillo sing a lovely serenade to the nursing mothers, 'Come close to me, Neneng, let me shower you with kisses,' with the toddlers bringing flowers to each mother, climaxed by my grandchildren, Angelí and Larry Henares Esguerra and Uno Henares Angeles, bearing roses to you and being hugged and kissed in return.  Then the most gracious gesture of all, which moved everyone to tears --- you motioned all the nursing mothers and fathers to come to you, all in a line, and you shook each hand, blessed each baby and kissed each nursing mother.  And your speech was the best on breastfeeding I have ever heard yet. Congratulations, Madam President."

*The President's Speech (in part) during the Launching Ceremony of the National Action*

*Plan for Infant & Young Child Feeding and World Breastfeeding Week*

*Monday, August 01, 2005, Rizal Hall, Malacañang*

Thank you, Secretary Duque and congratulations for your commitment to breastfeeding way back in 2002. Congratulations! Our co-host for this affair, Dr. Alipui of UNICEF and Dr. Velayudan of World Health Organization; our very important leaders of Congress, Senator Gordon who's also Red Cross; Congresswoman Bondoc who is Vice Chairman of the Committee on Health; Congressman Kintanar and Congressman Mandanas; Mayor Atienza who is launching this very important breastfeeding program for the City of Manila; Former Secretary Larry Henares and my consultant; Fr. Reuter; the different government officials who are here today; *ang ating mga nanay; ang ating mga* (and our mothers, our) breastfeeding mothers *saka mga anak nila* (their children); advocates of breastfeeding in the Philippines; ladies and gentlemen,

*Noong isang araw, inilunsad natin ang matagal nang pinaghandaang programang... Programa para sa mga bata ng siglo beinte uno. Ang tinawag natin dito, dahil ang hangarin natin na ang bata ng siglo beinte uno ay matalinong bata, tinawag natin sa programang ito "Bright Child." At ang mga programa ay mga programa para masigurado na matalino ang bata sa siglo biente uno. Kaya yung mga programa makakasigurado na siya ay matalino ay nagsisimula pa kung nasa tiyan ng nanay. From the point of conception hanggang ang bata ay labingpitong taong gulang.*

A few days ago, we launched our program which we had prepared for a long time, a program for the child of the twenty-first century. We call this program "Bright Child." This program will ensure that children will be intelligent for the twenty-first century. And so to guarantee that they will be bright, the program should start from the womb. From the point of conception until the child is 17 years old.)

We're determined to enable our children to have a strong start as the future builders of this nation. The positive impact of our national breastfeeding program will be felt not only by the newborn of this generation but all generations of Filipinos.

As he reported to you earlier, Secretary Duque in my behalf is working on the national breastfeeding program together with the World Health Organization, the UNICEF all their NGO partners and local governments. And we have all noted the valiant efforts, special mention of Mayor Atienza to make Manila the first city in the world to spearhead the cause of breastfeeding.

*Mga batang naririto ngayon, kayo'y matatalino at malusog dahil sa bitaminang nanggaling sa gatas ng inyong mga ina.* (To the children that are present today, you are intelligent and healthy because of the vitamins that comes from your mother's milk.) I am also... I was also a breastfeeding mother, but not exclusive. If I had been exposed to this program and this advocacy when I was a new mother, I would have fed... breastfed my children exclusively up to age of six months. But since even for all my education, *kahit na nagtapos ako ng PhD, nung ako ay nanganak hindi ko alam itong dapat six months exclusive breastfeeding. Kaya kung alam ko lang sana ginawa ko sana yon kaya alam ko na nung panahong yon kulang na kulang ang impormasyon. Kaya naman ngayon at ako ay merong pagkakataon na yung ibang mga nanay ng kasalukuyang henerasyon ay may mas alam tungkol dito kaysa sa akin,* (even though I finished my PhD, when I gave birth, I was not aware of the importance of breastfeeding exclusively for six months. Had I known, I would have done the same. I realize now that during that time, there was a dire lack of information on breastfeeding. And since I have the opportunity to make a difference, I commit that the mothers of the present generation will be provided with more knowledge about breastfeeding compared to what I knew then.)

I am pleased, as president and mother, to proclaim August 1 to 7 as World Breastfeeding Week. *Nanggaling rin sa aking karanasan tungkol sa pagkukulang ng impormasyon nung ako ay batang nanay.* (This came from my experience, my lack of knowledge on breastfeeding when I was a young mother.) It's time to actively promote mother's milk for the good of the child, for the good of the mother, the good of the nation.

*Kasi si doktora nung nagsimula kayo ng inyong*

*advocacy eh nanganak na ako, tapos na. Kung sana nandoon kayo noon,* (When Dr. Clavano started her advocacy, I had already given birth to my children. I would have wished you were there,) I would have known better.

*Lahat nito ay bahagi ng ating programang "Bright Child" o matalinong bata. Dapat exclusive breasfeeding sa unang anim na buwan, at dapat patuloy pa rin ang breastfeeding hanggang dalawang taon. Pagpasok naman sa day care o pre-school hanggang grade one, pasok na rin ang ating healthy start program o tinatawag nating masiglang pasimula na nagbibigay ng masustansiyang almusal sa mga eskwela. Ang programang Bright Child o matalinong bata ay kasama ang edukasyon, kalusugan, nutrition, pati na rin espesyal na atensiyon sa mga anak ng mga dukha, para higit na lumapit tayo sa ating mga hangaring magkaroon ng higit na malusog at matalinong batang pilipino sa mundong mas lalong dumidiin ang kumpetensiya.*

(These are all part of our "Bright Child" Program. Breastfeeding should be exclusive for the first six months and it should be continued up to two years of age. When the children enter daycare or pre-school until grade one, our healthy start program commences or what we call the vigorous start that provides a healthy breakfast in the schools. The Bright Child program mobilizes efforts on education, health, nutrition even special attention to children of the very poor so that we will be closer to our goals of having healthier and more intelligent Filipino children in a competitive world.)

Fr. Reuter, thank you very much for praying for us today.

The breastfeeding program benefits the national economy because if all lactating mothers at any given time breastfeed their infants exclusively up to six months, we would save the country 57 million dollars worth of milk formula imports per year. *Kasi sa alam ko, sa lahat ng ating iniinom na gatas, isang porsiyento lamang ang* (From what I know, of all the milk we consume, only one percent is) produced in the Philippines. Ninety nine percent (is) imported. *Kaya yung dairy industry natin, siguro naman yung iniinom ng mga adults na gatas kasama ng kape siguro hindi naman sila mawawalaan ng bumibili ng kanilang produkto. Kaya ang iniinom tuloy ng mga batang maliit imported lahat.* (With the milk that the adults drink with their coffee, the dairy industry will not lose their consumers. However, the milk that young children drink is all imported.) So we spend a lot of money. And if the mothers will exclusively breastfeed we will also have less pollution in our rivers and in our garbage because less milk cans, less plastic bottles, less used rubber in our garbage dumps.

But even beyond the peso impact, our most potent reasons lie in the child's own health and well-being. Now I know even when I was young, even then I knew that mother's milk enhances the children's brain capacity and produces more intelligent individuals. And that even then I knew that it bonds the mother and the child, and it protects both from illness. I knew that, that's why I decided that at least I would partially breastfeed. What I didn't know is that it is better to exclusively breastfeed.

That's why I congratulate Mayor Atienza who I understand has committed to set up lactation stations in all over the City of Manila. And I hope other local governments will do the same.

*Sa edukasyon naman, tuloy ang programing ng day care na siya ay responsibilidad ng mga local governments. Nagtayo na rin tayo ng halos tatlumpung libong silid-aralan,* (In education, the daycare program will continue as the responsibility of the local governments. We also built 30,000 classrooms,) more than the average in the past *at masasarado na natin ang classroom gap sa grade school sa susunod na limang taon basta dalawang shift ang gagamitin natin at limampung estudyante sa bawat silid aralan ang ating bilang* (and we will be able to close the classroom gap in grade school in the next five years as long as we conduct two shifts with fifty students in every classroom).

*Ang mga bagong buwis na sinimulaan nating kubrahin ay ginagastos natin sa mga ganitong bagay. Pati na rin sa pag-ibayo ng kalidad ng edukasyon* (The new taxes that we had started to collect are being spent on these priorities including the improvement of the quality of education) because as we have a bright child through nutrition, breastfeeding, breakfast program, we want to strengthen their brain power and competitive power by strengthening education in English, math and science.

I thank the UNICEF, the WHO for helping the

Philippines promote breastfeeding. I thank all the NGOs involved in this campaign for their tireless advocacy of this program. And I thank the congresswoman and the congressmen for your great interest in this very, very important program for the health of our children and our nation.

I am instructing the DOH and its agency partners, the council for the welfare of children, and I ask all local government units, plus the DepEd and the DSWD, *pati na rin yung* (including) Philippine Information Agency to prepare their moves to bolster the program's success.

*Maraming salamat sa inyong lahat.* (Thank you very much to all of you!)

**Note: Eventually, the Congress passed a law making the month of August of every year, "National Breastfeeding Awareness Month."**


**III. Revised Implementing Rules and Regulations of EO 51**

The National Milk Code (EO 51) was signed into law by President Corazon Aquino in 1986, to fulfill our obligation to the 1981 WHO/UNICEF International Code on the Marketing of Breastmilk Substitutes. For twenty years the Code was honored more in the breach than in the observance because the Implementing Rules and Regulations (IRR) allowed for exemptions to be granted through the Inter-Agency Committee. Finally upon the initiative of breastfeeding advocates such as Henares, Henares-Esguerra and Andaya-Castillo," and the UNICEF under Dr. Nicholas K. Alipui, and the office of President Arroyo, the Department of Health was moved to fast-track the 12th version of the IRR.

Undersecretary Alexander A. Padilla was appointed to head the Bureau of Food and Drugs Technical Working Group (BFAD-TWG) that discussed and discarded 11 versions of the IRR. The personal participation of the breastfeeding advocates and Dr. Alipui himself accomplished in 6! months what could not be accomplished in the last 20 years. Alleged improprieties and violations of the US Foreign Corrupt Practices Act by milk companies were reported to the US Department of Justice and the US Securities and Exchange Commission, attempts at lobbying and arm-twisting by US government officials, as well as by the American Chamber of Commerce were assailed and condemned by the Philippine Press.  But the tipping point was the 800+ signature-petition campaign of Children for Breastfeeding Inc. and Nurturers of the Earth Inc. that was supported by most of the national leaders, including past president Fidel Ramos, 20 out of 23 senators, 76 congressmen, and all of the Catholic Bishops' Conference, the entire main stream Protestant churches, the Buddhist organization and 80 non-government organizations.

The final IRR was signed on May 15, 2006, issued and published by the Department of Health on June 22, 2006, as Administrative Order No. 2006-0012, "Revised Implementing Rules and Regulations of Executive Order 51, otherwise known as The Milk Code, relevant International Agreements, Penalizing Violations thereof and for other purposes." It was to take effect later on July 7, 2006.  The battle is won, but the war is never really over.

The milk companies filed a case before the Supreme Court (SC) against the Department of Health, requesting a Temporary Restraining Order (TRO) against the implementation of the IRR, which was denied on July 11.

On the next celebration of World Breastfeeding Week on August 14, 2006 in Malacanang, the Revised IRR was launched during the 25th and 20th Anniversary of the International and National Code on the Marketing of Breastmilk Substitutes and the other Related Products. The support that the President gave to breastfeeding advocates further emboldened them to pursue the cause."

Then on August 16, 2006, two days after the launching of the IRR in Malacañang, the Supreme Court, on the eve of the retirement of Chief Justice Artemio Panganiban, suddenly, inexplicably and without hearing the side of the breastfeeding advocates, issued a Temporary Restraining Order, until the issues are finally resolved.  Not only that, the Supreme Court under Chief Justice Reynato Puno, refused to accept the Intervention of breastfeeding advocates; and refused as well to accept the offer of the Unicef and the WHO to act as friends of the Court, as *amicus curiae.*

A whole year after, on June 19, 2007, during the first hearing of the case before the

Supreme Court, a glimmer of hope appeared. The Supreme Court Chief Justice Puno challenged the contention of the milk companies that the Department of Health may derive its powers only from national laws passed by the legislature. Two other sources of power were cited: (1) International Treaties and Covenants upon Senate Ratification, and (2) the police power mandated by the Constitution and the Administrative Code. This hope was bolstered by the discovery that Wyeth Philippines had secretly violated the procedure for the recall of 4 million cans of contaminated formula milk a year before, duly exposed by Nurturers of the Earth Inc. and Children for Breastfeeding Inc. with the help of principled whistle-blowers within Wyeth.

Three and half months later, on October 9, 2007, the Court rendered its final judgment. The TRO was lifted, and the IRR was now in effect. Only two provisions were stricken off: the first provision was the total ban on advertising. However, the approval of an Inter-Agency Committee (IAC) of EO 51 on advertisements is still necessary. To give the breastfeeding advocates a meaty role in helping implement the revised IRR, the President appointed Andaya-Castillo as Presidential Consultant on Infant and Young Child Feeding, and issued an Executive Order that made her a part of the IAC to represent the Office of the President.

The second provision that was stricken off by the Supreme Court is the provision on the administrative sanctions on violators of the Code (although the ultimate weapon of canceling the permit for repeated violations is still in force). The rest is VICTORY. The milk companies' claim of "Legal Parameters," long accepted by the BFAD, were struck down one after another.

The result is one of the most stringent regulations ever imposed on the milk companies and this happened only under the Arroyo Administration. The SC ruled that the DOH's power to regulate embraces ALL breastmilk substitutes, even those sold to children beyond two years of age. That power may be exercised through the Inter-Agency Committee, to effect a total ban on all advertisements that undermine Breastfeeding; to impose labeling requirements that warn of the hazards of formula milk; to forbid the Milk Companies from ever contacting mothers, pregnant women and health workers with their propaganda or "gifts of any sort"; to forbid all kinds of nutritional claims, deceptive brand names and use of baby pictures in their advertisements, on the basis of their "total effect"; to forbid milk donations even to the Red Cross, especially those with pending expiry dates, and those that need energy for boiling and clean water for mixing, usually unavailable during disasters; to forbid milk company representation in policy making bodies. The real victory lies in the public awareness generated by Henares-Esguerra's and Andaya-Castillo's Non-Government Organizations.

The President also appointed Henares–Esguerra as a member of the Governing Board of the National Nutrition Council to pursue the policy not only of breastfeeding but also the consumption of indigenous foods for complementary feeding.

The Department of Health (DOH) also recognized the Philippine Lactation Resource and Training Center (PLRTC, jointly established by Children for Breastfeeding Inc. and Nurturers of the Earth Inc.) as an institutional partner of the DOH for the education and training regulation of lactation consultants, breastfeeding counselors, health workers and breastfeeding advocates. Further, the DOH affirmed the PLRTC as an accredited Monitoring Entity for the enforcement of the Milk Code and its revised IRR. Further also, the DOH endorsed the course offered by PLRTC titled "Breastfeeding, Infant and Young Child Feeding and Care: Reviving Indigenous Nurturing Practices."

To make sure that all physicians and health workers follow the law, the Arroyo Administration launched the DOH's "Guidelines for Physicians for the Promotion, Protection and Support of Breastfeeding" on May 17, 2010. DOH Secretary Esperanza I. Cabral also issued in June 2010 the "Guidelines for the Inter-Agency Committee on the Revised Implementing Rules and Regulations of EO 51" to make sure there will be no exemptions to the National Policy of regulating milk advertisements and nutritional claims directed toward infants and children up to three years of age.

**IV.    Guinness World Records, Synchronized Breastfeeding Worldwide**

Because the P2 billion annual advertising budget of

the milk companies have exerted enough influence on the media to impose a news blackout on issues affecting breastfeeding, the breastfeeding advocates were forced to accept the advice of news editors who said that no advertiser can shut out news from (a) the front pages, (b) the international news agencies, (c) the Internet, (d) independent opinion makers, and (e) paid advertisements.

On May 4, 2006, in partnership with the City of Manila, Children for Breastfeeding Inc. and Nurturers of the Earth Inc., the Department of Health and UNICEF Philippines was accorded recognition by the Guinness World Record Ltd., for having broken the world record for the Most Number of Mothers Simultaneously Breastfeeding in a Single Site with 3,541 mothers in the City of Manila.

On August 25, 2006, the Department of Environment and Natural Resources, Green Army Philippines and Green Philippine Highways with the participation of Children for Breastfeeding, Inc. and Nurturers of the Earth Inc., was accorded recognition by the Guinness World Record Ltd. for having broken the world record for the Most Trees Simultaneously Planted in Multiple Sites, 653,143 trees by 516,317 citizen-volunteers along 3,917.83 kilometers of National Highways. When Secretary Angelo Reyes of the Department of Environment and Natural Resources was told that "a woman's breast is the nation's greatest natural resource and is worth your support," he responded by promising to plant food-bearing trees to support the movement to promote indigenous foods for complementary feeding in place of cow's milk.

On May 2, 2007, in partnership with the Department of Social Welfare and Development, and the Technical Education and Skills Development Authority (TESDA), Children for Breastfeeding Inc. and Nurturers of the Earth Inc., established the world record for Most Number of Mothers Simultaneously Breastfeeding in Multiple Sites with 15,128 mothers in 295 sites nationwide, as audited by Sycip, Gorres and Velayo accounting firm.

On August 8, 2007, Children for Breastfeeding, Inc. and Nurturers of the Earth in partnership with the World Alliance for Breastfeeding Action (WABA), conducted for the first time in the history of the world, the Synchronized Breastfeeding

Worldwide (SBW) with the participation of 16 countries, in 24 time zones, at 10 AM local time, over a period of 24 hours, like the celebration of New Year on the same day.

Yesterday, Manila,  today, the Philippines, and forever, the entire World, for the breastfeeding advocacy, as attested by 2008 Year 2, and 2009 Year 3 of the Synchronized Breastfeeding Worldwide.

Since 2007, the President hosted the launch of Synchronized Breastfeeding Worldwide in Malacanang.  On its second year 2008,  the launch was held in Beijing, China during the Olympics and was dubbed  as "Breastfeeding Olympics." With breastfeeding Chinese mothers in attendance, the Filipino athletes and the Filipino community, the President also gave an award to the Chinese policewoman who breastfed 9 babies after the Szechuan earthquake on behalf of WABA.  With the strict regulations of the Chinese government on crowd control, this was a phenomenal feat!

Some of the event's goals are:

• To establish the event as a form of universal prayer for peace and thanksgiving for the gift of motherhood and breastfeeding.

• To elevate the status of breastfeeding as a social norm and a status symbol even among professionals and the upper class.

• To encourage mothers to sustain breastfeeding as they attend the affair every year and reach the goal to breastfeed beyond two years.

**V.   Ripple Effect:   Breastfeeding Stations in SM Supermalls, Bare-Breasted Virgin**

After an incident in a mall wherein a courageous, empowered, single mother named Elizabeth Cariño quarreled with a guard who insisted she breastfeed her baby in the comfort room, Henares-Esguerra's reaction was: "It is about time that breasts are considered, not as sex objects to stimulate men's libido, but as the provider of food and nourishment for the future citizens of the land as God meant them to be."  She added that her father told her that in the 82 years that he has been a movie addict he has yet to see a Hollywood movie showing mothers breastfeeding their infants, because the Catholic League of

Decency and the Hays Office objected to them. Instead, bottle-feeding with cow's milk has been the norm, even in Walt Disney movies.

One of the most tender and moving scenes in literature, the climax of the novel *Grapes of Wrath* by John Steinbeck, wherein the heroine after losing her own baby, fed a starving old man from her breasts – was excised from the movie version because of the public outcry. Barbara Walters, the famous journalist, was outraged that a mother seated beside her in an airplane, breastfed her baby without hiding her breast. The head of Makati Medical Center, confronted with a statue of the Virgin Mary suckling Baby Jesus, kept putting a napkin over her breast. The Catholic Bishops and Mayor Atienza asked that breastfeeding babies be hidden from public view. "It is about time we react," Henares-Esguerra said.

Convincing (a) Catholic *Cardinal* Ricardo Vidal to approve the layout of Mama Mary bare-breastfeeding Baby Jesus, (b) SM Supermalls to allow nursing mothers to breastfeed anywhere and at any time in all their malls (the Breastfeeding Stations are for those who want privacy) and (c) the City of Manila to break the Guinness World Record, resulting in publicity of a plethora of women baring their breasts everywhere in the Internet, on television and print media all over the world -- have the greatest effect of all.

Suddenly we see pictures of bare breasts of nursing mothers being shown everywhere without the usual protests by religious leaders and self-appointed moral guardians. The breast should not be a sex object to stimulate libido. As the source of nutrition for babies, it is not only natural, it is desirable and ennobling. A US senator even introduced amendments to the Nudity Law allowing the baring of breasts for breastfeeding.

On March 14, 2006, SM Supermalls partnered with Children for Breastfeeding, Inc. and Nurturers of the Earth, Inc. to set up Breastfeeding Stations in all its 34 SM malls serving tens of thousands of mother-child pairs nationwide.

Most gratifying of all is the regular inauguration of Breastfeeding Stations in each and every one of the 34 SM Supermalls in the country, three of which is among the 11 largest in the world. It is a whole day affair that starts from 7:00 AM up to 10:00 AM, when Children for Breastfeeding and

Nurturers of the Earth speak to some 100 to 300 SM employees that includes (1) the Maintenance Crew and janitors, (2) the Security Force, (3) Mall tenants, and (4) Administrative staff. Then the Supermall opens up to the public, while the non-government organization (NGO) leaders are entertained and given a tour. After lunch at 1:00 PM to 3:00 PM, the NGOs continue to give lectures to pregnant and nursing mothers from communities around the SM Supermall including the SM clients and those invited by the NGOs. Then at 3:00 PM to 5:00 PM, the formal program and launching of the Breastfeeding Station occurs.

Convincing SM Supermalls to build Breastfeeding Stations was a wonderful way to get businessmen to realize that they have a Social Responsibility to the family and the people. Businessmen like Ramon Jacinto offered the use of his radio and TV studio for the movement free of charge and Washington Sycip lent the services and facilities of Sycip, Gorres and Velayo accounting firm to audit, pro-bono three Guinness Record attempts.

Eventually, Republic Act 10028 or the "Expanded Breastfeeding Promotion Act of 2009," signed by President Arroyo last March 16, now provides tax incentives to all government agencies and private establishments that provide lactation stations for working mothers.

Eventually, on June 23, 2008, three years after Ricardo *Cardinal* Vidal approved the baring of the breasts of the Blessed Mother, the official Vatican organ, L'Osservatore Romano, called for artists to depict the Blessed Mother baring her breasts to feed Baby Jesus, to emphasize the humanity of the Son of God, that truly, the Word was made Flesh.

### VI. Virgin Mother's 12 Apostles, and other Exhibits

On the second WBW celebration in Malacañang on August 14, 2006, Children for Breastfeeding, Inc. and Nurturers of the Earth, Inc launched two Photo Exhibits: "Beauty, Brains and Breastfeeding," by Henares-Esguerra's cousin, Pancho Escaler; and "Apostles of the Virgin Mary," by Blow-Up Babies Photo Studio of Henares-Esguerra's nephew, Quark Henares. Both exhibits depict role models for breastfeeding mothers, which were formally launched in Malacañang, then toured in all

SM Supermalls, in Congress (both Senate and the House) during hearings on Breastfeeding, government offices, schools, hospitals and many other venues.

The Photo Exhibits of Role Models in the Breastfeeding Movement, who are rich, beautiful, glamorous working mothers, serve to convince the hoi-poloi (the common masses) that breastfeeding is a privilege, more than an obligation, that bottle-feeding is NOT acceptable even to those who are educated and who could afford the expense of formula milk, and that working outside the home is not an obstacle to breastfeeding.

Above all, they give a positive image of a breastfeeding mother, with full and erect breasts that elicit envy and admiration battling the myth that breastfeeding can disfigure a woman's body. For this, UNICEF Philippines issued a heartfelt Commendation to Children for Breastfeeding, Inc.

The Breastfeeding Movement is fortunate in being able to partner with Marissa Gonzales, also known as "Marigonz," a multi-awarded jewelry designer and an internationally acclaimed artist, who represented the Philippines at the 2007 Global Art Exhibit in Vienna, Austria, with her artworks exhibited in prestigious museums and galleries in Great Britain, Italy, Netherlands, Germany, Belgium, Luxembourg, USA, Brazil and such cities as London, San Francisco, and Amsterdam, who made available her inventory of more than 100 paintings depicting women's breasts and other subjects, as well as jewelries "for a cause," such as movement bracelets, movement pendants and movement key chains, intending to sell these artworks here and abroad, to help fund the Children for Breastfeeding, Inc. and her own advocacy, Philippine Art Central for Community Empowerment foundation. Such paintings have been twice exhibited in Malacañang Palace, preparatory to bringing them abroad for marketing.

There is also a series of exhibits depicting the "Seven Acts of Kindness" that children are urged to follow to provide community support for breastfeeding mothers.

Appropriate awards were also given in the presence of the President for such role models as the Breastfeeding Queen, Dr. Susann Roth, Breastfed Princess Mikaela Fudolig (16-year old *summa cum laude* from UP), Breastfed Princess

Sierra Isabelle A. Castillo (scholar and member of the UP Singing Ambassadors) and the five Breastfed Princes, the Tagala Brothers (Jonathan, David, Jimmy, Daniel and Samuel) who each play several musical instruments; and other awards for Public Health Initiatives.

### VII. Mobilizing Government and non-Government Organizations

Under the Macapagal-Arroyo administration, breastfeeding advocates like Henares-Esguerra and Andaya-Castillo find themselves inextricably linked in partnership with Secretary Francisco T. Duque III's Department of Health and Dr. Nicholas K. Alipui's UNICEF Philippines. Through the President's support, their partnership with government agencies that were seemingly remote from their advocacy became possible. It also created a ripple effect on their partnership/networking with other sectors:

1. National agencies like Secretary Jesli Lapus' Department of Education, Secretary Esperanza I. Cabral's Department of Social Welfare and Development, Secretary Angelo Reyes' Department of Environment and Natural Resources, Secretary Boboy Syjuco's Technical Education and Skills Development Authority (TESDA), Secretary Carlito Puno's Commission on Higher Education and Development (CHED), the National Anti-Poverty Commission (NAPC), Lorna Fajardo's PhilHealth Insurance, Cecile B. Gutierrez's TESDA Women's Center, Ricardo Saludo's Civil Service Commission, Cerge Remonde's Philippine Information Agency, Office of President Gloria Arroyo in Malacañang -- dealing directly with their highest officials.

2. Legislative bodies like the Senate Committee on Health and Demography, the House Committee on Health, the House Committee on Trade and Investment, all the senators and many Congressmen and women – appearing in most of their public hearings.

3. Local government organizations like Mayor Atienza's City of Manila and James Marty Lim's Liga ng mga Barangay sa Pilipinas, Ben Hur Abalos' Union of Local Authorities of the Philippines (ULAP), League of Mayors, City of Baguio.

**4.** Church organizations like the Catholic Bishops Conference, the Protestant United Churches of Christ, the Buddhist Universal Wisdom Foundation, and others.

**5.** Professional Associations with whom Henares-Esguerra has signed Memoranda of Agreement, or is affiliated with -- such as Philippine Pharmaceutical Association, La Salle University Medical Association, Philippine Medical Association, the UERM Medical Center which recognized Henares-Esguerra as one of the Fifty Most Outstanding Alumni in the 50 years of its existence in 2007, and the UERM Alumni Association which recognized Henares-Esguerra as one of the three Most Outstanding Public Health Advocates in Community Work in 2008. Henares-Esguerra also organized the Philippine Academy of Lactation Consultants, an affiliate society of the Philippine Medical Association, which is composed of multi-specialty professionals. She organized this group to be able to get the support of the doctors and to have a venue for Continuing Medical Education on lactation.

**6.** Non-Government Organizations with whom Henares-Esguerra signed Memoranda of Agreement or have Joint Projects with -- like Environmental Studies Institute, *Bantay Kalikasan*, Father James B. Reuter of the Catholic Media, Sister Pilar Verzosa of the Pro-Life Movement, Our Lady of La Leche Movement's Remedios Gonzales, Lola Grande Foundation for Women and Children headed by Sylvia Lichauco de Leon, four Rotary Clubs, SM Supermalls, DZRJ and RJTV, NU-107, among many others; Jaycee International Senate which together with the Department of Health, PhilHealth and Philippine Charity Sweepstakes Office, recognized Henares-Esguerra as one of the Ten Outstanding Filipino Physicians of 2008; Soroptimist International Philippines Region voted Henares-Esguerra as the national awardee for the 2010 Ruby Award for Women Helping Women; and Tintin Bersola-Babao for choosing both Henares-Esguerra and Andaya-Castillo as recipients of the Parentin NATURE award for their exemplary contribution to a back to basics way of nurturing our children and dedicated work in the field of parenting.

**7.** International Organizations with whom Henares-Esguerra signed Memoranda of Agreement, such as UNICEF Philippines, Guinness World Record Ltd.; World Alliance for

Breastfeeding Action (WABA, Malaysia, which awarded Henares-Esguerra and Andaya-Castillo each a Gold Medal for their organizations for launching the  Breastfeeding Olympics in Beijing and other breastfeeding advocacy activities in 2008); Framework Convention Alliance (Mary Assunta, Geneva); Public Health Advocacy (Richard Daynard, Boston); Global Alliance for Incinerator Alternatives (GAIA); International Baby Food Action Network; and Soroptimist International of the Americas for choosing Henares-Esguerra as one of the three finalists for the Ruby International Award of 2010 - Women Helping Women.

**8.** The Science Community, embodied by Secretary Estrella F. Alabastro's Department of Science and Technology, Mensa Philippines, and the Philippine Science High School, for evidence-based scientific research, largely through the efforts of Children for Breastfeeding's new Science Officer, Balik-Scientist Custer C. Deocaris, PhD.

**9.** Individuals who supported the IRR with their signatures, gathered by Children for Breastfeeding and Nurturers of the Earth, more than 800 of them, including President Fidel V. Ramos, 20 out of 23 senators, 76 Congressmen, Bro. Mike Velarde of El Shaddai, all of the bishops of the Catholic Bishops Conference, the Buddhist Foundation including two Tibetan monks, ex-Solicitor General Francisco Chavez.

Also, the NGOs have conducted lectures in such varied organizations like Philippine Air Force, the Association of Pathologists, Miriam and Assumption Colleges, and medical centers like PGH, St. Luke's and the World City Medical Center; ZOTO and PRRM.

**VIII. Presidential Awards for Pioneering Breastfeeding Advocates:**

President Gloria Macapagal-Arroyo has seen it fit to honor pioneering breastfeeding advocates in their 90s, as Dr. Natividad R. Clavano who stunned the world with a 10,000-baby study in Baguio General Hospital that proved that exclusive breastfeeding resulted in a 95% drop in infant morbidity and mortality, and inspired Senator Edward M. Kennedy's Subcommittee on Health to demand that WHO/UNICEF sponsor the 1981 International Code on the Marketing of

Breastmilk Substitutes and other Related Products; Ms. Manuela G. Maramba, the first nutritionist in the Philippines who spoke against the importation of milk after World War II on the grounds that we can grow our own indigenous foods with higher nutritional value without being addicted to imported milk;  Dr. Fe del Mundo, iconic woman doctor who graduated from Harvard Medical School, pioneer pediatrician and national scientist.  And the President also spoke of others worthy of her Presidential award, such as Senator Edward M. Kennedy of Massachusetts, and Dr. Nicholas K. Alipui of UNICEF in the following speech:

PRESIDENT GLORIA MACAPAGAL ARROYO'S SPEECH DURING THE

2009 WORLD BREASTFEEDING CELEBRATION
Heroes Hall, Malacañang, August 27, 2009

Thank you. Thank you, Boboy for your introduction. Our other Cabinet members: Espie and Jing. And we have, I see too, former Cabinet members in our audience, my Dad's NEC chairman, the former NEDA Larry Henares, and former DOT Secretary Tony Gonzales. Congresswoman Bondoc, City Mayor Bautista, Elvira and the other leaders of the Breastfeeding Movement, ladies and gentlemen:

Welcome to Malacañang on this year's celebration of World Breastfeeding Month!  Since our proclamation in 2005, every year, we have held a program in Malacañan Palace to celebrate this very important month for mothers and infants. We do it to show our endorsement of the most economical way to nourish infants. We do it to support natural family planning practices because breastfeeding is indeed a safe method of natural family planning. We do it because we want only the best for the Filipino child, and that includes the best source of baby's nutrition -- mother's milk.

Breastfeeding as you have heard from our Department of Health representative is part of our five-year national program for Infants and Young Child Feeding. And for this cause let me say that our mentor is a gentleman I mentioned earlier, Larry Henares, my late father's chairman of the National Economic Council.

It is not only women who can be advocates of the breastfeeding movement. In fact, aside from Secretary Henares, there is an outstanding American gentleman who played a key role in the international movement to make people aware, more aware of the benefits of breastfeeding. We offer the deepest sympathies of the Filipino people to the family of that gentleman, the late U.S. Senator Edward Kennedy, who just passed away yesterday. And it is fitting we hold this celebration today also to commemorate his memory and his contributions.

Senator Kennedy, Edward Kennedy was the youngest of the famous Kennedy brothers who contributed much to the U.S. advancement in human rights, in standing up to the Soviets during the Cold War, and in asserting the superiority of democracy over totalitarianism. Aside from what he did in common with his brothers, among Senator Edward Kennedy's greatest achievements were accomplished as chairman of the U.S. Senate Committee on Health, Education, Labor and Pensions. In this role he served the Philippines and the world when he chaired a session in 1979, that is 30 years ago, of the U.S. Senate Sub-Committee on Health to hear the testimony of a Filipina doctor, Dr. Natividad Clavano, about a 10,000-baby study on the experiences of the General Hospital in Baguio City. The study had shown a 95 percent decrease in infant mortality as the result of exclusive breastfeeding.

Reacting to this and related findings, Senator Edward Kennedy hurled a challenge to the World Health Organization. In two years' time, the WHO formulated the International Code on the Marketing of Breastmilk Substitutes and other Related Products.

For his singular role in promoting human rights and public health, including the passage of that International Milk Code, we honor the late Senator Edward Kennedy. And we will soon present to his family our highest Presidential award, through Special Envoy Dr. Elvira Lichauco Henares-Esguerra for the public health component of the award and Presidential Adviser Sonny Alvarez for the human rights component of the award.

We also recall the pivotal role played by Dr. Nicholas Alipui, who was in the audio visuals today, former UNICEF country representative to the Philippines and now the programme director of the UNICEF, his role was large in promoting breastfeeding in our country. So, also through Elvira, our special envoy, we will be awarding him the Order of the Golden Cross, rank of Maringal na Krus.

But, these are the men who have helped us very much in the breastfeeding movement. But let us not forget the women. We further commend Elvira and Dr. Nona Castillo for their herculean efforts, in fact, they have been behind the revival of interest in breastfeeding in the country. We also thank my cabalen Congresswoman Anna York Bondoc for today in the Philippines though we have a Milk Code, we have to strengthen that with a strong implementing rules and regulations which the Supreme Court has upheld. And now, thanks to the efforts in Congress of Anna, hopefully, those implementing rules and regulations can be institutionalized into a revised Milk Code.

Through the efforts of Larry, Elvira, Nona, Anna, our Cabinet members here, the breastfeeding movement has gained a lot of supporters in our country, including those in disaster prevention and mitigation -- and earlier, Elvira already acknowledged them -- the boy scouts, the nurses, the policemen, the firemen from different walks of life, that seem to have nothing to do with breastfeeding but a lot to do with disaster response. There is so much support for breastfeeding that, as pointed out earlier by Elvira, we even won the Guinness World Records for several first in breastfeeding. So, congratulations for all of that!

The more advocates we have, the stronger the movement becomes to reach out and convince every mother to breastfeed their child. The mothers who are the staunchest supporters of this movement are willing to breastfeed even infants who are not their own. We saw earlier the heroic effort, the heroic role that the Chinese policewoman played after the Sichuan earthquakes, when she breastfed nine of the surviving babies. Without her breastfeeding other mother's babies, those babies would also have perished in the aftermath of that earthquake. That is why, as you saw also in the audio visual, we presented to her the World Breastfeeding Gold Medal Award in Beijing last year.

So, once again, in closing, I thank and congratulate all of you for your support and leadership in the breastfeeding movement. And together, our message to the Philippines is -- and this is a message that was carried by our media because they always carry my speeches:

*Muli, tinatawagan natin ang sambayanan: suportahan*

*nating lahat ang Breastfeeding Movement. Ang gatas ng ina ay mas matipid at mas masustansya. Nakakatipid tayo, nakakatulong tayo sa natural family planning, at higit sa lahat mas nakasisiguro tayo na magiging malusog at matalino ang ating mga sanggol at anak." Mabuhay ang mga ina at mga sanggol ng Pilipinas! Maraming salamat sa inyong lahat.*

(Again, we call on the people, let us all support the Breastfeeding Movement. Mother's milk is less expensive and it is more nutritious. We save a lot, we also help in natural family planning and best of all, we can be sure that our infants and children will be healthier and brighter.

(Long live the mothers and children of the Philippines! Thank you very much to all of you!)

**IX. Urgent Legislative Measures and other Public Health Initiatives**

Having already enacted the Revised Implementing Rules and Regulations of EO 51 (National Code), the President wanted it to be enacted into law to ensure that no future administration may tamper with it for the benefit of milk companies, by certifying it as an urgent legislation.

The Breastfeeding Bill, which passed on third reading as House Bill No. 7022 "Infant and Young Child Feeding Act of 2009" (sponsored by Congresswoman Anna York Bondoc) adopted *in toto* [without change] in the Senate Committee Report No. 837 (sponsored by Senator Maria Ana Consuelo "Jamby" A. Madrigal), and certified urgent by President Gloria Macapagal Arroyo, supported by DOH, WHO and UNICEF and its constitutionality affirmed by the Supreme Court, was denied passage in the Senate during the *sine die* session on Friday June 4, 2010 based on a note objecting to it that turned out to be bogus.

The note, purportedly from Senator Pimentel, Senate Minority Floor Leader, who was absent at that time, was passed to Senator Miguel Zubiri, Senate Majority Floor Leader, relaying his objections against the bill. Respecting Senator Pimentel's will, Senator Zubiri, decided to lay aside consideration of the bill. However, Pimentel later denied that he was against the bill when he was frantically called by Congresswoman Anna York Bondoc, author of the House version.

On quite another matter, the legislative measure mandating the placement of **Graphic Warnings on labels of tobacco products**, as required by the Framework Convention on Tobacco Control which was ratified by the Philippine Senate in 2005, and supported by the President and the breastfeeding advocates, also failed to pass the legislature again and again due to opposition of the tobacco companies and industry.

To protect pregnant and breastfeeding mothers in particular, the public and environmental health in general, HEAL the Philippines' Hilarion "Larry" M. Henares Jr. led the organizing of an Inter-NGO support activity for the launching of the DOH Guidelines mandating the placement of graphic warnings on labels of tobacco products.

### X.  CONCLUSION: A Tribute for the President

This White Paper ends appropriately with a summarization of the accomplishments of the Arroyo Administration, in a speech of Special Envoy Dr. Elvira L. Henares-Esguerra, MD, FPDS, FABM, IBCLC, RPh:

Launching of the DOH Guidelines

for Physicians for the Promotion, Protection and Support for Breastfeeding

Presentation of the Memorandum of Agreement between DOST

and Children for Breastfeeding, Inc.

Malacañang Palace, May 17, 2010

President Gloria Macapagal-Arroyo, doctors and scientists, fellow breastfeeding and public health advocates, officials of the Department of Health and the Department of Science and Technology, and friends:

Today, we stand here as witness to a historic age, a golden age when one president's compassion and political will has reversed twenty years of frustration to usher in a new direction for Breastfeeding and Public Health, emphasizing the importance of optimal infant and young child feeding practices, its crucial role in national development and the means to reach our targets for the Millennium Development Goals of significantly reducing maternal mortality and the deaths of children under the age of five.  Many people, mostly doctors and scientists, have come here to support the breastfeeding movement.  We would like to let you know how President Gloria Macapagal Arroyo's support has empowered us to save the breastfeeding culture from the brink of extinction.

It started in 2005 with her issuance of Presidential Proclamation No. 1113, promulgating the Yearly Celebration of World Breastfeeding Week on August 1 to 7; the launching of the National Plan of Action on Infant and Young Child Feeding 2005-2010; a huge budget for the Hunger Mitigation Program providing funds for trainings and educational materials on breastfeeding; peaked with the issuance of the Revised Implementing Rules and Regulations of EO 51 in 2006, affirmed by the Supreme Court in 2007, bolstered by the Inter-Agency Guidelines of 2010 and the Department of Health Guidelines for Physicians on the Promotion, Protection and Support of Breastfeeding, that allow no exemptions to the National Policy of regulating milk advertisements for children up to three years of age, and forbidding nutritional claims that undermine breastfeeding; and climaxed with Presidential Awards honoring those who contributed to the Breastfeeding Movement here and abroad: Senator Edward M. Kennedy, Dr. Fe del Mundo, Dr. Natividad R. Clavano, Ms. Manuela G. Maramba, and Dr. Nicholas K. Alipui of UNICEF.

Thanks to your support, Madam President, we have averted the rapid decline of breastfeeding rates. Thanks to your support, the number of children who were never breastfed decreased from 13.2 % in 2003 to only 8% by 2008 and the duration of exclusive breastfeeding increased almost 4 times, from 24 days to almost 90 days. Thanks to your support, our country even received recognition from Save the Children as the first, the Number One, among 55 developing countries in providing basic health care to children cited in the State of the World's Mothers Report in 2007. Thanks to your support, the Philippine leaders of the breastfeeding movement also garnered national and international recognition for their dedication and commitment. But in view of the urgency of meeting our Millennium Development Goals, there is still much to be done.

We will exert all efforts to inform the public of their right to breastfeed inside and outside health facilities. The government has done its part. It is about time that we doctors live up to our responsibility. I am saying this because, the

National Demographic and Health Survey (NDHS) has shown that children born at home are more likely to breastfeed within an hour than those delivered in hospitals and health centers by doctors and health professionals, while 81 percent of breastfed children and only 48 percent of formula-fed children from 6 months to 2 years of age, are fed as frequently as recommended.

To address this, Health Secretary Esperanza I. Cabral compiled and codified all laws and regulations on Breastfeeding under the DOH Guidelines for Physicians for the promotion, protection, and support of Breastfeeding -- an epochal step that will mandate every physician to uphold Breastfeeding in their practice, according to the recommendations of the World Health Organization, UNICEF and our National Policies.

May I now call on Undersecretary Alexander A. Padilla, to join me in presenting to you the DOH Guidelines.

Presentation of the DOH Guidelines for Physicians for the promotion, protection,

and support of Breastfeeding to the President.

Thank you Undersecretary Padilla. Madame President, the Department of Science and Technology and the Children for Breastfeeding Inc., signed a Memorandum of Understanding through the assistance of Balik-Scientist Dr. Custer C. Deocaris when he joined our ranks. This Memorandum with DOST will strengthen the connection between the breastfeeding movement and the scientific community. We will encourage more evidence-based researches on the wonders of breastmilk and breastfeeding and independent peer reviews to verify the nutritional claims of milk companies involving all specialties of the medical profession.

May I now call on Sec. Estrella F. Alabastro and Director Jaime C. Montoya of the Department of Science and Technology to join me in presenting to you our Memorandum.

Presentation of the Memorandum of Understanding to the President

Thank you Sec. Alabastro and Director Montoya. Madam President, under your administration, we in the Philippines have established the best breastfeeding legal system in the world. We continue to build our castles in the air to the end that the Breastfeeding Movement may engulf all the rest of the nations worldwide, as the cheapest and most far- reaching strategy for the alleviation of poverty, and as the Social Capital that will ensure the life-long health and well-being, the emotional stability and intellectual development of the future citizens of this planet.  We build our castles in the air and continue to build foundations under them.

We continue to plead, plan, plot, and build -- hammer, hack, hold and build – push, pull, push and build -- and build and build and build, up to the stars till the universe shall know of our strength.  So that when all the stories have been told and all the songs have been sung, and all there is to be has become, we the Breastfeeding advocates of today may well turn to the children of tomorrow and say, we have not lived in vain.  We have not lived in vain.

To our Breastfeeding Champion, the Most Breastfeeding-friendly President thus far, *maraming, maraming salamat po Madame President! Mabuhay kayo, Mabuhay ang Pilipinas!* **To God be the Glory!** Thank you very much to all!

### XI.  The Non-Government Organizations' Profiles
### Children for Breastfeeding, Inc.

Children for Breastfeeding, Inc. was conceptualized by two breastfeeding advocates and International Board Certified Lactation Consultants (IBCLC) Elvira L. Henares-Esguerra, MD, FPDS, FABM, IBCLC, RPh (President, Children for Breastfeeding) and Nona D. Andaya-Castillo, IBCLC and Director, Nurturers of the Earth.

Since 1996, Nona had helped hundreds of mothers breastfeed their children and had been monitoring the violations of milk companies and medical professionals against the laws that protect breastfeeding. While Elvira was pregnant with her third child Larry, she met Nona and requested for her professional services. The two became very close friends and are now working as partners in promoting, protecting and supporting breastfeeding.

In 2002, the IBCLCs established the First Breastfeeding Clinic in a private hospital in the Philippines for indigent patients. They had observed that parents were unaware of the risks of formula feeding. Even if they were made aware of it, many resorted to mixed feeding and consequently, full formula feeding due to strong social pressure and massive advertisements that deceive mothers to believe that formula milk can replace mother's milk. There were 27 mothers who showed up during the first class and only one was breastfeeding! The following week, that sole mother was told by her doctor to stop breastfeeding due to the medication that the doctor prescribed.

Alarmed by the realization that the formula feeding culture is so deeply ingrained, they saw the need to educate children, the future generation of parents on the superiority of breastfeeding. The exposure of children to mothers who breastfeed will help them internalize that breastfeeding is the norm, the gold standard in infant and young child feeding. A concrete example is when children breastfeed their dolls when they see their mothers breastfeed. Hopefully, this will instill in their young minds that breastfeeding is the most natural and beautiful way of nurturing, when they become parents themselves.

The IBCLCs put up Children for Breastfeeding, Inc., an organization that promotes breastfeeding to children and youth by mobilizing them to perform the **Seven Acts of Kindness to Pregnant and Breastfeeding Mothers**. They were both inspired by the way Elvira's older children Angelí and Gabriel, supported her during her pregnancy, birthing and breastfeeding Larry. Children for Breastfeeding won the 2003 International Ford Conservation and Environmental Grants with their project: Mobilizing Children to Promote Earth-friendly Parenting. Their family story was documented in a film titled "Waiting for the Fifth Player" that was shown by the Catholic Media during the Fourth World Meeting of Families in Manila, January 2003.

### Nurturers of the Earth, Inc.!

Nurturers of the Earth is a support group for vegetarians and earth-friendly parenting. It organizes events, meet-ups and cooking classes for vegetarians and those who want to become vegetarians.

There are two types of members: Vegetarians and Vegetarians-in-Progress (VIP). The group was started by Nona D. Andaya-Castillo, an International Board Certified Lactation Consultant (IBCLC) in 2004 who has been a vegetarian since May 1991. Many of her patients as a lactation consultant were told by their doctors to stop breastfeeding because either they were sick or their babies were sick.  Wanting to breastfeed, these mothers agreed to change their lifestyles and went into natural healing using food and massage as medicine.  Later on, applicants from other sectors have joined the group and attended their events.

**Philippine Lactation Resource and Training Center**
TESDA Women's Center, Gate 1, TESDA Complex
East Service Rd., SLEX, Taguig City, Philippines
(632) 701-4429 and (632) 701-4430
thebreastfeedingclinic@yahoo.com.ph
www.breastfeedingphilippines.com

**HEAL the Philippines Foundation**

**Henares Environmental Action and Livelihood for the Philippines**

HEAL the Philippines was established by the family of Hilarion M. Henares Jr. to advocate for protection of the environment and response to climate change; to promote, protect and support Public Health initiatives, especially for breastfeeding as the least costly strategy for the alleviation of poverty and as the Social Capital to ensure the life-long health and well-being, the intellectual development and emotional stability of the future citizens of this nation and this planet; to build infrastructures and establish programs for community-based livelihood activities; to provide scholarships to poor but deserving students;  to advocate Consumer Protection against Corporate Greed.

It was established to perpetuate the memory of Cecilia Roensch Lichauco-Henares, the late wife of Hilarion (Larry), business-woman (toys, children's costumes, stock-market, real estate), who all her life spent her resources giving aid to the disabled, and sending indigent children through high school and college, on condition that she was not told who her beneficiaries are, and they are not told who their benefactress was.  HEAL the Philippines Foundation was set up by her children and their spouses: Ronnie and Ida, Atom and Vicki, Elvira and Bert Esguerra, Danby and Kim, Juno and Tonichi Chuidian, Rosanna and Eric Angeles.

ooooo

# CHAPTER THREE:
# Prince Mahidol Award Nomination Form

**I. NOMINEE: Dr. Elvira L. Henares-Esguerra, MD, FPDS, RPh, IBCLC**
**Director, Children for Breastfeeding, Inc.**

**II. MAILING ADDRESS**     Please check the box
Office     **Home  X**
Address:     **2198 Paraiso Street,    Dasmarinas Village**
City     **Makati  City,   Metro Manila**
Country     **Philippines**
Postal Code **1222**
Phone     **(632)  844  2390     (632)  671  3143**
TeleFax     **(632)  810  3372     (632)  671  6258**
e-Mail     **larryh@mydestiny.net**
**larryh@zpdee.net**
**children_for_breastfeeding@yahoo.com**

**III. STATEMENT OF THE NATURE OF THE WORK AND ITS RELEVANCE TO THE OBJECTIVES OF THE AWARD**
We are honored to nominate Elvira L. Henares-Esguerra, 52 years of age, natural born Filipino, for The Prince Mahidol Award on the strength of her character, integrity and dedication to the medical profession, and the impact of her advocacy of **breastfeeding, pro-life, earth-friendly parenting and environmental protection** to the national development in general and to public welfare in particular. **Dr. Elvira is a Public Health Advocate of Breastfeeding**, which is considered an urgent imperative by the United Nations, WHO, UNICEF and by the Official National Policy of at least 181 countries of the world.

Most doctors achieved success in their one chosen field, earning the patronage of their patients and the admiration of their peers. Elvira is not one of them. She is involved in many fields: a pharmacist (University of the Philippines Diliman), a doctor of medicine (University of the East Ramon Magsaysay Memorial Medical Center), a dermatologist (Makati Medical Center), and an International Board Certified Lactation Consultant (a well-established profession in countries like the USA, Australia, Canada).  But she spent the first years of her adult life being a mother and a housewife, who was unable to breastfeed her first two children for as long as she wanted to because hospital practices and her friends did not encourage her to do so.  By the time her third child was born, she became a stronger breastfeeding advocate and asserted her rights, knowing that Breastfeeding is best for her child.  Aware that Breastfeeding is not merely a **gender** issue that does not excite the interest of the national leaders, Elvira emphasized and campaigned that Breastfeeding is a **public health** issue, an **economic** issue, an **ecology** issue, a **political** issue, and above all, a **human rights** issue, that should move the national leaders to be informed, to be concerned, and to be involved.

It is a **public health** issue because breastfeeding is the gold standard that provides immunity from childhood diseases, and contains nutrients that guarantee health, emotional stability and intellectual development that no breastmilk substitutes could ever hope to provide.

It is an **economic issue** because breastfeeding is the most far-reaching and cheapest strategy for the alleviation of poverty, and while breastmilk is free and inexhaustible, massive importation of cow's milk and milk products divert resources that might have been used to encourage agricultural production of indigenous foods more nutritious than cow's milk, and build more educational and housing facilities.

It is an **ecology** issue because breastfeeding does not require clean water, fuel, non-biodegradable containers as breastmilk substitutes do.

It is a **political** issue because it pits powerful multinational corporations, oftentimes with the help of the US government, against weak governments and  breastfeeding advocates.

Above all, it is a **human rights issue** because it addresses the issue of the right of women to equality and empowerment, and the right of children, as defined in the Convention on the Rights of the Child, to the best nutrition and care available, and finally because it provides the SOCIAL

CAPITAL by which the future citizens of the world may survive, prosper, and contribute to the betterment of all humankind.

The malpractices and unethical marketing methods of milk companies have largely resulted in almost total loss of the breastfeeding culture in the modern world especially in the poorest nations that can ill afford it, and has resulted in the epidemic of juvenile diabetes, allergic reactions, life threatening diarrhea, and chronic diseases such as obesity, adult diabetes and vascular disease, caused by lack of breastfeeding. *This sad state of affairs resulted in the frantic efforts of the World Health Organization and the UNICEF to promulgate the:*

*1.    1981 **International Code** on the Marketing of Breastmilk Substitutes and Related Products," to which all nations in the world now subscribe;*

*2.    2002 **Global Strategy** on Infant and Young Child Feeding;*

*3.    Various World Health Assembly Resolutions that are passed upon by Health Ministers of all nations.*

*Earlier, the 1990 **Innocenti Declaration**, and the 1990 **Convention on the Rights of the Child** were ratified by more nations than any international agreement in the history of the world. This has also precipitated a **worldwide boycott of Nestle and Wyeth** Nutritionals that started in 1939, waxed off and on, and is still in full effect today.*

President Corazon Aquino under the Freedom Constitution, signed into law the National Code on the Marketing of Breastmilk Substitutes and other Related Products (Executive Order or EO 51) in 1986 as a sign of commitment to the International Code, but for the next 20 years, this national law whose spirit is to protect breastfeeding, was honored more in the breach than in the observance, because there were no Revised Implementing Rules and Regulations (RIRR) with teeth strong enough to enforce it in the face of blatant violations by milk companies.   The Bureau of Food and Drugs had been conducting public hearings that were never scheduled publicly. Under the watchful eye of a Nestle member of the Department of Health's Technical Working Group (TWG), 11 versions of a draft RIRR were composed, discussed, quarreled over, and rejected during the last 20 years.

**As a result, the duration of exclusive breastfeeding in**

the Philippines plummeted down to an average of 24 days, instead of six months (180 days) recommended by World Health Organization. The exclusive breastfeeding rate also went down to only 0.5% in the National Capital Region. This precipitous rate was also prevalent in other regions of the country as well. It is in this context that Dr. Elvira L. Henares-Esguerra and her group started their campaign to revive, protect, promote, support and sustain the culture of Breastfeeding in the Philippines that created national and international impact.

### IV. JUSTIFICATION FOR NOMINATION

Give objective evidence of the impact of the medical research, health service to a large number of people

To restore the Breastfeeding culture, Elvira Esguerra and her group faced an uphill battle, from which they eventually emerged victorious. The following they regarded, not as objections to close the doors of the mind, but as obstacles to be overcome with grit and determination:

A. The national leadership and the government bureaucracy, especially the Bureau of Food and Drugs, were not concerned enough to be sympathetic to the cause.

B. Formula milk feeding was considered normal, in the movies and in real life, where the exposure of breasts for infant feeding is equated with exposure of breasts to incite male libido, in nudity laws.

C. With their $60 million advertisement annual budget, the milk companies were able to impose a news blackout on the media to prevent public awareness of the problem.

D. There is lack of expertise in Breastfeeding to train lactation consultants, to monitor violations of the laws that protect breastfeeding, to empower maternity wards and breastfeeding clinics, and to enlarge the army of breastfeeding advocates.

E. There is a sad lack of role models to raise the image of nursing mothers from a poor woman who cannot afford to buy formula milk, to a modern liberated woman balancing the requirements of career and motherhood.

F. There is a need to institutionalize the

Breastfeeding Movement to continue long beyond our normal lifetime.

G.      The times demand a new kind of leader to fight this battle.

**A.      How to attract the interest and cooperation of national leaders?** Elvira got the attention of the national leaders when she presented statistics that she was able to wangle from the National Economic Development Authority (NEDA) which showed that the yearly importation of milk and milk products into the Philippines has reached $400 million yearly, an amount equal to 10 times the average yearly plunder of our resources by the former Philippine President Ferdinand Marcos in the 14 years of Martial Law.  This milk importation was worse because it represented a yearly expenditure out of our dollar reserves far into the future without any foreseeable limit.  Since breastfeeding is practically free, Elvira and her group said, **"breastfeeding is the cheapest, most effective and most far-reaching strategy for the alleviation of poverty."**  It was a new concept, a new approach to the problem, breastfeeding as an economic issue instead of a public health issue nobody was interested in.

**Elvira and her group came up with <u>research studies</u> that proved to be the turning point of the fight against the milk companies**.  In the Philippines where the per capita Gross National Product (GNP) income is only $1,320 (¼ that of Malaysia's $4,970, 1/20 of Singapore's $27,580, and 1/25 of the USA's $33,412), where half the population are living below the poverty line, fully 30% of the family income is spent on formula milk.  The milk companies import $57 million of formula milk and sell it at SEVEN times the import cost, or $399 million to the public.  Because they are not breastfed, 16,000 Filipino babies die every year, and funeral and medical expenses total $80.7 million.  Thus the total cost to the Filipino people of formula milk is $399 million plus $80.7 million or $480 million every year, including 16,000 babies dead every year, more than the American casualties from terrorist attacks and the war in Afghanistan and Iraq combined.  **Compared to this, the cost of Breastfeeding is almost zero.**  According to the UNICEF, <u>"When Baguio General Hospital (a Philippine Hospital located in the northern mountainous province) stopped purchasing formula</u>

milk and compelled all mothers to breastfeed, the number of infant diarrhea cases dropped by **94** percent, while the number of deaths due to infection plummeted by **95** percent."

Think of the economic consequences from the viewpoint of the balance of payments. The Philippines imports **$400 million a year of milk and milk products,** enough to finance an additional 22 million classrooms a year, an additional 880,000 housing units a year, and more than 1/3 of the $1.2 billion needed yearly to service our foreign loans. Thus this massive diversion of resources is wreaking havoc on our economy, adversely affecting all our plans for housing, education and the alleviation of poverty. On the other hand, not only is Breastmilk free, its supply is inexhaustible. And indigenous foods from local agriculture offer better calcium and nutrition content than imported cow's milk, for which Asians have lactose intolerance.

The President heard about this and ordered the National Anti-Poverty Commission to hold hearings on the economic consequences of the loss of the breastfeeding culture, followed by a full-fledged Presidential Cabinet Meeting where the demands of Elvira's breastfeeding advocacy group were heard and approved. President Gloria Macapagal Arroyo invited Elvira's entire family to dinner at Malacañang and the rest is history. Elvira and her group initiated public hearings in the Philippine Senate and Congress to discuss the issue and to expose the unethical marketing practices of milk companies.

Elvira was able to entrench her way into the Technical Working Group of the Bureau of Food and Drugs (BFAD). For **20 years** the 1986 National Code on the Marketing of Breastmilk Substitutes and other Related Products (Executive Order or EO 51) had 11 versions of the Revised Implementing Rules and Regulations (RIRR) drafted, considered and disapproved. Elvira and her group took a new direction with the 12$^{th}$ draft and with the personal attendance and intervention of Dr. Nicholas K. Alipui, former Country Representative of the UNICEF, had it approved **within 6½ months, from February 28, 2005 to September 16, 2005**. Challenged in the Supreme Court, the new RIRR was finally affirmed by the Supreme Court on October 9, 2007.

This novel research on the economic consequences of the loss of the breastfeeding culture by Elvira's group, was the tipping point in the successful breastfeeding advocacy in the Philippines.

    **B.**    **How to "normalize" Breastfeeding?**  There are many acts of discrimination against mothers who breastfeed in public. One such mother was Ms. Elizabeth Cariño, a product of a broken illicit relationship, and feeling rejected as a baby, she was entrusted to the care of her maternal grandmother who died when she was 16 years old and left her totally alone to fend for herself.  At the age of 19 she became pregnant by a rich man's son.  She decided to bear the child as a single mother.  After she gave birth, her boyfriend advised her to put up the child for adoption by his parents.  Her doctor told her, "Your mother never mothered you, you do not know what it entails to be a mother." In response, she swore she will never do to her child what her parents did to her.  "I am going to be a good mother!!"  she exclaimed.

    One day, she was in a shopping mall, breastfeeding her child.  She noticed that passers-by were averting their gaze as though she was doing something indecent and shameful.  A security guard approached her and suggested that she breastfeed her baby in the toilet where she will cause no embarrassment.  "Do you eat in the bathroom?" Elizabeth demanded to know.  "No," said the security guard, confused. "Well my baby will be fed anywhere and anytime he wants!" With that she popped out the other breast, offered the nipple to her baby and said, "Go ahead, call the police.  I dare you!"

    This courageous, empowered single mother reported the incident to Dr. Elvira L. Henares-Esguerra, breastfeeding advocate.  Elvira's reaction: **"It is about time that breasts are considered, not as sex objects to stimulate men's libido, but as the provider of food and nourishment for the future citizens of the land that God meant them to be.  Elvira's father says that in the 80 years that he has been a movie addict he has yet to see a Hollywood movie showing mothers breastfeeding their infants, because the Catholic League of Decency and the Hays Office objected to them. Instead bottle-feeding with cow's milk has been the norm, even in Walt Disney movies.  One of the most tender and moving scenes in literature, the climax of the novel Grapes of Wrath by John Steinbeck, wherein the heroine after** losing her own baby, fed a starving old man from her breasts – was excised from the movie version because of the public outcry.  Barbara Walters, the famous journalist, was outraged that a mother seated beside her in an airplane, breastfed her baby without hiding her breast.  The head of Makati Medical Center, confronted with a statue of the Virgin Mary suckling Baby Jesus, kept putting a napkin over her breast.  The Catholic Bishops asked that breastfeeding babies be hidden from public view.  It is about time we react," Elvira said.

The first thing she did was to ask Father James B. Reuter SJ, former teacher of her father, to convince Cardinal Ricardo Vidal to approve a layout of the Virgin Mother openly breastfeeding Baby Jesus with an exposed breast, with the tagline, "If breastfeeding was good enough for Baby Jesus, then breastfeeding is good enough for your baby."  It was duly approved by the Cardinal on October 2005 for the campaign to break the Guinness World Record for Simultaneous Breastfeeding.  Less than 3 years later, the ultra-conservative Vatican caught up with Elvira when on June 23, 2008 *L'Osservatore Romano*, the official newspaper of the Holy See, published two articles on art that encouraged "artists to uncover Virgin Mary and show her breastfeeding Baby Jesus.... The Virgin Mary who nurses her son Jesus is one of the most eloquent signs that the word of God truly and undoubtedly became flesh."

Elvira did not stop there.  With the experience of Elizabeth Cariño in mind, she approached a friend, schoolmate and carpool-mate in her college days at the University of the Philippines, Ms. Annie Silva-Garcia, vice-President of SM Supermalls (which have built three of the ten biggest malls in the entire world), with a proposition; "Annie, Henry Sy's SM Supermalls always considered itself family-oriented.  As such they refused to show any bold sex films in their theaters.  Since together they represent 60 percent of the market, the bold sex film business collapsed entirely.  I propose you do the same for breastfeeding.  Welcome pregnant and breastfeeding mothers into your malls.  Give them parking space, first priority in queue lines, comfort rooms, and the same consideration and facilities that you are required to do under law for the disabled.  Allow them to breastfeed anytime, anywhere they want in the entire mall. For those who want privacy, build them Breastfeeding Stations with facilities for breastfeeding and for expressing milk."

Within two months the SM Supermalls approved the budget and invited Elvira to partner with SM in a **project to build Breastfeeding Stations in all their 32 malls throughout the nation**, starting with Megamall (in the vicinity of Elvira's residence) and Mall of Asia. This project got newspaper front-page treatment and was announced on TV and radio. This became the opening salvo that spelled doom for the news blackout on breastfeeding. **Currently, these breastfeeding stations have been serving thousands of mothers and children nationwide.** Each breastfeeding station is launched in a grand fashion including an early-morning orientation on the importance of supporting breastfeeding to security and janitorial personnel, mall tenants, mall managers and administrative staff. The decision of the biggest malls to put up breastfeeding stations upon the appeal of Dr. Elvira served as a precedent. Several other malls owned by other establishments followed suit, thus changing public perception and attitude towards breastfeeding.

C.    **How to break the news blackout imposed by the $60 million annual budget of the Milk Companies on the print and TV media?** A newspaper editor said: "It is easy for advertisers to install a gatekeeper on the inside pages of the paper. To bypass him, you have to send your message via (1) front page news, (2) paid advertisements, (3) independent columnists, and (4) international news agencies.

Elvira and her group moved heaven and earth to change the attitude so prevalent in the present culture: the embarrassment of exposing breasts for feeding the baby, a natural act made unnatural through the influence of multinationals.

1.    PRESIDENTIAL    PROCLAMATION.    Elvira convinced President Gloria Macapagal-Arroyo to issue Presidential Proclamation No. 1113, officially promulgating the annual celebration of World Breastfeeding Week during August 1-7 of every year **observing the international standard of ethics of not partnering with companies that produce or sell milk and other products covered by the International Code**

**like baby foods, bottles, teats, and pacifiers**. To serve as a signal to the entire nation to celebrate this occasion, with the President leading the country, Dr. Elvira's Children for Breastfeeding Inc., a non-political, non-government organization, has been in charge of organizing the Ceremony in the Presidential Palace (Malacañang) since 2005 to date, capturing the headlines with the help of the Presidential Press Corps.

2.   GUINNESS   WORLD   RECORD   ON SIMULTANEOUS BREASTFEEDING IN A SINGLE SITE. Elvira's Children for Breastfeeding Inc. in partnership with the City of Manila, the Department of Health, the UNICEF and Nurturers of the Earth Inc., set out to break the Guinness World Record for Simultaneous Breastfeeding in a Single Site, established in Berkeley, California, in 2002, with 1,130 mothers. On May 4, 2006 she broke the record with 3,541 Manila mothers.

3.   GUINNESS   WORLD   RECORD   ON SIMULTANEOUS BREASTFEEDING IN MULTIPLE SITES. Then a year later on May 2, 2007, together with the Department of Social Welfare and Development and Technical Education and Skills Development Authority (TESDA), Elvira established a new World Record for Simultaneous Breastfeeding in Multiple Sites, 295 sites in the Philippines nationwide with 15,128 breastfeeding mothers. The total number of mother-child pairs actually reached 22,500 mothers in 590 sites but the Guinness World Record stipulated that there should be no less than 25 mother-child pairs in each site so the record number was reduced.

4.   GUINNESS   WORLD   RECORD   ON   TREE-PLANTING.  And for good measure, on August 25, 2006, to promote her project of providing indigenous foods as a source of calcium in place of imported milk, Elvira partnered with the Department of Environment and Natural Resources (DENR) to break the Guinness World Record for Most Trees Planted Simultaneously, with 653,143 trees planted by 516,137 persons along 3,917 kilometers of the National Highways of the Philippines.

5.   SYNCHRONIZED   BREASTFEEDING WORLDWIDE (SBW). On August 8 of 2007, in partnership with World Alliance for Breastfeeding Action (WABA), Elvira

sponsored **Synchronized Breastfeeding Worldwide (SBW)** with 16 countries and more than 10,000 mother-child pairs participating.   This is a YEARLY activity that is like the celebration of New Year, scheduled at the same local time, for a period of 24 hours across 24 time zones on the same day around the world.  The following year, **on August 9, 2008, she launched the invitation to the 2008 SBW in Beijing China, with President Gloria Macapagal Arroyo in attendance, appropriately billed as *The Breastfeeding Olympics* that occurred last October 11, 2008. The next SBW is scheduled for October 2, 2009, where the Philippines aims to break its own Guinness World Records for Breastfeeding in a Single Site and Multiple Sites in different Time Zones.** For Elvira's Breastfeeding Advocacy:  Yesterday Manila, Today the Philippines, and the entire World!

**All of a sudden the whole world was flooded with pictures of mothers baring their breasts to nurture their babies, openly, proudly and with delightful impunity, in front pages, in the Internet, in the international new agencies, and in many opinion columns.**  A United States senator even introduced amendments to the Nudity Law to exempt breastfeeding mothers.  In 2008, the Vatican pleaded for more artists to depict the Virgin Mother with bared breasts.

6.     If parents need to be educated on the benefits of breastfeeding to both mother and child as well as its positive social, ecological and economic consequences, parents also need to be informed of the hazards associated with formula-feeding. Because of their relentless media exposes' on the industrial accidents happening in other countries and formula milk contaminants like Enterobacter sakazakii, several whistle-blowers from Wyeth secretly approached the group of Dr. Elvira in May 2007 and gave them a complete documentation of **the sale of 4 million cans of contaminated milk products in 2006 that Wyeth tried to cover up.**

Dr. Elvira and her group courageously approached the Department of Health and called a press conference to inform the public despite the possible danger to their lives. Months before their expose' on the contaminated milk, one of the government lawyers who was fighting a case filed by milk companies against health officials was shot dead with his son. It happened the same day that Dr. Elvira and other advocates were in front of the Supreme Court to show their support to the said government officials.

Another incident that educated the public on the hazards of formula-feeding unfortunately claimed the lives of 86 infants from January to May of 2008 in Makati City Hospital, a government–run health facility.   Dr. Elvira took part in the investigation of the infants' deaths and pointed out that early initiation of breastfeeding could have prevented the onset of sepsis, a major cause of the deaths. This observation was supported and incorporated in the final report of the Fact-Finding Committee that also blamed lapses in infection control.

And from there on, Elvira's Advocacy bypassed the Milk Companies' news black-out and she was invited to present her views in all the media, radio, TV, print, and the Internet.

**D.     How to train the experts to carry on the Breastfeeding Movement?**

1.     A member of the international organization of medical doctors based in the USA, **Academy of Breastfeeding Medicine**, Elvira founded in 2004, the **Children for Breastfeeding Inc.** primarily to mobilize children and the family in support of the breastfeeding mother, and in general to promote, protect, and revive the breastfeeding culture.

2.     In 2002, she established **The Breastfeeding Clinic** the very first to be established in an exclusive private hospital to render service to indigent pregnant and nursing mothers.

3.     On July 26, 2004, she and her partner (Nona D. Andaya-Castillo, a non-doctor and mass communication graduate) took the examination of the International Board of Lactation Consultant Examiners (IBLCE), passed it and was awarded the right to use the title **International Board Certified Lactation Consultant (IBCLC),** and thus established their qualifications as Breastfeeding experts. The two IBCLCs have recently re-certified and will be recognized as such until 2014.

4.     In 2005, Elvira established the **Philippine Academy of Lactation Consultants Inc.,** an affiliate of the Philippine Medical Association, to institute breastfeeding as a part of the Continuing Medical Education (CME) of physicians. For the past three years, during the Annual Conventions, Elvira

organized the Continuing Medical Education of Physicians on Breastfeeding: 2007 - "The Imperatives of Breastfeeding"; 2008 - "The National Code on the Marketing of Breastmilk Substitutes and other Related Products or EO 51, and the Revised Implementing Rules and Regulations, as affirmed by the Supreme Court"; 2009 - Lectures on the relevance of Breastfeeding in the following subjects of (1) Diabetes, (2) Obesity, (3) Infectious Diseases, (4) Bone Health, (5) Ear Diseases, (6) Environment.

5.      In 2006, she established the **Philippine Lactation Resource and Training Center** in partnership with Nurturers of the Earth, Inc. and TESDA to set official national training standards and school curricula on breastfeeding counseling, and to actually train breastfeeding counselors, advocates, and National Code monitors. The training center is recognized and accredited by the Department of Health as a Training Institution, and as a Monitoring Entity.

6.      She established the **Grand Coalition Against Corporate Greed** to broaden the battlefront, and especially to counter the financial might of milk and tobacco companies, Genetically Modified Organism manufacturers and the big business polluters of the environment, and to protect public health, the environment and consumer welfare. Experts from other activist organizations now lend their expertise and experience in advocacy, legal litigation and lobbying to the Breastfeeding Movement and to each other.

E.      **How to create Role Models of Breastfeeding Mothers to change the image of nursing mothers from a poor underprivileged woman who cannot afford to buy formula milk, to a modern liberated woman balancing the requirements of career, motherhood and breastfeeding?**

Probably the most heartbreaking and pathetic statements we have ever heard from a nursing mother is "I breastfeed because I cannot afford to buy Promil (a formula milk brand) for my baby." It is a statement born of ignorance and the persistent propaganda of milk companies that their formula milk is superior to breastmilk and claims it breeds geniuses. Indeed so prevalent is this view that in the Metro Manila area where milk propaganda is most prevalent, the most popular item stolen by shoplifters is formula milk, and the most popular consumer item being bought, second only to the cell phone cards, is formula milk.

As a matter of fact, the more educated and the more well-heeled the mother is, the more she resorts to bottle-feeding "in order to preserve her figure, and in order to be able to be free to work and pursue her social life outside the home." Dr. Santiago del Rosario, an Obstetrics-Gynecologist who was a former president of the Philippine Medical Association, actually boasts (he boasts!) that only 20 percent of his patients breastfeed their babies.

How then should we create Role Models of Breastfeeding Mothers to change the image of nursing mothers from a poor ignorant woman who cannot afford to buy formula milk, to a modern liberated woman balancing the requirements of career and motherhood?

Elvira and her group launched another campaign, **"I Can Work Because I Breastfeed"** to show that it is possible to breastfeed while pursuing a career, by expressing breastmilk for storage. DJ Llabres is a stewardess flying the international route, who expressed her breastmilk and sent it back by the return flight for her husband to pick up in the airport when it arrived. Marites Sobeng, an insurance agent, doing a lot of fieldwork in her job, expressed her breastmilk, and brought it home everyday. Pamela Magallon, an event organizer, sometimes stayed out of her home for more than 24 hours on a job, in which case, she expressed her breastmilk and gave it to her husband to bring home to their child. All of these breastfeeding mothers worked better with the assurance that their infants were getting the best of care.

Another campaign launched the **"Seven Acts of Kindness,"** a 7-day celebration and encouragement of **Faith** (lighting a candle in church and praying for children who die of malnutrition), **Nutrition** (bringing calcium-rich vegetables for a nursing mother to eat), **Medicine** (give herbal tea or massage a nursing mother), **Economics** (contribute your loose change to the Breastfeeding Movement), **Ecology** (offer a flower or a glass of water to a breastfeeding mother), **Empowerment** (congratulate Breastfeeding Mothers for breastfeeding), and **Love** (embrace a breastfeeding mother to show your appreciation), designed to empower and mobilize children and the family to support breastfeeding mothers.

Two photo exhibits of beautiful and talented mothers were also created:  one **"The Virgin Mary and her 12 disciples"** by Blow-Up Babies Photo Studio of Elvira's nephew, Palanca Literary Awardee and movie director Quark Henares; and the other, **"Beauty, Brains and Breastfeeding"** by Pancho Escaler, Elvira's cousin, a well-known photographer displaying 17 glamorous mothers highly placed in social circles.  The first is a joint project of Elvira's Children for Breastfeeding, Inc. and the UNICEF, and features the Virgin Mary exposing her breast to feed Baby Jesus, and 12 Filipino nursing mothers who continue to breastfeed their infants two years and beyond, for which they were properly commended by Dr. Nicholas K. Alipui, former head of UNICEF Philippines, as **admirable exemplars one can identify with.**   The second featured Society Women who breastfeed their babies exclusively for six months –- **celebrities one can look up to and emulate.**  WHO's recommendations are for Exclusive Breastfeeding for six months, and continued breastfeeding for two years and beyond, complemented with fresh and nutritious indigenous food instead of imported follow-up cow's milk. These two exhibits were first unveiled in the Presidential Palace with President Gloria Macapagal Arroyo in attendance, then went the rounds of all the SM Supermalls, in the Congress, Senate, Department of Education, PhilHealth Insurance, Civil Service, various schools and city halls.

Children for Breastfeeding Inc. under Elvira L. Henares-Esguerra and its partner, the Department of Education under Jesli Lapus, searched for a beautiful role model who is breastfeeding her children up to 2 years of age and beyond. There are many such Filipina women celebrities, but invariably they are tempted to accept millions of pesos, which milk companies gleefully offer for the endorsement of their products even if they have breastfed. Dr. Elvira was able to convince Susann Roth, Doctor of Medicine, Doctor of Philosophy and Master of Public Health, to be a role model, who agreed to sign a contract never to endorse milk products, be photographed breastfeeding her two babies in tandem, and was crowned Breastfeeding Queen of the Philippines by President Gloria Macapagal Arroyo, on Valentine's Day 2009.

Elvira also chose Breastfed Princesses, Mikaela Fudolig, breastfed for two years who entered college at 11 years old and at 16 graduated *summa cum laude*, BS in Physics with a near perfect grade, and was chosen Valedictorian of the entire Batch 2007 of the University of the Philippines and Isabelle A. Castillo, 20, breastfed by her mother and grandmother, UP scholar and soprano of UP Singing Ambassadors, and the five (13 to 22 years old) Tagala Brothers, Breastfed Princes of the "Vegetarian Voices and Violins" -- concert musicians who individually can play the violin, the viola, the cello, the saxophone, flute, piano, the guitar and sing and compose songs as well. This is to counterbalance the milk companies' false nutritional and health claims of breeding geniuses.

**F.    How to institutionalize the Breastfeeding Movement to continue and endure long beyond our normal lifetime.**

As a Breastfeeding Advocate, Elvira finds herself inextricably linked **in partnership with Secretary Francisco T. Duque III's Department of Health and Dr. Nicholas K. Alipui's UNICEF Philippines.** Yet she dares to think "out of the box," and to further institutionalize her Breastfeeding advocacy, Elvira broadened her team **to involve others seemingly remote from her advocacy:**

• **Local government** organizations like Mayor Atienza's City of Manila and James Marty Lim's Liga ng mga Barangay ng Pilipinas.

• **National agencies** like Secretary Esperanza Cabral's Department of Social Welfare and Development, Secretary Angelo Reyes' Department of Environment and Natural Resources, Secretary Boboy Syjuco's Technical Education and Skills Development Authority (TESDA), Secretary Carlito Puno's Commission on Higher Education and Development (CHED), the National Anti-Poverty Commission, Lorna Fajardo's PhilHealth Insurance, Cecile B. Gutierrez**'s** TESDA Women's Center, and President Gloria Macapagal Arroyo's Office of the President in Malacañang -- dealing directly with their highest officials.

• **Legislative** bodies like the Senate Committee on Health and Demography, Senate  Committee on Women, Children and Family Relations, the House Committee on Health, the House Committee on Trade and Investment, all the senators and many Congressmen and women – appearing in most of their public hearings.

• **Church organizations** like the Catholic Bishops Conference, the Protestant United Churches of Christ, the Buddhist Universal Wisdom Foundation, the *Dating Daan* religious organization, and others.

• **Professional Associations** with whom Elvira has signed Memoranda of Agreements, or is affliliated with -- such as Philippine Pharmaceutical Association, La Salle University Medical Association, Philippine Medical Association.

• **Non Government Organizations** with whom Elvira signed Memoranda of Agreements or have Joint Projects with -- like Environmental Studies Institute, *Bantay Kalikasan*, Father James B. Reuter of the Catholic Media, Sister Pilar Verzosa of Pro-Life Movement, Our Lady of La Leche Movement, four Rotary Clubs, SM Supermalls, DZRJ and RJTV, NU-107, among many others.

• **International Organizations** with whom Elvira signed Memoranda of Agreements, such as UNICEF Philippines, Guinness World Record Ltd.; World Alliance for Breastfeeding Action (WABA, Malaysia); Framework Convention Alliance (Mary Assunta, Geneva); Public Health Advocacy (Richard Daynard, Boston); Global Alliance for Incinerator Alternatives (GAIA), Baby Milk Action.

• **Individuals** who supported the RIRR with their signatures, gathered by Elvira's Group, more than 800 of them, including President Fidel V. Ramos, 20 out of 23 senators, 76 Congressmen, Bro. Mike Velarde of El Shaddai, all of the bishops of the Catholic Bishops Conference, the Buddhist Foundation including two Tibetan monks, ex-Solicitor General Francisco Chavez.

It is amazing how far Elvira has gone to promote and protect breastfeeding. The roles she played in securing a Presidential Proclamation for the annual celebration of World Breastfeeding Week, in the finalization of the new RIRR to enforce the National Code, and in the National Plan of Action on Infant and Young Child Feeding, her breaking the Guinness World breastfeeding records (in one site, in multiple sites and in world-wide synchronization), Breastfeeding stations in all SM

Supermalls – all define the **SCOPE**, **MAGNITUDE** and **BREADTH** of her advocacy.

But it is not enough. She knows that she now must **INSTITUTIONALIZE** Breastfeeding, give it relevance in the lives of all the people and define the **DEPTH** of her commitment so that the movement will continue to grow in the years to come, long after she is gone.

What is needed is **EDUCATION** at all levels -- to integrate the culture of breastfeeding **(1)** into all Nursing and Medicine courses, **(2)** into Health related courses in college, **(3)** together with all extension classes and *practicum*; **(4)** in health related subjects at the vocational level; **(5)** the Continuing Medical Education (CME) of doctors already practicing. These will definitely be done together with the **Philippine Medical Association, the TESDA and the Commission on Higher Education and Development (CHED)**, with two of whom Elvira has already a Memorandum of Agreement. On February 13, 2009, she signed a Memorandum of Agreement with the **Department of Education** to introduce Breastfeeding in as many subjects as possible in the **(6)** pre-school, **(7)** elementary, **(8)** high school level, and **(9)** alternative learning systems for out-of-school adults.

According to Education Secretary Jesli Lapus, this is part of his department's overall "Exemplar Program" to inculcate values and develop role models, not only to revive the Breastfeeding culture in their country, but also to inculcate the values that will promote youth resistance against the use of tobacco and illegal drugs, graft and corruption, and the abuse against women, children and the environment.

**G.     What kind of leader is needed to fight this battle?**

A perfect example of a nationalist, Elvira, slated by her parents to be a diplomat, could not bring herself to leave the country, preferring to serve her people in the grassroots as a hands-on doctor and breastfeeding advocate.

A perfect specimen of a health enthusiast, a God-loving citizen, and a doctor, Elvira does not drink alcohol, she does not smoke, she does not gamble, she does not take illegal drugs.

Perfectly at ease with kings and servants, Elvira put away her Mercedes Benz to take the bus to school, she stayed in the dormitory or single bed-space in preference to her own large room at home, in Europe she backpacked and stayed in the homes of ordinary people instead of expensive hotels.  Elvira steps out of her comfort zone to experience what it is to be poor or ordinary, so that she may better serve the people.

A perfect innovator, she thinks "out of the box" to find new and better solutions.

A perfect role model, she "walks her talk" and breastfeeds her six year old child anytime he wants ("If I am not embarrassed, Mama, why should you be?" said her son).

All her accomplishments became possible because she is always willing to work long, hard hours with unwavering passion and commitment.


**V. AWARDS AND HONOURS RECEIVED**

2008 Ten Outstanding Filipino Physicians

**2008 September 29, Given by Jaycee Senate International, Department of Health, Philhealth, Philippine Charity Sweepstakes Office**

2008 Outstanding Public Health Advocate in Community Service

**2008 December 19, UERM Memorial Medical Center Alumni Association**

2008 World Breastfeeding Week Gold Medalist

**2008 August 09, World Alliance for Breastfeeding Action, Beijing, China**

2007 One of the 50 Most Outstanding Alumni of her school

**2007 June 14, 50th Year Anniversary Celebration, UERM Memorial Medical Center**

Elvira enrolled in the UERM to take up medicine, and graduated in 1986.  In 2007, on the 50th anniversary of the founding of UERM, the school chose Dr. Elvira Lichauco Henares-Esguerra as **one of the 50 greatest alumni among the 15,000 graduates of the school, for her advocacy of Breastfeeding**, "transcending the narrow confines of her specialty to embrace the concerns of all humanity."

**2007 May 2,** Guinness World Record, Simultaneous Breastfeeding, Multiple Sites

**2006 May 4,** Guinness World Record, Simultaneous Breastfeeding in a Single Site

**2006 August 25,** Guinness World Record on the Most Trees Planted Simultaneously

**To break the news black-out imposed by milk companies with their multi-million advertising budget, Elvira broke into the front pages, television, radio and the Internet by breaking** Three Guinness World Records.

**2006 June 22 to December 31,** Project Cooperative Agreement with the UNICEF : **Awarded to Elvira's Children for Breastfeeding, Inc., a non-government organization by the UNITED NATION'S CHILDREN'S FUND (UNICEF), an international inter-government organization established by the General Assembly of the United Nations – for the project:** Bringing Back the Breastfeeding Culture: Celebrating Breastfeeding Week and Beyond, **the project cost of PhP 1,609,200.00.**

**2004 January, 2003 Ford Conservation and Environmental Grants Program: In 2004 she and her Children for Breastfeeding Inc. won an environmental award and funding for her advocacy from the Ford Motor Co.**

2003, January, **Catholic Family of the Year, made into a film by Father James B. Reuter S.J.**

2002, September, **Nominated for the WABA Hall of Fame:** In April, 2002, an article and Power Point Presentation "Waiting for the Fifth Player" delivered at the WABA Regional Asia- Pacific international conference in Kuala Lumpur, earned her and her family a **nomination to the WABA Hall of Fame** in September; and inspired Father James B. Reuter SJ to make a movie depicting her family as the **Catholic Family of the Year** at the time Pope John Paul II was to visit the Philippines for the 4th World Meeting of Families in January of 2003.

**1982, University of the Philippines, Plaque of Appreciation for Service to Hanggan, Bae, Laguna.** In Bae, Laguna, where she had her practicum, she was awarded by the landlord and tenants of the barangay a special plaque for her unique role in improving the community, the first and only one to receive such honor.

**1977-1978, University of the Philippines,** In UP where she was enrolled as a Pharmacy student, Elvira was designated one of the Corps Sponsors of the UP Vanguards, along with her sister Juno.

**January 1974, World Youth Day, New York City, USA,** Designated a Youth Delegate to the United Nations

**Fall of 1973, Santa Cruz, California, USA,** 2nd Place, Voice of Democracy Oratory Contest, USA Countrywide

1974 June, Commencement Exercises, Santa Cruz, California, USA, Fall of 1973, Santa Cruz, California, USA, Honored with Elvira Henares Day, Morello Preparatory High School, In the school year 1973-74, she earned a Youth for Understanding (YFU) scholarship to the United States, where she was enrolled in a private Catholic school, Morello Preparatory High School in Santa Cruz, California, she distinguished herself by being the only foreign student, chosen for one whole day (Elvira Henares Day) to hold the stage, in response to an American's remark that "the Philippines belongs to the United States." Elvira spoke extemporaneously of the history and culture, the hopes and aspirations, and the mating rituals of her people. She showed a map of the Philippines, and a large flag that was the twin of the one first displayed on June 12, 1898, in Kawit, Cavite, a gift of General Aguinaldo to Elvira's great grandfather, Don Daniel Maramba. She played the guitar and sang traditional Filipino songs and modern songs composed by her brother Ronnie. She taught her classmates how to manipulate the wooden sticks and lent them costumes for the *Tinikling* dance, put on a Maria Clara dress and danced the *Tinikling* and the *Pandanggo Sa Ilaw* for her schoolmates. From there on, Elvira was the darling of the school, whose handwriting, spoken English, assertive ways, and academic straight A's, they considered admirable. She won the Voice of Democracy contest, second place in the entire United States, and made the front pages in Manila. She was designated a delegate to the United Nations on World Youth Day, spending three weeks in New York, one of the 18 chosen from all over the United States. She was asked to speak in the graduation ceremonies of her school with a valedictory address, alongside the valedictorian. She was on top of the world!

1973, Assumption Convent School, Manila, Philippines,

**Second Place, School Oratorical Contest,** Most of her siblings are scholars, orators and social leaders of their respective classes. Elvira in the Assumption Convent was unfortunate in having Imee Marcos, daughter of the Martial Law President, as a classmate, and has always played second fiddle to her in oratorical contests. The Voice of Democracy Oratorical Contest though where the Henares children excelled, was cancelled during Elvira's time, Martial Law.

**VI. EDUCATIONAL BACKGROUND**

**DIPLOMAS AND LICENSES:**

**May 16, 1982** **B.S. in Pharmacy, University of the Philippines**

**Oct. 17, 1984, Passed the Board,** Pharmacy Registration Number: 25653

**June 1982 to April 1986, Doctor of Medicine, UERM Medical Center**

**May 1986 to April 1987, Senior Internship, Makati Medical Center**

**Jan. 6, 1988, Passed the Board,** Physician's Registration Number: 63820

**Jan. 1988 to Dec.1992, Dermatology Residency, Makati Medical Center**

**Apr. l6, 1997, Diplomate, Board of Dermatology,** CME # 97-00213

**November 2001** **Fellow** **Philippine Dermatological Society**

**July 26, 2004, took Exam, International Board of Lactation Consultant Examiners (IBLCE)**

**October 15, 2004, Accredited International Board Certified Lactation Consultant,** BCLC Number: 204-53539

**CONTINUING MEDICAL EDUCATION:**

**Nov. 17-29, 2008, Outreach Course on Infant & Young Child Feeding**

**Institute of Child Health in London and WABA, Penang, Malaysia**

October 22-26, 2008, 13th Meeting, Academy of Breastfeeding Medicine, Working towards being a Fellow, Dearborn, Michigan, USA

October 11-14, 2007, 12th Meeting, Academy of Breastfeeding Medicine, Working towards being a Fellow, Fort Worth, Texas, USA

July 2007, Speaker and Participant, State of the Art Summit on Mother Support, World Alliance for Breastfeeding Action, Chicago, Illinois, USA

July 2007, Speaker and Poster Presenter, 50th Anniversary Conference, La Leche League International, Chicago, Illinois, USA

July 2003, Speaker and Facilitator, 2003 International Conference, La Leche League International, San Francisco, California, USA

July 2003, Participant, Dermatologic Surgery, University of California, La Jolla, San Diego, USA

October 2002, Participant, Trainers' Training Course on Breastfeeding Counseling and Complementary Feeding, New Delhi, India

September 2002, Resource Speaker and Performer for Pantomime Mums, Global Forum 2, World Alliance for Breastfeeding Action (WABA), Arusha, Tanzania, Africa

September 2002, Participant, WABA-UNICEF Colloquium on HIV and Breastfeeding, Arusha, Tanzania, Africa

July 2002, Participant, First Asian Congress on Vegetarian Nutrition, Manila, Philippines

April 2002, Speaker (son Gabriel) and Participant, Asia-Pacific Global Initiative, on Mother Support, Kuala Lumpur, Malaysia

**VII. POSITIONS OCCUPIED**
**DERMATOLOGY PRACTICE:**
**January 2004 to present, Dermatology Consultant,** MD Eastwood, Eastwood City, Libis, Quezon City

**January 2004 to present, Dermatology Consultant,** Medical Plaza Ortigas, Ortigas Center, Pasig, MM

**April 2003 to January 2006, Dermatology Consultant, Clinica Manila,** Megamall, Mandaluyong, Metro Manila

**January 2001 to present, Dermatology Consultant,** Skin and Cancer Foundation, Medical Plaza Ortigas, Ortigas Center, Pasig, MM

**August 1997 to present, Active Consultant in Dermatology,** Makati Medical Center, Makati City, MM

**May 1995 to September 1996, Dermatology Consultant, Clinica Manila,** Megamall, Mandaluyong, Metro Manila

**1988 to present , Member,** Makati Medical Society, Philippine Medical Association

**BREASTFEEDING ADVOCACY:**

2007 July to present, Partner and Project Manager, World Alliance for Breastfeeding Action, **Runs Synchronized Breastfeeding Worldwide, Sabay-sabay Sumuso sa Nanay**

2006 September to present, Co-Founder and Co-director, Philippine Lactation Resource and Training Center, **in partnership with Nurturers of the Earth, Inc. and TESDA to set official national training standards and school curricula on breastfeeding counseling, and to train breastfeeding counselors, advocates, and National Code monitors. This organization is recognized and accredited by the Department of Health as a Training Institution, and as a Monitoring Entity.**

2006 September to present, Founding Member, Grand Coalition Against Corporate Greed, **Composed of health, anti-tobacco, environment and consumer advocacy groups, pooling their resources, experience and expertise in advocacy, legal litigation and lobbying to combat corporate malpractices.**

2006 June 22 to December 31, Partner, Project Cooperative Agreement with the UNICEF, **Done between Elvira's Children for Breastfeeding, Inc., a non-government organization and the UNITED NATION'S CHILDREN'S FUND (UNICEF) for the project: Bringing Back the Breastfeeding Culture: Celebrating Breastfeeding Week and Beyond, the project cost of PhP 1,609,200.00.**

2005 August to present, Founder, Board Member, CEO, Philippine Academy of Lactation Consultants, Inc., **An affiliate society of the Philippine Medical Association that advocates breastfeeding among medical professionals, and conducts the Continuing Medical Education (CME) on Breastfeeding.**

2004 December to present, Active member, working to be a Fellow, Academy of Breastfeeding Medicine, USA, **A worldwide organization of physicians dedicated to the promotion, protection and support of breastfeeding and human lactation. It unites members of the various medical specialties with this common purpose through: physician education, expansion of knowledge in breastfeeding science and human lactation, facilitation of optimal breastfeeding practices, encouragement of the exchange of information among organizations.**

2004 May to present, Co-Founder, Director and CEO, Children for Breastfeeding, Inc. **Conducts lectures, trainings and counseling on indigenous nurturing practices including breastfeeding and initiates campaigns and projects to promote, protect and support breastfeeding, mobilizes children to promote earth-friendly parenting.**

VIII. PUBLICATIONS

**The Advocacy Group of which Elvira is the leader is composed of three people all differently involved in other pursuits. These are (1) Elvira L. Henares-Esguerra, the doctor as the leader of the movement under Children for Breastfeeding, Inc., (2) her partner Nona D. Andaya-Castillo, the mass communicator, vegetarian and environmentalist who heads Nurturers of the Earth, Inc. and is the Presidential Consultant on Infant and Young Child Feeding, (3) Hilarion M. Henares Jr. of HEAL the Philippines, Inc., Elvira's 85-year old father, who is an economist, industrialist and the Presidential Consultant on National Affairs (to President Gloria Macapagal Arroyo), whose word is sacrosanct in government and public circles.**

Most of the speeches, long formal reports and magazine articles are **the result of close collaboration of the three of them.** But those who face the public wear different faces, in pursuit of a strategy they call *"in globo,"* that is attacking the problem from different directions, by presumably independent sources wearing different hats. They have agreed that all public speeches and press statements are delivered by Elvira under her own byline. All magazine articles published are under the byline of Nona. And all the formal reports are submitted with complete set of Exhibits, under the byline of the most knowledgeable and credible of the Group, her father, Hilarion M. Henares Jr.

Some of the Formal Reports submitted to the government, co-authored by Dr. Elvira L. Henares-Esguerra, Nona D. Andaya-Castillo, and **Hilarion M Henares Jr.,** delivered by the latter, under his own byline, are:

1.    **Economic Consequences of the Loss of the Breastfeeding Culture**, May 4, 2005, before the Senate Committee on Health and Demography.

2.    **Three Milk Companies Most Guilty of Malpractice**, May 25, 2005, before the National Anti-Poverty Commission.

3.    **Report to the Cabinet on Breastfeeding,** June 14, 2005, in behalf of the Secretary of Health, and Children for Breastfeeding, Inc.

4.    **Overwhelming Support for the IRR from your bitterest enemies,** October 27, 2005, Memo to President Gloria Macapagal Arroyo.

5.    **Nestle is the Worst Enemy of Breastfeeding: Why it is imperative to keep away from Nestlé**, November 1, 2005, to the President of the Philippines and her Cabinet.

6.    **Complaint Against Wyeth Philippines, guilty of illegal, unethical and immoral behavior,** November 13, 2005, to the President of the Philippines and the Secretary of Health.

7.    **Soliciting the Support of Chief Justice Hilario Davide,** January 14, 2006, Memo to UNICEF head, Nicholas Alipui.

8.    **The Milk Wars** (in 2 parts), January, 2006, submitted to WABA International.

9.    **Report on the 2007 Discovery of the Wyeth 2006 sale of 4 million cans of contaminated milk a year before,** 2007 to the Department of Health and Bureau of Food and Drugs.

10.    **Statement for the joint committee of House Committee on Health and the House Committee on Trade and Industry,** December 9, 2008.

Some of the magazine articles and papers co-authored by Dr. Elvira L. Henares-Esguerra, Hilarion M Henares Jr., and

**Nona D. Andaya-Castillo,** published under the byline of the latter, are:

1.    **"I Am Able To Work Because I Breastfeed,"** published November, 2005, Baby Magazine.

2.    **"Health and Nutrition: Nurturing Healthy Mothers and Babies through Indigenous Foods,"** submitted at Global Session, La Leche League International, 50th Anniversary Conference, July 22, 2007.

3.    **"Children for Breastfeeding: Mobilizing Children to Perform the Seven Acts of Kindness,"** a Poster Presentation, La Leche League International, 50th Anniversary Conference, July 20-23, 2007.

4.    **"Follow-up Milk is Not Necessary,"** Baby Magazine, September 2008.

5.    **"Breastfeeding Beyond Two Years: It is Normal!"** Baby Magazine, January 2009.

6.    **"Eight Optimal Goals in Infant and Young Child Feeding,"** Baby Magazine, May 2009.

Elvira established the Philippine Lactation Resource and Training Center, to encourage and produce local **evidence-based studies, led by Cochrane-trained researchers,** on various aspects of Breastfeeding and Earth-friendly Parenting. Most of the papers that appear under her by-line are Statements issued in Public Hearings, and Speeches on various subjects to large audiences. But here we submit three of her original works that made an impact on the breastfeeding movement:

1.    **Waiting for the Fifth Player**, the story of the birth of her third child and how she made breastfeeding her apostolate.  This resulted in her family's nomination to the WABA Hall of Fame, and a movie of Father James B. Reuter SJ depicting her family as the Catholic Family of the Year at the time Pope John Paul II was to visit the Philippines.

2.    **The Seven Acts of Kindness**, which is the standard ritual of her Breastfeeding Movement, now being introduced in schools to involve the children as well.

3.    **Economic Consequences of the Loss of the Breastfeeding Culture in an Underdeveloped Country: and other Tipping Points in the Successful Advocacy of Breastfeeding:** A Poster Presentation submitted to the 13th Annual International Meeting of the Academy of Breastfeeding

Medicine, October 23-26, 2008, Dearborn, Michigan, USA.

### IX. NOMINATED BY
Last name                                                    **DUQUE**
First name                                                **FRANCISCO III**
Middle initial                                        **T.**
Title                                                         **Doctor of Medicine**
Position                                              **Secretary of Health**

**Department of Health, Philippines**      **Republic of the  Philippines**

Address                                           **San**                **Lazaro Compound**

                                                        **Tayuman, Sta. Cruz**
City                                                       **Manila**
Country                                             **Philippines**
Postal Code                                       **1003**
Phone                                              **(632) 711  9502**
                                                       **(632) 743  8301 to 23**

Fax                                                      **(632)  493  5280**

e-Mail
**ftduque@co.doh.gov.ph**
**(SIGNED – see hard copy))**

### X.  LETTER OF REFERENCE # 1
11 May 2009
The Secretary General
Prince Mahidol Award Foundation
Bangkok, Thailand
Dear Sir/Madam,
Warm greetings from the Philippines!

I am Undersecretary Alexander Padilla of the Department of Health and I am pleased to know that our Secretary of Health Francisco T. Duque has nominated Dr. Elvira L. Henares-Esguerra, a nationally-recognized International Board Certified Lactation Consultant to the Prince Mahidol Award Foundation.

In 2006, Dr. Elvira established the Philippine Lactation Resource and Training Center (PLRTC) as the national headquarters of her projects that included simultaneous breastfeeding in single and multiple sites, the yearly national celebration of World Breastfeeding Week and the establishment of breastfeeding stations in SM Supermalls, the largest chain of malls in our country.

PLRTC has promoted not only breastfeeding but also the appreciation and use of indigenous foods with the objective of ensuring food security and self-sustainability for our people. Her organization upholds international recommendations and covenants while at the same time adapts these to the Filipino culture. I met many mothers that they empowered during several affairs that Dr. Elvira and our Department have jointly organized.

The Center has trained and mobilized many advocates, breastfeeding counselors, and monitors of the implementation of the laws that protect breastfeeding.

A feisty lady doctor who comes from a family of nationalists, Dr. Elvira has initiated Senate and Congress hearings and bravely gave her testimonies against milk companies that have violated the Philippine laws that protect breastfeeding. Despite apparent danger, Dr. Elvira also exposed the sale of 4 million cans of contaminated milk to innocent Filipino children last 2007.

I am looking forward to the results of the Prince Mahidol Awards and her success!

Yours sincerely,
(SIGNED – see hard copy)
Undersecretary Alexander A. Padilla
Department of Health, Philippines


## XI.  LETTER OF REFERENCE # 2

The Secretary General
11 May 2009
Prince Mahidol Award Foundation
Bangkok, Thailand
Dear Sir/Madam,
Warm greetings from the Philippines!  I am Dr. Bu C. Castro, former President of the Philippine Medical Association (PMA) in 2004-2006; President, Philippine Society of Pathologists from 1997 -1998 and President of the Philippine Association of Forensic Medicine from 2000-2003. Currently, I

am the President of the Coalition of all the Philippine Health Organizations which was launched last April 29, 2009.

During my presidency in PMA, I had the privilege of assisting Dr. Elvira L. Henares-Esguerra in instituting the Philippine Academy of Lactation Consultants (PALC) as an affiliate society of the PMA with the objective of securing Continuing Medical Education (CME) on Breastfeeding in as many activities of the PMA as possible especially during the conventions.

While she was leading a national campaign to revive the breastfeeding culture, she diligently fulfilled all the requirements in affiliating PALC to the Philippine Medical Association including the recruitment of 30 medical doctors as the initial members of the organization. Later on, PALC became the lead organization in initiating the Continuing Medical Education on Breastfeeding that started during the 100th Anniversary Conference of the PMA last May 2007 and continues every year to this day.

It is amazing how far Dr. Elvira L. Henares-Esguerra has progressed in her advocacy of Breastfeeding.  A doctor of medicine, a pharmacist, a dermatologist and a International Board Certified Lactation Consultant, she accomplished in 6 ½ months what took the government 21 years to accomplish – usher into effect the rules and regulations that gave teeth to the National Milk Code of 1986 that was honored more in the breach than in the observance, through all the hearings in the Senate, House, the Bureau of Food and Drugs, the National Anti-Poverty Commission, the Presidential Cabinet, and the Supreme Court. She broke three Guinness World Records on Breastfeeding and Tree-Planting, and broke the nudity taboos on exposing breasts for breastfeeding practically worldwide, won at least three awards as outstanding physician, and still managed to earn a living as a dermatologist and her family's love as a trusted wife and a doting mother of three children, and international renown as a world traveler and a world advocate of Breastfeeding.

No one deserves the Prince Mahidol International Award than Dr. Elvira L. Henares-Esguerra, a Filipino, an Asian, a woman doctor who "transcended the narrow limits of her specialty to embrace the broad concerns of humanity."

(SIGNED – see hard copy)

Bu Castro, doctor and lawyer,

President of the Coalition of all the Philippine Health Organizations

ooooo

# STAGE AND SHADOWS

**I. BIG BROTHER** (A movie in Super 8, color and sound) 1970

*Scene at the Luneta (take advantage of President Marcos' Inaugural ceremonies).—Huge crowds cheering and haunting "Big Brother! Big Brother!". Medium shot of President Ronnie Henares surveying crowd. Fade in martial music, soldiers and tanks pass in review. Titles flash on the screen super-imposed on scenes of marching men.*

BIG BROTHER
Starring  RONNIE HENARES and
YEYETTE ALBERT
and introducing Danby Henares and Juno Henares
based on a short story "I Am Nothing"

*Scene at Luneta continues, fade in chant "Big Brother, Big Brother!" Ronnie motions for silence.*

**Ronnie***: My countrymen, I will be brief. For many years our just claims to the territory of Sabah have been ignored by the Federation of Malaysia. The time has come for action, not words.  My countrymen, we are at WAR! I therefore call on all Filipinos…

*Cheers drown out his words, and chanting begins anew, "Big Brother! Big Brother!" Close-up of Ronnie, as he continues talking; the words are not heard, but his thoughts are articulated on the soundtrack.*

**Ronnie***: (stream of consciousness)* Whatever reason I gave for the war with Malaysia is strictly for the history books, nothing but plausible pretexts. In all history there is but one root cause for conflict that persisted right back to the dim days of the jungle. When two monkeys want the same banana that is war.

*Back to close-up of Ronnie.*

**Ronnie***: (stream of consciousness)* Stupid fools! I can never be sure whether they hate me. One thing I am certain they fear me. Everyone fears me. Everyone without exception. I see to it one way or the other that everyone does. It is good to be feared. It is an excellent substitute for other emotions I have never known.

*Sudden cessation of chants, sudden flashback to picture of a child hysterically crying, being beaten by his parents.*

*Ronnie: (stream of consciousness)* When I was a child, I feared my father long and ardently, also my mother. Both of them so greatly that their passing came as a vast relief. *(back to close-up Ronnie)* Now it is my turn. This is the natural law, fair and logical. What is gained from one generation should be passed on the next. What is denied should likewise be denied.

*Flashback to picture of Ronnie as a young man raping a terrified Yeyette. Scene must be suggestive, not explicit.*

*Ronnie: (stream of consciousness)* I wanted Yeyette, and I took her. The strong always takes from the weak. She gave me obedience and fear, but never love. As long as I remember, form my very earliest years, love had never been forthcoming, not from Yeyette my wife, not from anyone, never, never, never!

*Flashback to picture of Danny weeping on his mother Yeyette's shoulder. He is in soldier's uniform. His father is ordering him to join the Armed Forces.*

*Ronnie: (stream of consciousness)* Yeyette bore me a son. Danny is weak, like his mother. My son, a weakling! I ordered him to join the Armed Forces, knowing fully well the inevitability if war with Malaysia. The war will make him strong. For our army is strong enough to conquer Malaysia.

*Cut in scene of war and carnage. Sound of artillery and cries of wounded.*

*Ronnie: (stream of consciousness)* It is the law of nature that the weak must give way to the strong. A sensible law. The Malaysians received my ultimatum and replied with protest and what they called an appeal to reason. In accordance with my instructions, our Armed Forces rejected this as unsatisfactory and the attack was on. The Malaysians pleaded for reasonableness that means they want us to go soft. Life is not made for soft.

*Cut in, Ronnie home, met by the maid, escorted to the room. He sees his wife reading.*

*Ronnie*: Danny is being promoted to captain. *(No answer)* Well, aren't you interested?

*Yeyette*: Of course, Ronnie. *(Puts aside book)*

*Ronnie*: What's the matter with you?

*Yeyette*: The matter? Nothing is the matter with me. Why do you ask?

*Ronnie*: I can tell. And I can guess. You don't like Danny being out there. You disapprove if me sending him away from you. You think of him as your son and not mine. You…

*Yeyette*: You're rather tired, Ronnie. And worried.

*Ronnie*: I am not tired, Neither am I worried. It is the weak who worry.

*Yeyette*: The weak have reason.

*Ronnie*: I haven't

*Yeyette*: Then you're just plain hungry. Have something to eat. It will make you feel better. *(She pours a cup of coffee and hands it to him)* There has been another letter from Danny.

*Ronnie*: Yes? I know he's happy, healthy and in one piece. If anything went wrong, I'd be the first to learn of it.

*Yeyette*: *(hands letter to Ronnie)* Don't you want to see what he says?

*Ronnie*: *(doesn't reach for it)* Oh, I suppose it's all the usual chit-chat about the war.

*Yeyette*: I think you ought to read it.

*Ronnie*: Do you? *(He takes the letter)* Why this particular letter should calls for my attention? Is it any different from the other? I know without looking that it is addressed to you. Not to me. To you. Never in his life has Danny written a letter specifically to me.

*Yeyette*: He writes to both of us.

*Ronnie*: Bah! Then, why does he always start with "Dear Mother"?

*Yeyette*: Probably, it just hasn't occurred to him that you would feel touchy about it.

*Ronnie*: Nonsense!

*Yeyette*: Well, you might as well look at it as argue about it unread.

   *Ronnie reads the letter. Off screen, the voice of Danny speaks.*

***Danny****:* Better tell you, I've become a willing slave for a Malaysian girl. Found her in what little was left of the village of Pori, which had taken a pretty bad beating from our heavy artillery. She was all alone and, as far as I could discover, seemed to be the sole survivor. Mom, she's got nobody. I'm sending her home on the hospital plane "Mayon". The captain was dubious, but dared not refuse the son of President Henares. Please meet her for me and look after her until I get back.

***Ronnie****: (flings letter on the table)* That imbecile! how dare he? The eyes of the world are on him. As a public figure, as the son of his father, he is expected to be an example. And what of some designing little skirt who is quick to play upon his sympathies. An enemy female!

***Yeyette****:* She must be pretty.

***Ronnie****:* No Malaysian are pretty. Have you taken leave of your sense?

***Yeyette****:* No, Ronnie, of course not.

***Ronnie****:* Then, why make such pointless remarks? One idiot in the family is enough. *(He punches his fist into his other palm)* At the very time when anti-Malaysian sentiment is at its height, I can well imagine that effect on public opinion if it became known that we were harboring an especially favored enemy alien, pampering some painted and powdered bitch who has dug her claws into Danny. I can see her mincing proudly around, one of the vanquished who became a victor by making use of a fool. Danny must be out of his mind.

***Yeyette****:* Danny is twenty one.

***Ronnie****:* What of it? Are you asserting that there's a specific age at which a man has a right to make a fool of himself?

***Yeyette****:* Ronnie, I did not say that.

***Ronnie****:* You implied it. Danny has shown an unsuspected strain of weakness. It does not come from me.

***Yeyette****:* No, Ronnie, it does not.

*Ronnie: (stares at her)* I'll bring this madness to a drastic stop. If Danny lacks strength of character, it is for me to provide it *(picks up phone)* There are thousands of girls in the Philippines. If Danny feels that he must have romance, he can it at home.

***Yeyette****:* He is not home. He is far away.

*Ronnie: (speak into phone)* Has the hospital plane, "Mayon" left Borneo yet? *(Yeyette looks up; he pauses to listen, and drops phone into cradle)* I would have had her thrown off, but it's too late. The girl is due here tomorrow. She's got a nerve, a blatant impudence. It reveals her character in advance. *(he pauses, mind working).* That scheming baggage is not going to carve herself a comfortable niche in my home, no matter what Danny thinks of her. I will not have her, see?

**Yeyette***:* I see, Ronnie.

**Ronnie***:* If he is weak, I am not. So when she arrives, I'm going to give her the roughest hour of her life. By the time I've finished, she'll be more than glad of passage back to Borneo on the next plane. She'll get out in a hurry and for keeps. *(Yeyette is silent)* But I'm not going to indulge in a sordid dramatic fracas in public. I won't allow her even the satisfaction of that, I want you to meet her at the airport, and then bring her to my office immediately. I'll cope with her there. Understand?

**Yeyette***:* Yes, Ronnie.

*Cut in shot of Malacañang, and then office of Ronnie. He sits impatiently drumming his fingers.*

**Intercom***:* Two people want to see you sir, Mrs. Henares and Miss Tatiana Aleli.

**Ronnie***:* Show them in *(Ronnie's face hardens, he stands up, turns back to the door, his hands behind his back. Off-screen, the door opens and closes. Yeyette speaks off-screen)*

**Yeyette***:* Ronnie? *(Ronnie whirls around)*

**Ronnie***:* Well, where is she?

**Yeyette***: (close-up, she smiles)* This is she.

*(Camera zooms out to reveal a little girl with doll, Ronnie is shocked, he sits down)*

**Yeyette***:* Well, Ronnie?

**Ronnie***:* Leave her with me for a few minutes, I'll call you when I have finished. *(Yeyette smiles and leaves)*

**Ronnie***:* Come here, Tatiana…round this side, please near to my chair. You're able to speak, aren't you? *(she nods vaguely)* But that isn't speech. *(she stares vacantly)* Are you glad you're here or sorry? *(No reaction).* Well, you're glad then? *(vague nod)* You're not sorry to be here? *(vague nod)* Would you rather stay or go back? *(she looks up with haunting eyes)*

**Ronnie***: (to intercom)* My wife please. *(Yeyette comes in)*

Take her home.

*Yeyette*: *(sweetly)* Home, Ronnie?

*Ronnie*: *(snaps)* That's what I said. *(he watches as they leave)*

*Fade in sala comedor. Ronnie is eating. Tatiana with her doll on the floor. She seems to live in a private world of her own. Ronnie is bothered of the silent figure, he couldn't eat.—He leaves the table to talk to her.*

*(Yeyette opens the door, spies the two and smiles)*

*Yeyette*: Are you two having a private gossip?

*Ronnie*: As if we could! *(he leaves, and slams the door)*

*Fade in, Ronnie at his office at home. He is staring out of the window watching Tatiana with her doll in the garden.*

*Intercom*: Yes, sir.

*Ronnie*: Get me Dr. Fernandez. *(he looks out again)*

*Intercom*: Dr. Fernandez on the line, sir.

*Ronnie*: Dr. Fernandez, I am saddled with maladjusted child. My son took a fancy to her and shipped her from Borneo. She's getting in my hair. What can be done about it?

*Fernandez*: I'm afraid I can't help you very much, sir.

*Ronnie*: Why not?

*Fernandez*: I'm a physicist, sir. You need a child psychologist.

*Ronnie*: Who's the best in the country?

*Fernandez*: Dr. Marquez

*Ronnie*: How can you get him to my home?

*Fernandez*: in 30 minutes, sir.

*Ronnie*: I want him here in 15 minutes.

*Fernandez*: Yes, sir.

*(Close up of fingers drumming on the desk)*

*Intercom*: Dr. Marquez is here to see you. Sir.

*Ronnie*: Let him in.

*(Dr. Marquez comes in)*

*Ronnie*: Dr. Marquez?

*Marquez*: Yes, sir.

*Ronnie*: Dr. Fernandez briefed you about my problem?

*Marquez*: Yes, sir.

*Ronnie*: Come here by this window. There she is.

*(They look out. Zoom to child. Zoom out to reveal Dr. Marquez approaching the child. He tries to talk to her, pretending conversation with doll. Ronnie watches from the window. Yeyette comes in and joins Ronnie.)*

**Yeyette**: Who's our visitor, Ronnie? Or is it no business to mine?

**Ronnie**: Some kind of a mind specialist. He's examining Tatiana.

**Yeyette**: Really?

**Ronnie**: Yes, really.

**Yeyette**: I didn't think you were interested in her.

**Ronnie**: I am not. But Danny is. Now and again I like to remind myself that Danny is my son.

*(Yeyette looks at him and smiles. She kisses him. He is surprised, and she leaves. He stares out of the window, then sits down on his desk, fingers drumming. Close-up of fingers, zoom out to reveal Ronnie.)*

**Intercom**: Dr. Marquez wants to see you sir,

**Ronnie**: Let him in *(Marquez enters)* Well, where is she?

**Marquez**: the maid took her. Said it was her bedtime.

**Ronnie**: Oh!

**Marquez**: I've a playful little game for dealing with children who are reluctant to talk. Nine times out of ten it works.

**Ronnie**: What is it?

**Marquez**: I persuade them to write. Strangely enough, they'll often do that, especially if I make a game of it. I cajole them into writing a story or essay about anything that created a great impression on them. The result can be revealing.

**Ronnie**: And did you…?

**Marquez**: Excuse me, sir. Before I go further, I'd like to impress upon you that children have an inherent ability many authors envy. They can express themselves with remarkable vividness in simple language with great economy of words. They create telling effect with what they leave out as much as what they put in. *(pause, looks at Ronnie)* You know the circumstances in which your son found this child?

**Ronnie**: Yes, he told us in a letter.

**Marquez**: Well, bearing those circumstances in mind, I think you'll find this exceptional in the way of horror stories.

*(hands him sheet of paper)* She wrote it unaided. *(he stands up to leave)*

**Ronnie**: You're going? What about your diagnosis? What treatment do you suggest?

**Marquez**: Beg your pardon, sir. You are an intelligent man. *(indicates sheet of paper)* I think that is all you require. *(leaves)*

*Ronnie looks at the sheet of paper. Music. Close-up of paper.*

*"I am nothing. I am nobody. My house went bang my cat was stuck to the wall. I wanted to pull it off. They threw it away!"*

*Ronnie reading sheet with horror in his eyes, zoom to his eyes. Montage of screaming Tatiana, explosion, cat on the wall, "Nothing"; explosion, Tatiana screaming; flashback of Ronnie as a child being beaten by parents; Yeyette screaming as Ronnie towered over her; Danny weeping; explosions, war scenes; Tatiana screaming—Ronnie, asleep on desk wakes up screaming in cold sweat. He stands up, like a drunken man, staggers to room of girl. Music. He tiptoes in, look at her, and tenderly tucks her in. Fade out.*

*Fade in Ronnie's desk at the house.*

**Intercom**: Prime Minister Yokosawa of Japan on an urgent unscheduled visit, sir. May I let him in?

**Ronnie**: Of course *(the Prime Minister enters)* Mr. Prime Minister, this is certainly a pleasant surprise.

**Yokosawa**: Mr. President, I'm sorry to have come without due notice, but I was in such a hurry.

**Ronnie**: Sit down. What can I do for you?

**Yokosawa**: I received a call from Prime Minister Ghazali of Malaysia. He said his country was involved in a serious dispute with your country. He appealed to me to intercede as a disinterested neutral.

**Ronnie**: Oh, so that is why you came.

**Yokosawa**: Yes, Mr. President. There was nothing for me but to come as fast as I could and hope for the best. The role of peace-maker appeals to those with any claim to be civilized.

**Ronnie**: Does it?

**Yokosawa**: It does to us. We called at Kuala Lumpur on the way here. The Malaysian still wants peace. They're losing the battle in Borneo. Therefore we want to know one thing: Are we too late?

     *Camera zooms to the eyes of Ronnie, he closes his eyes as if to shut out pain.*

**Ronnie**: *(stream of consciousness)* Too late? Yes or no? Yes means victory, power, glory... and empty victory like my victory over Yeyette, Danny and Tatiana. No means, well...

     *Camera zooms out to reveal Big Brother's Face. Off camera, Yokosawa's voice fade in*

**Yokosawa**: Are we too late?

**Ronnie**: *(slowly)* No. no it is not too late.

**Yokosawa**: You mean, Mr. President...

**Ronnie**: Your trip has not been in vain. You may negotiate.

**Yokosawa**: On what terms?

**Ronnie**: The fairest to both sides you can contrive. Malaysians are neighbors and blood brothers. It would please me if Malaysian and the Borneo territories agree to a union between our two countries, with common citizenship and joint development of natural resources. But I don't insist upon it. I merely express a wish—knowing that some wishes never come true.

**Yokosawa**: The preposition will be given serious consideration all the same time. *(stands up)* You're big man, Mr. President.

**Ronnie**: Am I? I'm trying to do a bit of growing in another direction. *(looks out of the window, long shot of Tatiana)* The original one kind of got used up.

**Yokosawa**: I must leave now, Mr., President.

**Ronnie**: Yes, yes. Thank you for coming, Mr. Prime Minister.

     *Prime Minister Yokosawa leaves, Ronnie looks out of the window; zooms to Tatiana, she has her eyes closed. She opens eyes, sits upright; zooms out, Ronnie approaches her, puts doll aside, sits beside her. She stares vacantly ahead.*

**Ronnie**: Tatiana, why are you nothing? *(no answer)* Is it because you have nobody? *(no answer. He is almost desperate trying to reach her)* Nobody of your own? *(no answer, he cries out)* Not even a kitten?

**Ronnie**: *(he gives up, sighs and mutters of himself)* Since I was very small, I have been surrounded by people. All my life, there have been lots of people. But none were mine. Not one was really mine. Not one. I, too, am nothing.

*Tatiana looks at him sympathetically puts her hand on his hand shyly. The dam breaks. Music. He snatches her on to his lap, hugs her. She weeps now as she never wept before, not as a woman does but like a child, with great racking sobs. He is weeping too as he rock and strokes and murmurs, "Tatiana, Tatiana." Yeyette comes and puts her arms around both.*

**Ronnie**: *(stream of consciousness)* This is victory. Not empty, but full victory.

*Camera zooms out to encompass the whole garden showing the tableau of Ronnie, Yeyette, and Tatiana.*
**-THE END-**

### II. MANG SERAPIO        (1972), by Juno Henares

1.      Fade in on shadowy figure, back lighted and huddled over what appears to be a baby. He is singing a sad lullaby:

"*Ito na Neneng, matulog ka na*
*Nandito ang tatay mo nagbabantay sa iyo*"

2.      The camera moves around the man, medium close-up and the lullaby is sung all throughout the credits that follow:

a.)      Atom Henares Production of Mang Serapio
b.)      Suggested by Paul Dumol's stage masterpiece
"*Ang Paglilitis Kay Mang Serapio*"
c.)      Screenplay by Juno Henares and Ateng Zaragosa.

3.      The song continues as the camera pans out of the windows where a blind beggar cocks his ears and mimics rocking baby, while a second dumb beggar condemns the act with inarticulate sounds and gestures.

4.      **CORDAPIO**, a lame beggar comes upon the two and asks: "*Mga pare ko, nariyan ba si Mang Serapio?*" the two beggars nod and gesture towards Serapio's room.

5.      **CORDAPIO** calls out "*Mang Serapio!*" **SERAPIO's** voice answer, "*Ano yon?*"

**CORDAPIO** tells him, "Ipinapatawag ka ng Boss."

**SERAPIO** emerges from the room. He is lame, a bit stupid, with dreamy look on face.

6.    *"Halika na.   Naghihintay ang Boss"*, says **CORDAPIO**.

Both leave…Dissolve to…

7.    **BOSS** (*one eyed beggar*), close-up, speaking:

*"Alam mo, Mang Serapio, baguhan ka pa dito. Marami ka pang dapat malaman. Ang patakaran ditto, lahat ng kita sa isang araw ay ibibigay sa kapisanan."*

8.    **SERAPIO**, absentmindedly, *"Lahat?"*

9.    **BOSS**: *"Oo lahat! Ang ibang kasamahan mo rin araw-araw ay cuarenta peso ang binibigay, nguni't ang sa iyo ay sampo lamang. Napakaliit naman ata. Bakit?"*

10.    **SERAPIO** does not answer. **CORDAPIO** answers for him:

*"Boss, bigyan natin siya ng pagkakataon. Alam mo naman, baguan pa lang siya rito."*

11.    **BOSS**: *"Sige. Pero mayroon pa akong ipaala-ala sa kanya. Una, huwag kang gumawa ng gulo sa pulis. Pangalawa, huwag umalis sa puestong ibinigay sa iyo. Pangatlo, ibigay mo lahat ng kita mo sa kapisanan, at doon na kunin ang lahat mong pangngangailangan, pagkain, gamut, lahat."*

12.    As the **BOSS** stands up, he adds:

*"Oo nga pala, baka sakali makakita ka ng sanggol sa basurahan. Maraming nangyayaring ganyan eh. Malaking tulong sa iyo yan, lalo na kung bulagin at pilayin."*

13.    **SERAPIO** is horrified. **CORDAPIO** drags him off saying:

*"Aalis na kami, boss. Huli na kami."*

**BOSS** answers:

*"O sige, lakad na, "* takes **CORDAPIO** aside,

*"Cordapio, kailangan bantayan mo iyan. Balita ko eh, nagtatago iyan ng pera mayroong ginagastahang iba."*

(Aloud): *"Sige lumakad na kayo."*

14.    They walk to their post. On the way, we see different kinds of beggars. A beggar with musical instruments. One with no legs selling sweepstake tickets. Another with rented child. A series of blind and lame beggars, while **CORDAPIO** makes appropriate remarks:

*"Tingnan mo yong mga lintik na iyon. Nakakatawa ano? Pero sinadya nila iyan na magpabulag at nagpapilay upang mas malaki ang kitain. Kung gusto mo eh, magpabulag din tayo."*

**SERAPIO** answers: *"mahirap yata iyan eh."*

15.    The two take up their positions in a street corner, replacing two other beggars whose turn just ended. They beg. **CORDAPIO** suddenly contorts himself into a pitiful sight, and gestures to **SERAPIO** to do the same.

16.    **SERAPIO** laughs and gets into the act. Many people come to put money into his hand. Suddenly a woman comes into the picture back lighted and bends to give him money.

17.    Music of the lullaby. **SERAPIO** starts. He stares at the woman, murmurs, *"Sol, Sol, mahal ko."* She is startled .He grabs her hand and cries out *"Sol, asawa ko, bumalik ka rin."* The girl screams, while **CORDAPIO** tries to extricate the girl from **SERAPIO's** clutches. The girl screams louder. A policeman's whistle is heard.

18.    Policeman's whistle. The girl screaming. Sound of policemen shouting and running. **CORDAPIO** wrenches **SERAPIO** away and drags him from the girl. They run. Policemen follow. The chase. They hide in an alley corner. The policemen runs past, misses them.

19.    Panting, **CORDAPIO** hisses, *"Naloloko ka ba? Bakit mo ginawa iyon?"* **SERAPIO** covers his face and sobs.

20.    **CORDAPIO** looks concerned: *"Napapano ka ba?"*

21.    **SERAPIO** sobs and moans: *"Sol! Sol!"* He is inarticulate. The scene dissolve to a flashback:

22.    Face of the woman Sol, screaming in childbirth. The midwife turns to **SERAPIO** (still a young man) *"Serapio, madali, tumawag ka ng doctor. Hindi makalabas ang bata, dinudugo si Sol."*

23.    **SERAPIO** rushes off the street, trying to stop vehicles; the cars careen dangerously past him. The car lights blind him. A screech of brakes, he is struck by a car. Zoom to his face: *"Sol! Sol! Ang anak natin!"*

24.    Zoom to face of **SERAPIO** as a beggar still screaming.

**CORDAPIO** slaps and shakes him:

"*Mang Serapio! Huminahon ka. Ano bang nangyayari sa iyo?*" **SERAPIO** does not answer.

"*O, tena. Kailangang malaman ito ni Boss.*"

25.     Door opens in a bodega. Night time. **CORDAPIO** and **SERAPIO** enter. They stare at:

26.     A circle of light at the center of the bodega, with one stool in the middle. Around are beggars of all descriptions, the lame, the blind, the dumb, the diseased, all staring at them. Am authoritative voice from a silhouetted figure intones, "*Mang Serapio, lumapit ka.*"

27.     **SERAPIO** hesitates. He is pushed forward by **CORDAPIO**. He moves to the center of light. He looks around frightened. The voice again:

"*Umupo ka Mand Serapio!*" He sits on the stool.

Pan to accusing faces of the beggars.

28.     The **BOSS** speaks, "*Mang Serapio, lumabag ka sa ating batas.*"

Serapio starts to speak, the boss shouts:

"*Tumahimik! Makinig ka. Sa iyong ginawa siguradung ikaw ay mapaparusahan. Hindi ba, mga kasama?*"

29.     **SERAPIO** asks "*Pero boss, ano ang aking pagkakasala?*"

The **BOSS** answers:

"*Ikaw ngayon Serapio ay aming lilitisin sa iyong maraming kasalanan. Una, tinakot mo iyong babae at ikaw ngayon ay pinaghahanap ng mga pulis. At pati kami napahamak tuloy dahil sa iyo. Hinuhuli tayong lahat.*"

**SERAPIO** is dumbfounded.

30.     **BOSS**: "*Pangalawa, ikaw ay nagtatago ng pera na dapat mapunta sa kapisanan. Mandaraya ka sa iyong mga kasamahan. O nandito ang iyong baul. Nakakandado. Iyan ang katibayan na ikaw ay talagang nangungupit ng pera.*"

31.     **SERAPIO**: "*Ha? Ang aking baul! Wala kayong karapatan na kunin yan iyan.*"He starts to move towards it. He is stopped by two beggars and pinned down. "*Walang laman iyan! Wala kayong karapatan.*"

32.     The **BOSS** moves towards Serapio, clutches his hair and shouts:

"*Walang utang na loob, magtigil ka!*"

**SERAPIO**: "*Walang laman iyan…*"

**BOSS**: *"At ang pangatlo, ikaw ay may alagang bata. Iyan ay labag sa ating batas. Kailangan na kung may anak kayo, dapat ay i-abuloy sa kapisana. At bulagin, pilayin, upang lalaki an gating malilikom na pera."*

33.   **SERAPIO**: *"Ngunit siya'y aking anak! Ang aking mahal…mahal na anak!"*

34.   **BOSS**: *"Ah, kalokohan. Wala na iyan sa ating kapuspalad na nilalang sa ibabaw ng lupa."*

35.   The camera pans to a woman with maimed child.

**BOSS**: *"Tingnan mo ang babaing iyan. Siya'y bulag at bingi. Wala nang pag-asa sa buhay. May anak siya, aming binulag. Ngayon doble ang kanyang kinikita."*

36.   **SERAPIO**: (screaming) *"Hindi! Hindi!"*

37.   The **CROWD** shouts: *"Ang pera! Ang pera! Buksan ang baol!"*

38.   **BOSS**: *"Serapio, nasaan ang susi?"*

39.   **SERAPIO**: *"Huwag! Huwag! Wala kayong karapatan!"*

40.   **BOSS** to **CORDAPIO**: *"Cordapio, hala sige basagin ang baol."*

41.   **SERAPIO**: *"Mga walang hiya! Huwag ninyong buksan!"*

42.   **SERAPIO**: *"Mga walang kayong kaluluwa! Sige, pagtulung-tulonga ninyo ako! Isusubong ko kayong lahat sa pulis. Ibubunyag ko kayong lahat sa pulis. Ibubunyag ko lahat ng kalokohan sa kapisanang ito. Sasabihin ko kung anong ginagawa ninyo sa mga bata."*

43.   Sudden silence. The **CROWD** steps back, shocked. The **BOSS** says: *"Serapio, pag-ginawa mo iyan, hindi ka manin mapapatawad. Ipapahamak mo kami na iyong mga kasamahan?"*

44.   **SERAPIO**: *"Talaga, mga hayup kayong lahat."*

The **CROWD** screams: *"Taksil! Magnanakaw! Mandaraya!"*

45.   **BOSS** signals for silence: *"Serapio, ikaw ay nagkasala. Tinakot mo ang ating mga parokyano at ipinahamak mo kami sa pulis. Nangungupit ka ng pera ng kapisanan. May alaga ka pang bata. At ngayon pinagbabantaan mo kami na*

*magsusumbong sa pulis. Inaamin mo sa ang iyong pagkakasala?"*

46.    **SERAPIO**: *"Hindi! Kayo ang may pagkakasala Ninakaw ninyo ang aking baul! Akin iyan! Kawawa ang aking mahal na anak!"*

47.    **BOSS** turns to the crowd: *"May pagkakasala ba o wala?"*

The **CROWD** shouts back: *"Mayroon! Mayroon!"*

48.    **BOSS**: *"Serapio, ikaw ay napatunayan na nagkasala sa ating batas. Kaya ikaw ay dapat lamang na parusahan. Kaya, Serapio, ihanda mo ang iyong sarili. Ito ang martilyo para durugin ang iyong mga buto. Katulad niyan!* (A lame beggar lurches forth and cackles) *Ito ay taga at kutsilyo para pumutol ng dila* (dumb beggar holds out his tongue, cackling). *At ito ay ice-pick. Ito ang pinakamasakit sa lahat! Iyan ay pang-ukit ng mata* (a blind beggar comes forth, cackling) *At iyan din ang mangyayari sa iyong anak pagnahanap naming."*

49.    **SERAPIO**: *"Hindi! Hindi! Maawa kayo sa akin at sa aking anak.* (cries)

50.    **BOSS** addresses the crowd: *"Mga kasama, anong gagawin natin sa kanaya?"*

51.    A **BEGGAR** answers: *"Bulagin!"* The rest of the **CROWD** takes up the cry: *"Bulagin! Pilayin ang kanyang anak! Bulagin!"* The surge forward and crowd over Serapio with ice picks. **SERAPIO** screams and screams.

52.    **CORDAPIO** succeeds in opening the box. **SERAPIO** still screaming. **CORDAPIO** takes out a doll, with a picture of Sol on the chest. He stares at it in disbelief. He whispered, *"Hindi! Manyika!"* He glances at the crowd, shouts: *"Manyika! Ang laman ng baul, Manyika!"*

53.    The **CROWD** stops, stares. They leave **SERAPIO** moaning on the ground.

54.    **SERAPIO**: *"Ang anak ko! Nasaan ang anak ko?"* He crawls around, blindly groping for the box. **CORDAPIO** drops the doll. The crowd steps back. **SERAPIO**, groping and crawling: *"Ang anak ko! Nasaan?"*

55.    **SERAPIO** finds the doll on the floor. He cradles it lovingly, *"Anak! Anak! Nandito na si Itay, Hindi ko sila*

*papayagan na ikaw ay saktan. Ssh, matulog kana, matulog kana."*

56.    Pan to the faces of the guilt-stricken **BEGGARS**. One drops his bloody ice-pick. Another wipes his bloody hands on his short.

57.    **SERAPIO** looks up, his eyes are bloody holes. He cradles the doll and sings his sad lullaby, *"Ito na Neneng, matulog ka na.—Ito ang tatay mo nagbabantay sa iyo."*

58.    One by one, the beggars leave till only **SERAPIO** is left within the circle of light.

59.    The music takes up the lullaby song and more credits appear on the screen on top of the still picture of Serapio with doll

60.    The End. Fade out.

### III.  MOMENT OF DECISION

Specially written by Hilarion M. Henares, Jr. and staged on the occasion of the Presidential Award for the Outstanding Mother of the Year presented to Doña Pelagia Garcia de Maramba at Malacañang, on December 7, 1953.

CAST OF CHARACTERS *(in order of their appearance):*

Doña Pelagia Garcia de Maramba played by Elfrida Regala de Maramba

Pacing Maramba, her eleven year old daughter, played by Lourdes K. Maramba

Don Pedro Sison, an intimate friend and political leader played by Felix K. Maramba, Jr.

Don Daniel Maramba, father and provincial governor played by Hilarion M. Henares, Jr.

Crowd of conventionists, offstage, played by the grandchildren.

*(Scene opens with Doña Pelagia sitting on the rocking chair. She is mending some socks. She glances through the window nervously once in a while, and goes back to her mending. No longer able to suppress her excitement, she lays down her mending and stands up and calls for Pacing.)*

***Pelagia****:* Pacing, Pacing, is everything all ready? *(Pacing enters through the left entrance).*

***Pacing****:* Yes, Nana?

***Pelagia****:* I said, is everything packed?

*Pacing*: But Nana, we have been packed since a week ago.

*Pelagia*: Yes I know, but did we not forget anything? Are you sure you packed the chinelas of your father?

*Pacing*: Yes Nana.

*Pelagia*: How about the kerosene lamp? You know how important that is in the farm.

*Pacing*: Oh Nana, you know we have gone through this several times before.

*Pelagia*: Oh yes, yes , I'm just little excited , that's all.

(*She goes back to the chair and resumes her mending; Pacing approaches her.*)

*Pacing*: What are you so excited about?

*Pelagia*: (*excitedly*) We're going back to the farm. Oh hija, you don't know what this means to me—to be back at the farm and at work again—your father and I and all the rest of your children—together at the last after all these years. Let me see… how old are you now?

*Pacing*: Nana, you ought to know. I am eleven years old.

*Pelagia*: Of course, of course, I ought to know, but there are quite a number of you—eight children—and some times I forget. Yes, you are eleven years old and soon, pretty soon, you will have to go to high school. Your brother Feling, is going to college now. He is going to the United States to study. Do you want to go to the States to study Pacing?

*Pacing*: No. Nana, I'd rather be with you.

*Pelagia*: (*laughs*) You say that because you are only eleven years old. When you grow older like your Atchi and Cuya, you will want to go to the States too. And you will need clothes and money for your board and lodging, money for your tuition and books…

*Pacing*: But where will we get the money, Nana?

*Pelagia*: Pacing, I know we did not have much money during these past three years. You see your papa is the governor of this province. As governor, he spends more money than he earns. We did not have much because we did not have time to take care of our farm. (*She brightens up*) But it will be different form now on. A few months from now on he will no longer be governor. And we will be going back to the farm again so we can earn enough money to send you and all the rest of your brothers and sisters to school. Why, today, Pacing, right now, this very moment, they are holding a convention to choose the man to succeed him. Think of it! No wonder I am so excited. It must be over now. Oh why don't they come? They should be here by this time.

(*The noise of the crowd coming from the distance is coming louder and louder. One can hear shouts of Mabuhay Gobernador Maramba! Mabuhay!*")

*Pelagia*: They're here, Pacing, they're here, Pacing...Go out to the kitchen and have them prepare coffee. Hurry! Hurry!

*Pacing*: Yes, Nana, *(exits on the left)*

(*Don Pedro comes in form the right exit. Pelagia comes*)

*Pelagia*: Pedro, Pedro, where's Daniel?

*Pedro*: He's outside talking to his leaders. He will be coming right in. This has been a great day, Doña Pelagia.

*Pedro*: Yes, it's over at last.

*Pelagia*: At last! At last! We can go back to our farm. Oh Pedro, you don't know how much this means to me. Do you know that for years I have gone through this kind of life...all this hectic politicking...we are through with all this. *(Pedro looks a little surprised.)*

*Pedro*: But Doña Pelagia, I don't think you understand...

*Pelagia*: Understand? Pedro, do you remember the revolution when Daniel went off to the mountains and I was left without help and support? I died a thousand deaths waiting for him! But I never suffered as much as I did during this last three years when Daniel was governor. I did not mind his being Municipal Mayor in the years before. I did not mind neglecting the farm and going through the endless, meaningless political chores. My children were very small then. But I have eight of them now and all of them are going to school. We have a responsibility towards these children and from now on we will discharge that responsibility—Daniel and I. Far, far away from the political scene, thank God.

*Pedro*: But Doña Pelagia, what I am trying to tell you is --I don't quite know how to say it.

*Pelagia*: What are you trying to say, Don Pedro? What happened at that convention?

*Pedro*: I don't think you will like this.

*Pelagia*: Like what, Pedro? Pedro, tell me—I want to know.

*Pedro*: Don Daniel has been nominated unanimously to another term.

*Pelagia*: Oh no! no.

*Pedro*: Yes, Doña Pelagia, the people clamored for him. You should have seen it…

The crowd went wild. They never even gave him a chance to speak. They raised him up on their shoulders—shouting and cheering, clamoring for his reelection.

*Pelagia*: *(in a small voice)* But he gave me his word. He said he will not run again.

*Pedro*: He must, Doña Pelagia, he must. He's the one called upon by the people to tackle the job. Can't you see, Doña Pelagia, he does not wholly belong to you. He belongs to the people of this province. They need him.

*Pelagia*: I need him too and so do my children. I won't have it, I tell you, I won't.

*Pelagia*: Tell your Don Daniel that with or without him I am going back to the farm. Tell him that.

*(No longer able to suppress her tears, she rushes into the left exit. At the same time from the right exit rushes in Don Daniel.)*

*Daniel*: Pelagia, Pelagia…

*(Goes after her. He is stopped by Pedro)*

*Pedro*: I don't think you should see her right now, Daniel

*Daniel*: Why, what happened?

*Pedro*: I told her you have just been nominated.

*Daniel*: You didn't! I wanted to tell her myself. Pedro, what have you done?

*Pedro*: I'm sorry, I did not know, I just told her that you were nominated. I did not expect her to react that way.

*Daniel*: It's no use. I tried to tell them at the convention that I couldn't accept the nomination. But they wouldn't even let me speak. Deep inside I knew she wouldn't be happy as long as I am in politics. And yet, in that convention…what's the use, I gave her my word that I would not run again.

*Pedro*: Daniel, deep in your heart you also know that you'd never be happy unless you give your life to your people. They need you. You know that. And I don't think you will ever fail them. You remember what happened when the big flood came and destroyed the rice harvest? Who else but you could have inspired that people to pick up their tools and start to build up again? Who else but you have the vision tyo plan a flood control project,,,.

*Daniel*: (*excitedly*) That flood control project can divert the flood waters and store them for irrigation. Think of it, Pedro, we can have an irrigation system so that rain or no rain our people can plant and grow rice. Pangasinan will not only be the granary, but also the garden of the Philippines. Pedro, we will need roads, more roads and bridges over which we can bring our produce to all parts of the province—nay, to all parts of the country. We will need railroads, too, and telegraphs and telephones.

(*All this time Doña Pelagia slips in unnoticed and watches her husband with fascination as he animatedly describe the plans he has for the future. Daniel stops and look at her, embarrassed. Pedro still unaware of the presence of Doña Pelagia is carried by Daniel's enthusiasm...*)

*Pedro*: Only you can do it, Daniel, only you!

*Daniel*: (*sadly*) No, Pedro, not I...not I, but the man who is going to succeed me. Go tell our leaders that I have decided to withdraw from the election.

*Pedro*: But...

*Daniel*: (*decidedly*) I have made up my mind. Neither you nor anyone else can change it. Go now, tell them I am out of the race.

*Pedro*: Won't you rather tell them yourself?

*Daniel*: (*sinks down on the rocking chair*) No! No! I cannot face them, I cannot!

(*Pedro leaves and Doña Pelagia approaches Daniel. She sits on the floor in front of Daniel and lays her cheek on his knee.*)

*Pelagia*: Daniel, Daniel, I don't know what to say.

*Daniel*: What else is there to say? In a few months I shall no longer be governor and we can go back to the farm... just as you always dreamed.

*Pelagia*: Daniel, as I watched you just now talking about things that you wanted to do, as I watched you, I knew...what I never wanted to believe...that there is one part of you that will never be mine. I don't think that you were ever cut out to be a farmer. At heart you will always be a leader to your people. I was a fool to think that I could drag you out of politics. It is in your blood and I don't think you will ever be happy knowing that you have failed your people when they needed you.

*Daniel*: But our children…they are going to college now…

*Pelagia*: And they will go to college! Because Daniel, I am going back to the farm! *(Daniel starts to speak but she puts her fingers on his lips.)* No, don't say a word! Let me continue. I am going back to the farm and run it! I can do it myself. I helped you clear that land when it was only a wilderness! I have worked on it when you fought in the revolution.

*Daniel*: But Pelagia…

*Pelagia*: Let's be practical. I can work. You know I can. You stay in Lingayen and serve out your term. I'll stay in the farm and wait for you every week-end. I will see to it that we will have enough money for your political expenses. And I will see to it that your children will get the education they are entitled to. Daniel…for the last three years I have been nothing but a burden to you. From hereon I will be truly your partner, your wife, and the mother of your children.

*(Daniel stands up, strokes her hair, in his eyes a new light of respect for Pelagia.)*

*Daniel*: You are truly wonderful woman, Pelagia.

*Pelagia*: Go, Daniel, Go to your people, they are waiting outside, and I'll be waiting here when you need me.

*(Daniel stands up, walks to the right exit and halfway he stops, turns around towards his wife, he smiles. Shouts of the crowds can be heard outside—"Mabuhay Don Daniel!" Pelagia stands up, sits down on the chair buries her face in her hands, and sob softly. The stage darkens, music fades in and voice of narrator is heard.)*

*Narrator*: Doña Pelagia Garcia de Maramba—for you this was the moment of decision. You were lost in the tears of uncertainty—for the first time in your life the heavy weight of responsibility fell on your frail shoulders—and you knew not whether you were right or wrong.

But the years proved kind to you. You saw your husband blaze a trail across the political horizon as a governor, as a congressman, as a respected senator of the

Commonwealth of the Philippines. In his lifetime, he was known as the Grand Old Man of Pangasinan. You watched him die amidst the roar of planes and the burst of bombs—alone save for his family, in a suite in Quezon Institute, worn out by a lifetime of sacrifice to the service of his people. You sanctified his death bed with a kind tearless resignation born of the wisdom of the ages. There was a halo on the moon that night. Amidst the pandemonium of a world gone mad, it seemed that there was one place that was blessed with eternal peace. That peace was in your heart, Doña Pelagia—for God knows you were a good wife.

Your husband left a name for your children to live up to. And you saw to it that they did. Thirty-five years will have come and gone since you made the decision of your lifetime. And your children? They are the products of your success as a mother.

*(The spotlight seeks out Lolita and each of the children in the audience as their names are called. Each stands as he is mentioned.)*

**Lolita** is your youngest child, a nutritionist of note. The United Nations gave her recognition by sending her to various countries of the East Asia to help in the world's fight against disease and starvation.

**Nicanor** is a guerrilla fighter, a leader among the underprivileged, a pioneer in the best traditions of the frontier, a man among men.

**Paz** is a housewife first and foremost. She married an army man, presently a Lieutenant Commander of the Philippine Navy. But her claim to distinction lies in her joy of motherhood, in the unquenchable humor with which she faces life, in her limitless capacity for love and compassion that extends far beyond her family circle.

Then comes **Tomas**, a small man with a big heart, a quiet man of honesty and integrity. One if the first of the CPA's, he is a beloved professor, trusted bank employee, a friend with an instinct for humanity. Of all your children he enjoys the widest circle of friends.

And now **Arturo**, a lawyer turned farmer who views life as an exciting game. He inherited from his father a profound understanding of people, a trait that served him well in his undertakings.

**Emilia** was a school teacher, a stern disciplinarian with a heart of gold. She is dead now, God Bless her soul. Her tragic death left four orphans all of whom are in good hands.

**Concepcion** is your eldest daughter, a national figure of her own right. Starting out as a champion of women's rights, she became a social and civic leader of note and is presently the President of the National Federation of Women's Club. A chemist, an inventor, an assistant to her engineer husband, she was voted Woman Industrialist of 1950

**Felix** is your eldest son, a proud son of a proud father, the Dean of Filipino Agricultural Engineers. Now retired after 31 years of government service, he has served in turn as Director of the Bureau of Plant Industry, as the General Manager of the Land Settlement and Development Corporation.

*(The real Doña Pelagia stands up from the front seat, faces the audience spotlighted.)*

**Doña Pelagia Garcia de Maramba**, today, on the 7th day of December, 1953, your countrymen gave you an award as an Outstanding Mother of the Year.

To your eight children, their children and their grandchildren, you will always be the best Mother in the world, now and for all the generation to come.

*(The music mounts to a climax on the tableau, and the curtain slowly closes.)*

**-THE END-**


**IV.   The Most Perfect Form   from the movie, Gigli w/ *Jennifer Lopez*, Ben Affleck**

**Man**: So I'm not your type, huh?

***Woman:*** *How did we get back there all of a sudden?*

**Man**: Relax. You're more woman than I know what to do with. I don't need to be dipping into the sisterhood. But I am just curious, because all of a sudden now, you say you've been with guys.

***Woman:*** *I have.*

**Man**: But they have their shortcomings?

***Woman:*** *Besides the fact that they give terrible head.*

**Man**: See, right there, that tells me something.  I know the guys you've been with obviously did not know how to bring home the pearls when they were diving for oysters.

*Woman: I was actually just joking.*

**Man**: Well since we're letting it all hang out now, let me tell you something else.  Okay.  When it comes to pleasing a woman, your girlfriends, they're just at a natural disadvantage.  It's like they might try hard, but they're not just backed up by millions of years of genetic engineering, programming, instinct.  Nature has evolved man for that purpose.  Satisfy.  Lead the pack.  That's why lesbians are always buying, spending their dough on, you know... sexual appliances, erotic monkey wrenches and shit, trying to compensate for what they don't have.  For what they're not getting.  The penis.  That's right.  Its very design tells you everything you need to know.  Forward motion.  With advancements.  Fucking progress into the dark deep mysterious unknown.  It's like adventure seeking, frontier conquering, obstacle eradicating...

*Woman: And you tried to create the impression you don't not read books.*

**Man**: You're settling for second best. That's what all I am saying.

*Woman:  So in review, you're saying that it is men that are at the top of the must-fuck pyramid.*

**Man**: That's all I'm telling you.

*Woman: Loving, caring, sensitive, giving men.*

**Man**: That's right.

*Woman:  You're entitled to your opinion.  But let us reconsider women for a minute.  Shall we?*

**Man**: Sure.

*Woman: Their form.  Neck.  Shoulders.  Legs.  Hips.  I think pretty cool.  Now as far as your famous penis goes, the penis is like some sort of bizarre sea slug or like a really long toe.  I mean it's handy, important even, but the pinnacle of sexual design?  The top of the list of erotic destinations?  I don't think so.  One's first impulse is to kiss what?  To kiss the lips.  Firm delicious lips.  Sweet lips.  Surrounding a warm moist dizzyingly scented mouth.  That's what everyone wants to kiss.  Not a toe.  Not a sea slug.  A mouth.  And why do you think that is, stupid?  Because the mouth is the twin sister, the almost exact look alike of the what? Not the toe. The mouth is the twin sister of the vagina. All creatures big or small seek the orifice. The opening. To be taken in, engulfed. To be squeezed and lovingly crushed by what is truly the all powerful, all encompassing... Now if it's design you're concerned with, hidden meanings, symbolism, power, forget the top of Mount Everest. Forget the bottom of the sea, the moon, the stars. There is no place, no where that has been the object of more ambitions, more battles than the sweet sacred mystery between a woman's legs that I am proud to call my pussy. So I guess it's just my round-about way of saying that it is the women who are in fact the most desirable form. Wouldn't you agree?*

**Man**: I agree.
***Woman:*** *And so do I.*
*April, 2004*


**V.   NOT IN VAIN by Atom L. Henares, La Salle Green Hills, 1969, Voice of Democracy**

The story was once told that St. Peter, worried about what was wrong with the world, commissioned St. Theresa to come down to earth and find it out.

The first thing of course St. Theresa did was to visit St. Theresa's College. A few days later, she dialed heaven to report: "Hello, St. Peter. This is St. Theresa. I know what's wrong with the world. Women! With their hot pants and mini skirts they willfully contrive to resist a man's advance and then block his retreat."

"St. Theresa, you don't find out what's wrong with the world in St. Theresa's College. Why don't you try Ateneo, Lyceum or the University of the Philippines?"

Two weeks later, the heavenly telephone rang again: "Hello, Peter baby. This is Terry. I know what's wrong with the world. These flower children with long hair, beards and sandals! They're the ones who wave placards. Break windows and cry for revolution. Peter baby, you better tell the Boss about these kids with long hairs, beards and sandals!"

St. Peter wasted no time telling his Boss: "Boss, you really have to do something about these young revolutionaries with long hair, beards and sandals!"

# *Heaven and Hell*

The Almighty looked at St. Peter and replied, "Have you forgotten, St. Peter? I had a Son too, and he had long hair, beard and sandals!"

Indeed, it may be said without being irreverent that Christ was a revolutionary of his time, an agitator with ideas dangerous to the status quo. His manifesto was the Sermon on the Mount; his crucifixion, a testament to the police brutality of his day.

Have you time right now, ladies and gentlemen, to meet revolutionists of our times? Look in on mass meetings and manifestoes, song and shouting, placards of protest, bonfires and barricades, strikes and demos, dated Planet Earth, 1969

From the student activities in Manila, to the Zengakeren in Tokyo, to KAMI of Indonesia; across the unpacific oceans to Berkeley, Harvard and Columbia; flash across the dark Atlantic, eastward against the grain of time to older worlds, in France and Czechoslovakia; as far south as South America, as far east as the Far East—you see very much the same faces.

Line them up in your mind's eye and observe. Who are they?

Here's one who is the despair of barbers, with "long beautiful hair, shining, gleaming, streaming, flaxen waxen"—a Jack who looks like Jill and smells like John.

Here's another who grazes in the grass, smoking pot and holding out a flower—one might say, a flower power pot.

There are others of course, who do take a bath and smell like a fresh Breeze, *"di lang malinis, amoy malinis pa."* And these are the one with the more intense look, who are sickened and outraged by our times, and who cry out for revolution!

Observe them. Note them well.

They are your sons and daughters, flesh of your flesh, blood of your blood, poured out of your loins and wrenched out of your wombs. They are the youth of our nation, the hope the fatherland, the future of our democracy.

According to a famous psychologist, the youth of today are as culturally distinct from their parents, as we Filipino are from the Eskimos.

We who are young indeed a breed apart from our parents. We are different. We are different in our art, our literature, in our moral outlook, in our political ideas, in our way of thinking and feeling and doing. Conditioned by the Atom, the

Computer and the Satellite, we have become the First Citizens of a shrinking New World, painfully conscious of the common humanity of man. We are in truth the first generation of the Universal Man.

A young college graduate on his way home on his first day in his new job, was waylaid by a gang of hoodlums in a crowded street in broad daylight. He clung to a lamp-post, screaming for help, legs broken and battered with a baseball bat, flesh ripped and rent by daggers and darts, screaming, till he slumped, twitching, into the silence of death. Death for no reason at all—senseless, brutal, insane—while a crowd of witnesses watched like a movie audience, fascinated.

The widowed mother of that young man sits alone in her room with his picture tonight, as she does every night, and remembers among other things how he struggled with the barber when he had his first hair cut and how she tired to calm him. And her thoughts burn like candles, quietly and slowly, and they trail into smoke, and are lost in shadows. To the mother, the death of her son is as deeply personal as the pain of her private grief.

But to us, the youth, the death of that young man is one with all that pains of human society, a sign and portent of malignant cancer.

Our president warns that we sit atop a social volcano. A vice governor is assassinated on the very steps of the provincial capitol. A movie star is abducted and ravished. A woman is butchered and hacked into bits like a hunk of beef. These and many more…

Signs and portents? This is no furtive tapping on the window sill, but clamorous pounding in the public square, blow after blow like a monstrous dropforge, beating into shape the times to come.

Do you wonder then that we who are young want a complete overhaul of human values and institutions?

You taught us peace and the brotherhood of man. Suffer us then to march in protest against violence and crime, foreign bases, unequal treaties and the horror that is Vietnam.

You taught us justice and human dignity. Suffer us then to grieve in anger for the Negroes in the United States, for the poor and the hungry among us, the friendless, the cheated and the beaten.

# Heaven and Hell

You taught us self-involvement. Suffer us then, since you have not given us the vote, to use the only means we have to advance our cause: demonstrations and confrontations.

You taught us the value of sacrifice. Suffer us then to suffer the brutality of those who would club us into silence, name-plates removed, with authority dangling from a gun hoster.

Suffer us "to dream the impossible dream, to right the unrightable wrong, to reach the unreachable star."

Yes, we are revolutionists. In a conformist society, we are the dissenters. In a frivolous society, we are the thinkers and the doers. In a society hypnotized by slogans and dogmas; we have a mind of our own and the courage to speak it out. In the Philippines jungle with its exhibitionist monkeys, idle peacocks, trained parrots and predatory hawks, we are the incaged lions.

Judge us by the enemies we make. Their names are Intolerance, Greed, Apathy, Servility; Opportunism in a coat and tie; Hypocrisy in a barong tagalong; Bigotry in a cassock; Poverty, Ignorance, Injustice—we fight them all, and we are proud of our wounds!

Ladies and gentlemen, in every generation there lies a dream, a dream of greatness enshrined in its own niche of time. No matter how secret or how small, it is a seed awaiting growth and fulfillment.

We of the Filipino Youth, born without an umbilical cord to the colonial past, we who have never known what it is to be under a foreign master, unhindered by the chains of the status quo, do hereby take up the challenge of change to fulfill our own dream of greatness. We lift our eyes above the far horizons, we lift them up to where faith prayers and visions have wing room, and build our castle in the air. We leave our castle in the air, and now we build foundations under them.

> *Plead, plan, plot and build.*
> *Hammer, hack, hold, and build,*
> *Yell, pull, push and build,*
> *And build and build up to the stars*
> *Till the universe shall know of our strength!*

So that when all the stories have been told, and all the songs have been sung, and all there is to be has become, then we the youth of today may well turn to the children of tomorrow, and say:

We have not lived in vain.
*We have not lived in vain!*

## VI.  The Many Faces of Christ

### Part 1. Ben Hur: A Tale of the Christ

There are many stories about how Jesus Christ affected the lives of people.  One such story in fiction is the story of Ben-Hur, as depicted in a magnificently filmed silent version made in black and white in 1926, starring Ramon Novarro and Francis X. Bushman.

It was the last of the great spectacles of the silent film, impossible to duplicate in these days of inflation, independent producers and constricted budgets.  Even the new version in 1959 starring Charlton Heston and Stephen Boyd pales in comparison, its sea battles done with miniature sets and small dolls.  The silent version had real sets, peopled by thousands of extras.  And the Nativity scenes which served as an overture to this master opus, were painstakingly tinted in color, by hand frame by frame.  A special orchestral score was composed for the movie, and it was shown complete with full orchestra in the big theaters, and with the magnificent Wurlitzer Organ in smaller theaters.

And in my opinion, the story was better told in the silent version than in the sound version, with a panorama of soundless tableaus that were simply breathtaking.  The scion of a rich family during the time of Christ, Ben-Hur's world was shattered when watching the parade of conquering Romans below, he accidentally loosed a tile that almost hit the Roman tribune.  His childhood friend Messala, a Roman soldier, was instrumental in sending his mother and sister to the Roman dungeons where they contracted leprosy.

Messala also had him dragged across the desert as a criminal -- where he met Jesus who gave him water to quench his thirst. -- and had him condemned as a galley slave in the Roman Navy.  In a sea battle Ben Hur rescued the Roman Commander who adopted him as a son and heir with a new name Arius.  In this capacity he had a chance to exact vengeance on Messala in a chariot race that is a classic in fictional literature.  Finding the mysterious preacher being proclaimed as the Messiah and the King of the Jews, he raised an army to fight the Romans and rescue the Man condemned to be crucified on a cross.  But he also found that His kingdom was not of this earth, to be founded on Love, Charity and Mercy. When the Christ was carrying his cross on the cobblestones of Jerusalem, Ben-Hur followed and found his long-lost mother and sister cured by the same Man who gave him water to drink in the desert.

The scenes of the Crucifixion provided a fitting Coda to this masterpiece.  See it on Laser Disc, available for rental in the Sunshine Video Shop in the Magallanes Commercial Center.

### Part 2.  The Four Versions of Judas Iscariot

Jorge Luis Borges of Argentina died without ever winning the Nobel Prize for Literature, but his admirers feels he should have.  He is probably the most interesting writer of this century. He wrote stories as short as one paragraph, so real and yet so other-worldly that its effect stays with you the rest of your life. There is the story of a Jew condemned to death by Hitler's Nazis, who discovered that time does not exist and asks God to suspend his execution.  God agrees, and when the time comes for him to be shot, "Ready, aim....," he lives a lifetime before the word "Fire!"  He dies and the time interval recorded was only one second.  He has another story about a man who dreams about a stranger who seemed so real, then discovers in the end that he himself is a dream of that same stranger.

But Borges' most shocking piece is one called "The Four Versions of Judas," wherein Borges argues that when God became Man to save mankind, He found no merit in only two days of suffering and being forever revered as the Messiah and the King of Kings.  No, Borges said, God's love for us requires the greatest sacrifice of all, that of being reviled forever as a Betrayer and the worst villain of all time.  Therefore, Borges says, Christ is really Judas Iscariot.

That is his fourth version of Judas.  The first three versions of course are standard fare, if I remember right:  (1) That Judas is really the villain who wanted to be a power in the service of the King of the Jews, was disappointed, and betrayed Christ;  (2) That Judas was really a mere hired hand assigned the role of villain by God himself, and is therefore blameless; (3) That he was really forced into the role against his will, and therefore, should be considered a victim of the powers-that-be.

The famous Cecil de Mille silent movie made in 1927, "The King of Kings" about Jesus Christ, opens with a lengthy and lavish orgy filmed in the original two-strip Technicolor process, crude but impresssive in 1927. Mary Magdalene is depicted as a courtesan, that is, an expensive prostitute. She is waiting impatiently for her favorite, the handsome Judas Iscariot, and is insulted to find out that her boyfriend Judas prefers the company of a lowly carpenter than her own. Imperiously she mounts her chariot drawn by zebras, a gift of the Nubian king, and goes to cow the carpenter, and instead finds herself purged of the seven deadly sins. Judas Iscariot is depicted as an ambitious nobleman who wanted to be the power behind the new King of Israel. He was disappointed to find out that Jesus sought not power but the goodness in the hearts of men, and he betrayed him. This resulted in the Crucifixion and death of our Lord, and his suicide out of despair.

### Part 3. The Many Faces of Christ

In the controversial film, "The Last Temptation of Christ," while dying on the cross, Jesus is asked by an angel if he wanted to suffer and die. Time stops while Jesus himself weakens and yearns to live an ordinary life as the husband of Mary Magdalene. He is taken from the cross, and re-lives his life, as a husband and father, to the very end. While he is dying of old age, he is visited by his Apostles. It is Judas who insists that Jesus perform his assigned role of sacrificial lamb, and Jesus finds himself in a time warp, back on the cross on Calvary, dying as he was meant to be, thus fulfilling his destiny and ours.

The story of Christ has been told many times in the movies, each accompanied by a storm of controversy. Once it was considered sacrilegious to even show His face, or even to show Him speaking, or tell the story except as depicted in the Bible. In the 1925 version of Ben-Hur, Jesus' face is never shown, only His hands raised in benediction. In the lavish 1927 production of Cecil de Mille's "King of Kings," the entire Jesus is shown. But because the Son of God is divine rather than human, Jesus exudes a kind of sacred boredom, "moving through darkened space radiating a divine glow by means of an ill-defined halo."

In the 1961 "King of Kings" Jeffrey Hunter portrayed Christ as a believable human being, with moving moments during the Sermon of the Mount. In the 1965 "Greatest Story Ever Told," Jesus is portrayed by Max von Sydow looking as if he was suffering from a terrific constipation. Probably because of an indigestible succession of cameo roles of big time actors like Charlton Heston, Angela Lansbury, Sidney Poitier, Jose Ferrer, Claude Rains, Telly Savalas and others, including (hahaha) John Wayne as a Roman Centurion supervising the Crucifixion.

"Jesus of Nazareth" by Franco Zeffirelli is a TV mini-series worth watching. Now there are many interpretations of Christ. As a human being subjected to sexual fantasies (in "The Last Temptation of Christ"). As a musical Superstar (in "Jesus Christ Superstar"). As an unconventional and austere Marxist hero in a beautiful film directed by a Communist, "The Gospel According to St. Matthew".

And also as a comic figure disguised as Brian, who was born next door to the manger, and whose life parallels that of Christ (in Monty Python's "Life of Brian"). Brian is wildly hilarious as he denies he is the Messiah and the crowd insists he is; and in the last scene at the crucifixion, Brian is cheered up by chorus line of criminals being crucified, singing "Always look at the bright side of life."

*April 4-8, 1996, ISYU*

ooooo

# THE HUMAN CONDITION

### I.  The joys of parenthood

To be a good father, one must first be a good husband. To be a good husband, one has to be a good son.  To be a good son, one has to have a good father.  And that is the root of the saying that the child is father to the man.  The good is often passed on from one generation to another till the end of time.

After our wedding, my wife and I decided that before we become parents, we have to wait two years to get to know each other.  And we did.  When we had our first child, a boy named Ronnie, we were ready to enjoy the pleasures of parenthood. He was followed by Atom, Elvira, Danby, Juno and Rosanna. First, we realized that our children were brought into this world without their express consent and definitely at our own pleasure; therefore we owe them more than they owe us.  We owe them a good life, nourishment for their bodies, education for their minds, a Christian upbringing for their characters.  They owe us of course, their love and obedience and loyalty.

Be that as it may, the stage was set for the grandest adventure of our lives.  The nice part about being children is that their early life is punctuated with milestones that seem to stretch out in time, as in slow motion, and prolong our parental pleasures – the smell of baby powder and baby lotion, the first time they sit up and crawl and stand up, the time they say their first words, their first alphabet, and walk and run, their first haircut and begin their schooling, ride their first bike, and get their first medal and diploma.  These are experiences to stick to our minds and our memories.

From there on their lives are already a repetition of the milestones, year after year in their school commencements. And the years come much faster, in fast forward mode, until we parents are rudely awakened to find they have already grown up, going on their first date, going abroad for graduate work, getting their first job and getting married.  This is the most trying period of parenthood, dealing with their teen-age years.

Our parental pleasures grow out of high hopes and great expectations that our children will become better than we parents are.  We take pride in their good looks, their sterling characters, and brilliant minds, and treasure every moment that the best in them become manifest, whether in the form of medals and good grades, or accounts of their kindnesses, their capacity to make friends and influence people, the love of their sweethearts, the skills they develop in photography, in writing, in computer work, etcetera – all that provide us with colorful anecdotes with which to regale our friends and other members of our family.

We parents must treasure every moment we spend with our children, and enjoy them to the outmost, even at the expense of our life's work, our means of livelihood, our life style. Why? Because we are given only a limited time to be parents, and sooner more than later, we will lose them to their grandparents who can devote more time and resources to their education and training. We will eventually lose them to their peers and friends, social acquaintances and business associates who will share their lives to the very end of their days.

By that time, we are ready to enjoy being grandparents to our children's children, which is even better, because as such we can enjoy the children even more, spoiling them with impunity without suffering the consequences, sending them home to their parents when they begin to be a nuisance, and doubly enjoy each milestone the punctuates their journey upon this earth.

But let me tell you the greatest lesson I have learned. To be a good son, a good husband, a good father and a good grandfather, one must be above all, a good man.

### II.  The Story of Two Miracles

After my daughter Elvira suffered two miscarriages, her children Angeli' and Gabriel, aged 8 and 6 respectively, asked: "Mama, why does God give us a baby and then take it away?" Desperate for answers, Elvira replied, "Maybe God does not think you want to share your toys, compete for parental attention, or give up part of your allowances or inheritances." They answered, "Oh mama, we do not care for material things, we will gladly sacrifice everything just to have a brother or sister! But we are still lucky. We have each other, while Tita Rosanna does not even have one child because she just can't have any. If God gives us only one child, no matter how much we want him, we would rather give him to Tita Rosanna who does not have one of her own." Elvira broke into tears and begged them, "Then children, pray, ask the Lord for a baby." Elvira now says that the prayers of her little ones, both named after angels, "must have touched God's heart, because He gave us not one but two babies, one for Rosanna and one for myself, both boys, the first of the Henareses to be born in the new millennium."

It was not easy. Elvira had one more miscarriage and had an operation in her left ovary to take out a cyst the size of an avocado. The operation almost killed her. By some miracle she survived with her left ovary intact, and this was the same ovary from which her son Larry was conceived. In the meantime Elvira got in touch with Inez Fernandez of Arugaan to help her prepare for the breastfeeding of the coming baby, something that she felt she failed to do with her first two children. She attended all the lectures with Angelí and Gabriel who by now constituted her support group pledged to nurse the new baby, who even learned how to pump breast milk for him. Not only that, both Angelí and Gabriel volunteered to serve in the Arugaan day-care center where they worked six hours three times a week, feeding babies, cleaning their poo-poo and wee-wee, changing their diapers, playing with them and putting them to sleep. They became role models for the children who call them Ate and Kuya. When the great day came, Angelí and Gabriel witnessed the actual birth of their baby brother in the delivery room, and carried the baby to their mother for his first feeding.

It was not easy for my youngest daughter Rosanna either. She had five miscarriages in as many years of marriage and despaired of ever having a child. She was diagnosed as having a strange affliction that forced her immune system to treat her fetus like a foreign object and expel it – an ailment she shared with Princess Diana, Maria Shriver Shwarzeneger and Sharon Cuneta. Expensive medicines, in refrigerated boxes, were carried by hand personally by Boy Saycon all the way from the United States for Rosanna's use. Her treatment proved successful. Her son Uno was born prematurely at seven months, weighing only 2 1/2 pounds, kept in an incubator and fed with a medicine dropper. She did not have enough milk, so her friends, led by Maricel Laxa, mobilized a group of mothers to provide milk for Uno with enough left over to feed the rest of the premature babies in Manila Doctors Hospital. The most beautiful sight in the world is that of Elvira and Rosanna nursing each other's babies – Larry sucking Rosanna's nipples to stimulate lactation, and Uno sucking Elvira's breasts to get the experience of full satisfaction with breast milk.

Rosanna spoke for her sister too when she sent the invitation for Uno's baptism, quoting the words of a song, "On the day that you were born, the angels got together, and decided to create a dream come true," with a note that said, "The Lord said 'Ask and ye shall receive.' We asked, and we asked, and we asked... and last year, we finally received. Thanks for believing." On September 16 and November 11, 2001, only two months apart, two miracles were born.
*April 11, 2002*


### III. I was there, I was there!

What is four days in the lifetime of a man?

Measured in terms of the humdrum routines of everyday living, four days can pass like four minutes, uncounted and unremembered.

But four days measured in terms of history made, of hopes and fears and Goliaths slain, of smiles and tears and bright suns that rise and fall scorching upon the earth, of prayers and visions and the grace of God showering its blessings on all of us, the meek and the humble at last supreme over the land --- such four days can add up to an entire lifetime, each minute counted and recounted in the vast storehouse of a man's memory.

I was there, I was there! I was at the Miracle at Edsa, along with the millions of waving, cheering, cursing, crying, singing, praying millions. So great grandchildren of the 21st Century, listen, the family was there.

Ronnie, the Number One son, was on TV with June Keithley, the most visible of us all; while wife Ida stayed home with 2 month old Christian who slept, ate and excreted throughout the Revolution. His ex-wife, Merce and children Celine and Ryan were watching Ronnie on TV in Portland Oregon.

Atom, the Number 2 son and favorite of Ninoy, his 5 year old son Quark and 2-year old daughter Crystal, found themselves in their neighbor Bongbong Marcos' house with its arsenal of high powered guns and crates of cash, moved out by armed men.

Elvira, the Number 3 child, our new doctor, was in the UERM Hospital emergency room, taking care of the wounded. Vicky, Ninoy's niece and Atom's wife, a doctor at the Makati Med, were among those who revived Mayor Yabut from a heart attack, and was there when the old boy died.

Danby, Number 4, was in Camp Crame with his girlfriends, as is usual, and Juno the Number 5, was in Glendale, California, with husband Tonichi Chuidian and son Tonic, watching TV and burning the long distance lines to Manila.

Rosanna the 6th and her friends were, between writing their theses, there on Edsa, in Channel 4, inside Malacanang Palace, and singing and dancing in the streets. Her mother Cecilia was moving house and glued to the radio.

I was there on the first day in the war room of General Ramos, with my computer making press statements, right in the eye of the storm. And on the last day I kept a date with history in the Club Filipino, right in the Presidential Table as Cory Aquino took her oath as the first woman president of the Philippines.

Look at the photo, at the lower left corner with my right forefinger on my cheek, that's me ... together with Monsignor Freddie Escaler SJ, Jose Diokno, Soc Rodrigo, Aurora Aquino, General Ramos and Cory Aquino.

That is my mark upon history. I was there.
*November 10, 1986*


**IV. From Caruso to Carreras, from shellac to CD**

With the coming of Luciano Pavarotti and Jose Carreras, as well as the Wednesday and Friday performances of Nomer Son and Elmo Maklit and their colleagues in the Captain's Bar of Mandarin Hotel, there is a revival of interest in classical music that has not been seen since the time of Enrico Caruso in the 1900s.

For one who has lived as long as I did, a whole lifetime bridged the phonograph record of Enrico Caruso I inherited from my parents, and the latest Compact Disc of Luciano Pavarotti and Jose Carreras.

When Thomas Edison invented the phonograph in 1877, the microphone and the speaker of today did not exist. A gramophone horn was used instead, the sound being recorded and reproduced through it. The phonograph record as we know it did not exist either; a cylinder wrapped with metal foil served its purpose. Later the cylinder was replaced by shellac discs (1887) which could record more music and was easier to manufacture and store, and which revolved on a turntable at the standard rate of 78 revolutions per minute (rpm).

This was the system used by Enrico Caruso, the King of Tenors, who recorded some 250 songs under the RCA Red Label, with the logo of a dog listening to His Master's Voice over a gramophone horn. Enrico Caruso died in 1921, and it was only in the late 1940s after the war that a radical innovation came into being. Dr. Peter Carl Goldmark of Columbia Records came to lecture in MIT on how he invented the Long Playing (LP) record. By substituting vinyl for the shellac, he made the record unbreakable and less prone to noise and scratch. By slowing down the rotation from 78 rpm to 33 1/3 rpm, and reducing the needle size to 1/3 of what it was, he was able to increase record time to 7 times, or 70 minutes instead of 10 minutes per 12 inch record. By using sapphire or diamond needles instead of steel, he was able to reduce record and needle wear. The industry now concentrated on developing hi-fidelity sound reproduction.

Electronic circuits were improved, but the weakest links were the mechanical portions of the system: the pick-up that converts the wiggles on the record to electric impulses, and speaker that converts the electric impulses to sound vibrations. The inefficient piezo-electric crystal was replaced by the electro-magnetic pick-up (pioneered by the GE high compliance variable reluctance pick-up) which was so light in weight that it also minimized record wear. Speakers were now housed in bass reflex cabinets to enhance the lower frequencies and were then installed in a series of multi-speakers, from small tweeters directly radiating its high frequencies, down to very large speakers in "dynamic suspension" reflecting the booming low frequencies off back walls. Later, up-and-down vibrations were added to the side-by-side vibrations of the needle, so two separate signals became possible, the left and right of the stereo (1958). Later circuit improvements gave birth to multiple speakers of "surround-sound."

To overcome the record's physical limitations, a "standard RIAA recording characteristic" was adopted, making the loudest sounds softer to keep the needle from swinging to the adjacent groove, and making the softest sounds louder to keep their volume above the noise and the scratch. Such loudest and softest sounds are then restored to their original volume when reproduced. Later noise reduction systems like the Dolby adopted the same principle.

The vibrating metal diaphragm in the old pickup reverberating through the gramophone horn, was replaced by an electronic circuit powered by vacuum tubes; then by transistors; then by Integrated Circuits (ICs) made of many transistors; then by microchips made up of many ICs.

In the 1990s an even more radical innovation came into the market. Before that, the analog method of recording was used; where physical wiggles on the platter corresponded to the sound vibrations. Now with the invention of the computer binary system, the recording was "digitalized," converting the original sounds into pulses and complicated mathematical formulas that could be converted back to sound vibrations. This is the principle of the Compact Disc (CD), where the needle is replaced by a laser beam.

The advantage of this CD system is that, firstly, the record never wears out, being touched only by a light beam. Secondly, all the noise and hiss which are analog signals, are completely eliminated. Thirdly, completely high-fidelity reproduction becomes possible, there being no necessity of compressing of the dynamic range, making the loud sounds softer and the soft sounds louder; moreover, the frequency range was extended from 100 to 5,000 cycles per second (cps or hertz) plus or minus 10 decibels, to one that more than matches the most sensitive human hearing, 30 to 30,000 cps plus and minus 0.001 decibels. Fourthly, the amount of music recorded on one side of the 5 inch CD record (80 minutes) is more than that of two sides of the 12 inch LP record (70 minutes).

Nicholas Negroponte, brother of US Ambassador John Negroponte and director of the MIT Media Lab, was once asked by a student how much music can be recorded on one side of a CD. Nick answered "If you change the laser beam from blue to red, you can increase the one hour CD capacity to five hours." The student countered, "I just put 5,000 hours of music on a CD, using compression techniques, and making use of the periods of silence between sound signals." A complete library of classical music on one Compact Disc? Amazing!
*November 28, 1994*

### V.    Blow by blow account of the Tokyo Incident between Manny and Zobel

Danny Gozo of the Ayala Companies e-mailed me in December: *Hi Larry, I just read you column "Make My Day" today and noted that you may have been fed wrong information about that "Tokyo hotel incident" supposedly between Fernando Zobel and Manny Pangilinan. I was there when it happened and quite frankly it looked to me more of a one way tirade from MVP to FZA. A good way to describe it is, "MVP lost it!". He was fuming mad about something, gesticulating and raising his voice. FZA, embarrassed by the excessive emotional outburst turned around and left. End of incident. It lasted no more than a minute. There were a lot of witnesses. It was therefore a surprise for us to read in a Manila newspaper that there was supposedly a "heated exchange." No such thing happened, it was a one-way tirade. "Loud and confrontational", best describes MVP, not FZA. Cheers Larry and Merry Christmas! Larry, (about the ads for your show)... While I cannot guarantee you any commitments right now, I am sure these commentaries won't come in the way of our recommendations... unless... of course we hear from" friends of you know who" and do an "Inquirer" on you! [That is supposed to be a joke!] Happy Holidays just the same, and keep on punching! Danny.*

Danny old boy, no problem, (1) the Ayalas are so kuripot, the ads, though welcome, won't amount to much anyway, (2) the Ayalas are so admirably courageous, they resisted political pressure and stuck with *Inquirer* when the chips were down, (3) I am the grandson of a revolutionary hero against Spain and I still carry the chips on my shoulder, but I'd like to recount an eye-witness account of the Tokyo Incident between Manny Pangilinan and Fernando Zobel and let the readers draw their own conclusions:

During the last visit of President Erap Estrada to Japan, while cocktails were hosted for the Japanese business community in the presidential function room of Hotel Okura, Manny Pangilinan and his friends, Napoleon Pol Nazareno, Boy Saycon and a third person left to take dinner at Seryna Steak House.  When they were in the lobby of Building B, they were accosted by Fernando Zobel asking a minute to talk to Manny.  In the crowded lobby, Danny says he was just 15 feet away.  This is the way it went:

Manny: "What can I do for you?"  Fernando: "It is about the interconnection between Globe and PLDT.  I think you and Augusto (Zobel, the brother of Fernando) should talk."  Manny: "Fernando, there is no problem there.  All Augusto has to do is to lift the phone and we can talk."

Fernando: "About the ads (that came out addressed to the Globe subscribers putting the blame of failed interconnection on PLDT) – they will only come out for two days."  Manny: "Fernando, we cannot resolve our differences through the newspapers.  When we talk interconnection, we should also talk about the interconnection between Globe and Smart."  Fernando: "That is not the issue."  Manny: "It is part of the issue because Smart is owned by PLDT."

Fernando (raises his voice): "Why are you making it hard for us?? (Since he is much taller than Manny, Fernando looked threatening to Manny, *parang nag dudura*).  Manny: "What do you mean, making it hard for you?  Smart has been writing letters to you asking for interconnection, and you just completely ignored it for almost a year.  What do you mean I am making it hard for you?  You stopped me at a lobby of a hotel, and asked me for a minute to talk to me, and I gave in to your request, and I am making it hard for you??"  Fernando (repeats): "So why are you making it hard for me?"  Manny (with a helpless gesture): "I do not want to discuss the issue."  And he walked away followed by his friends.

Fernando was left standing there.  He later recounted the incident to Tonyboy Cojuangco, Babes Romualdez, Al Tengo and Iggi Yenko, saying there was an altercation between him and Manny.  Everybody rushed to Manny in Lobby A for confirmation.  Manny reconstructed the entire story for them, saying there was really no altercation.  Manny and Fernando have been exchanging notes from their hotel room quite peacefully until this thing happened.  Manny lost his appetite and went up to his room while his friends Boy Saycon, Paeng Buenaventura and Nick Locsin went to dinner by themselves. According to Manny's friends, Danny Gozo and Rodolfo Salalima initiated the black propaganda against Manny after his Cebu speech drawing a parallel between Manny-Fernando and LapuLapu-Magellan.  They added that Augusto Zobel is even more confrontational and loud-voiced than Fernando.

*April 5, 2000 for the Post*

### VI.  Rah Rah Boys and Magnificent Loners

THE blinding blaze of suns and stars grow dim beside the brilliance of a single thought.  How true indeed! Like the time the apple fell on the head of Newton with a force directly proportional to its mass and acceleration. Like the time Archimedes was immersed in a bathtub, bouyed up by a force equal to the weight of the water he displaced.

Such moments produced flashes of inspiration, the brilliance of a single thought, that have illumined the mind of man forever -- the brilliant insight that brings about the decisive moment, the blinding instant of Truth, the turning point upon which history revolves.  Such a moment occurred when Rah Rah Boys (headed by Manglapus and Manny Manahan) wrote the famous speech of Magsaysay in Plaza Miranda, wherein Magsaysay recounted how he carried the bleeding mutilated body of Moises Padilla, killed by political goons, an allegory of our fallen democracy.  The story was not true. By the time Magsaysay viewed the body it was in rigor mortis and in an advanced state of decomposition.  But what a speech, it moved the audience to tears and to an iron resolve to bring down President Quirino.  A decisive moment.

Such a moment occurred with another group of Rah Rah Boys headed by Jaime Ongpin, Father Bernas, Vicente Jayme -- recruits in the fight against Marcos. The flash of inspiration, the brilliance of a single thought, the blinding instant of Truth, the turning point -- are still their ace.  The Convenor's Group with its fast track scenario, the Million Signatures for Cory, and probably the entire concept of Cory's candidacy are their doing. The Rah Rah Boys did it again!

Such a moment occurred with the Rah Rah boys of COPA (Council Of Philippine Affairs) headed by Pastor Saycon and Teodoro Benigno under whose aegis the campaign for the resignation of President Erap Estrada was initiated, coordinated and escalated.

Once we thought that Rah Rah Boys are incurable romantics, anachronisms from the Age of Chivalry, Don Quixotes forever tilting windmills, knights in shining armor looking for dragons to slay, fighting for empty platitudes like Democracy, God, Motherhood, Brotherhood, Goodness, Beauty, Truth, Honesty, Sincerity  -- which no one else disputes.  Rah Rah Boys we thought are rebels without a cause, fighting like hell for nothing.  And we can only speculate with a sense of loss how the history of our nation might have been different had the Rah Rah Boys supported the other breed of Magnificent Loners, such as Recto, Tañada, Diokno, Alejandro Lichauco, intellectual heirs of Jose Rizal, the great nationalist.  The Rah Rah Boys come in clusters, with the drive and enthusiasm of the mob, with the unpredictability of exploding stars.  The Loners stand in magnificent isolation and lonely splendor, dreaming impossible dreams and thinking dangerous thoughts, unafraid even when alone, deriving strength from the steady glow of the sun of Nationalism.

Together the Rah Rah Boys and the Magnificent Loners constitute a critical mass with an explosive potential for revolutionary change, as did happen when both supported Cory against Marcos.  When the brilliance of exploding stars merge with the steady life-supporting glow of the sun, strange alchemies occur.  Hopes and dreams are let loose upon the streets, and real revolutions occur.  Hopes and dreams are seductive sirens, jealous lovers and demanding masters.  We hope and dream only at our own risk.

*November 3, 2000 for the Post*

### VII.   Caltex strike ended racial discrimination

THE Caltex strike in April 1965 was the turning point of the Filipino struggle against discrimination in pay-scales and promotion in the foreign companies operating in the Philippines.

Supported by the National Economic Council (NEC of which I was chairman) which passed a resolution condemning racial discrimination, by the Dept. of Labor, labor unions and student activists who joined the picket line, and by Senators Pepe Diokno and Lorenzo Tañada who pushed through a bill on ``equal pay for equal work" in both houses in Congress, and eventual victory in the courts -- the Caltex strikers won the day.

The Diokno-Tañada bill was vetoed by President Macapagal upon representation of General Carlos Romulo of the Philippine Association, an American lobby group, and the American Embassy -- upon their promise that racial discrimination will end in foreign companies.

It is ironic that Filipinos who benefited most from the strike were those who opposed the strike.  J.P. Roxas, vice president and board member, attempted to pacify the strikers, as did his assistant Joe Mathay; both were booed.

Amaury Gutierrez, the one of the managers in the Bauan, Batangas refinery, was uninvolved in the strike; he became first President and Managing Director of Caltex Philippines in September 1982, and is now in Dallas, Texas, as Chairman of the Board of Caltex Philippines.

His successor Francisco Ablan was not involved in the strike either, and he became President and Managing Director on July 16, 1988.

The adage is true: They benefit most who stand and wait for others to do the fighting.

Yet the battle was won, and it was won by the Caltex Filipino Managers and Supervisors Association (CAFIMSA) led by Jose J. Mapa of Bacolod, distant cousin of Placido Mapa Jr. who then at the Citibank (then on to Malacañang's economic staff, to World Bank and back to government as DBP and PNB president).

CAFIMSA was organized by supervisors from the Marketing Operations of Caltex, who felt left out of promotions and salary increases, and felt humiliated by having to cater to the whims and caprices of the operations manager.  Soon the

CAFIMSA gained adherents among the supervisors in other departments, including those in the outlying depots, terminals and district offices in the Visayas and Mindanao.

And what a strike! The strikers even had their ``Batangas Navy,'' a crew of strikers operating motorized bancas to stop tankers from unloading at the refinery. With the help of nationalists in NEC, Labor Dept., Congress, labor unions and students, the battle was won after 45 days.

After the strike, adjustments in compensation and benefits were made. The positions of several supervisors were upgraded, both CAFIMSA members and non-members alike; and many got salary adjustments as well.

Pampangueño Federico Esguerra (like our editor, Federico Pascual, nicknamed Dick) remembers having been upgraded from Supervisory Clerk to Assistant Chief Accountant with a chauffeur-driven company car and an expense account -- equivalent to a 30 percent increase in salary.

The first Filipino Caltex president, Amaury Gutierrez, was appointed in 1982; his successor Francisco Ablan in 1988.

But the greatest result of the Caltex strike is the recognition by foreign companies that Filipinos no longer tolerate racial discrimination in their own country. Shell, Mobil and Esso immediately took steps to correct similar situations in their companies before their employees decided to go on strike. And soon the American banks and commercial establishments followed.

American neanderthals who insult Filipinos got their first taste of the Filipino boot. The American who insulted Jose Olbes was thrown out of a Cebu Clubhouse; he who insulted Epifania Lim, later to be Welfare Secretary, was deported; and an American embassy official was knocked out in front of PhilAmLife Auditorium by Labor Secretary Bernardino Abes for remarks against the President Macapagal.

Americans who were trained on the job by lowly-paid Filipinos rose to be big-shots in the States: Frank Zingaro, Vice President in New York; Jim Wolohan, V.P. Marketing; Raymond Johnson, Chairman of the Board of Caltex Petroleum Corporation, an overseas merger of Standard Oil of California and Texaco, Inc.

No colonial power can withstand the collective wrath of the Filipino people.
*August 24, 1988*

## VIII.  A HERITAGE OF SMALLNESS        an  epic speech by Nick Joaquin

Society for the Filipino is a small rowboat: the barangay. Geography for the Filipino is a small locality: the barrio. History for the Filipino is a small vague saying: *matanda pa kay mahoma; noong peacetime*. Enterprise for the Filipino is a small stall: the *sari-sari*. Industry and production for the Filipino are the small immediate searchings of each day: *isang kahig, isang tuka*. And commerce for the Filipino is the smallest degree of retail: the *tingi*.

What most astonishes foreigners in the Philippines is that this is a country, perhaps the only one in the world, where people buy and sell one stick of cigarette, half a head of garlic, a dab of pomade, part of the contents of a can or bottle, one single egg, one single banana. To foreigners used to buying things by the carton or the dozen or pound and in the large economy sizes, the exquisite transactions of Philippine *tingis* cannot but seem Lilliputian. So much effort by so many for so little. Like all those children risking neck and limb in the traffic to sell one stick of cigarette at a time. Or those grown-up men hunting the sidewalks all day to sell a puppy or a lantern or a pair of socks. The amount of effort they spend seems out of all proportion to the returns. Such folk are, obviously, not enough. Laboriousness just can never be the equal of labor as skill, labor as audacity, labor as enterprise.

The Filipino who travels abroad gets to thinking that his is the hardest working country in the world. By six or seven in the morning we are already up on our way to work, shops and markets are open; the wheels of industry are already agrind. Abroad, especially in the West, if you go out at seven in the morning you're in a dead-town. Everybody's still in bed; everything's still closed up. Activity doesn't begin till nine or ten - - and ceases promptly at five p.m. By six, the business sections are dead towns again. The entire cities go to sleep on weekends. They have a shorter working day, a shorter working week. Yet they pile up more mileage than we who work all day and all week.  Is the disparity to our disparagement?  We work more but make less.  Why?  Because we act on such a pygmy scale.  Abroad they would think you mad if you went in a store and tried to buy just one stick of cigarette.  They don't operate on the scale.  The difference is greater than between having and not having; the difference is in the way of thinking.  They are accustomed to thinking dynamically.  We have the habit, whatever our individual resources, of thinking poor, of thinking petty.

Is that the explanation for our continuing failure to rise -- that we buy small and sell small, that we think small and do small?  Are we not confusing timidity for humility and making a virtue of what may be the worst of our vices?  Is not our timorous clinging to smallness the bondage we must break if we are ever to inherit the earth and be free, independent, progressive?  The small must ever be prey to the big.  Aldous Huxley said that some people are born victims, or "murderers."  He came to the Philippines and thought us the "least original" of people.  Is there not a relation between his two terms?  Originality requires daring: the daring to destroy the obsolete, to annihilate the petty.  It's cold comfort to think we haven't developed that kind of "murderer mentality."

But till we do we had best stop talking about "our heritage of greatness" for the national heritage is -- let's face it -- a heritage of smallness.

However far we go back in our history it's the small we find -- the nipa hut, the barangay, the petty kingship, the slight tillage, the *tingi* trade.  All our artifacts are miniatures and so is our folk literature, which is mostly proverbs, or dogmas in miniature.

About the one big labor we can point to in our remote past are the rice terraces -- and even that grandeur shrinks, on scrutiny, into numberless little separate plots, only a series of layers added to previous ones, all this being the accumulation of ages of small routine efforts (like a colony of ant hills) rather than one grand labor following one grand design.  We could bring in here the nursery diota about the little drops of water that make the mighty ocean, or the peso that's not a peso if it lacks a centavo; but creative labor, alas, has sterner standards, a stricter hierarchy of values.  Many little efforts, however perfect each in itself, still cannot equal one single epic creation.  A gallery full of even the most charming statuettes is bound to look scant beside a Pieta or Moses by Michelangelo; and you could stack up the best short stories you can think of and still not have enough to outweigh a mountain like War and Peace.

The depressing fact in Philippine history is what seems to be our native aversion to the large venture, the big risk, the bold extensive enterprise.  The pattern may have been set by the migration.  We try to equate the odyssey of the migrating barangays with that of the Pilgrim, Father of America, but a glance of the map suffices to show the differences between the two ventures.  One was a voyage across an ocean into an unknown world; the other was a going to and from among neighboring islands.  One was a blind leap into space; the other seems, in comparison, a mere crossing of rivers.  The nature of the one required organization, a sustained effort, special skills, special tools, the building of large ships.  The nature of the other is revealed by its vehicle, the barangay, which is a small rowboat, not a seafaring vessel designed for long distances on the avenues of the ocean.

The migrations were thus self-limited, never moved far from their point of origin, and clung to the heart of a small known world; the islands clustered round the Malay Peninsula.  The movement into the Philippines, for instance, was from points as next-door geographically as Borneo and Sumatra.  Since the Philippines is at heart of this region, the movement was toward center, or, one may say, from near to still nearer, rather than to farther out.  Just off the small brief circuit of these migrations was another world: the vast mysterious continent of Australia; but there was significantly no movement towards this terra incognita.  It must have seemed too perilous, too unfriendly of climate, too big, too hard.  So, Australia was conquered not by the fold next door, but by strangers from across two oceans and the other side of the world.  They were more enterprizing, they have been rewarded.  But history has punished the laggard by setting up over them a White Australia with doors closed to the crowded Malay world.

The barangays that came to the Philippines were small both in scope and size.  A barangay with a hundred households would already be enormous; some barangays had only 30 families, or less.  These, however, could have been the seed of a great society if there had not been in that a fatal aversion to synthesis.  The barangay settlements already displayed a Philippine characteristic: the tendency to petrify in isolation instead of consolidating, or to split smaller instead of growing.  That within the small area of Manila Bay there should be three different kingdoms (Tondo, Manila and Pasay) may mean that the area was originally settled by three different barangays that remained distinct, never came together, never fused; or it could mean that a single original settlement; as it grew split into three smaller pieces.  Philippine society, as though fearing bigness, ever tends to revert the condition of the barangay of the small enclosed society.

We don't grow like a seed, we split like an amoeba.  The moment a town grows big it becomes two towns.  The moment a province becomes populous it disintegrates into two or three smaller provinces.  The excuse offered for divisions is always the alleged difficulty of administering so huge an entity.  Philippine provinces are microscopic compared to a US state.  The government of Maryland, the size of the Philippines does not complain that it can't efficiently handle so vast an area.  We, on the other hand, make a confession of character whenever we split up a town or province to avoid having of cope, admitting that, on that scale, we can't be efficient; we are capable only of the small.  The decentralization and barrio-autonomy movement expresses our craving to return to the one unit of society we feel adequate to: the barangay, with its 30 to a hundred families.  Anything larger intimidates.  We would deliberately limit ourselves to the small performance. This attitude, an immemorial one, explains why we're finding it so hard to become a nation, and why our pagan forefathers could not even imagine the task.  Not E pluribus unum is the impulse in our culture but Out of many, fragments.  Foreigners had to come and unite our land for us; the labor was far beyond our powers.  Great was the King of Sugbu, but he couldn't even control the tiny isle across his bay.  Federation is still not even an idea for the tribes of the North; and the Moro sultanates behave like our political parties: they keep splitting off into particles.

Because we cannot unite for the large effort, even the small effort is increasingly beyond us.  There is less to learn in our schools, but even this little is protested by our young as too hard.  The falling line on the graph of effort is, alas, a recurring pattern in our history.  Our artifacts but repeat a refrain of decline and fall, which wouldn't be so sad if there had been a summit decline from, but the evidence is that we start small and end small without ever having scaled any peaks.  Used only to the small effort, we are not, as a result, capable of the sustained effort and lose momentum fast.  We have a term for it: *ningas cogon*.  Go to any exhibit of Philippine artifacts and the items that from our "cultural heritage" but confirm three theories about us, which should be stated again.

First:  that the Filipino works best on small scale--tiny figurines, small pots, filigree work in gold or silver, decorative arabesques.  The deduction here is that we feel adequate to the challenge of the small, but are cowed by the challenge of the big.  Second:  that the Filipino chooses to work in soft easy materials -- clay, molten metal, tree searching has failed to turn up anything really monumental in hardstone.  Even carabao horn, an obvious material for native craftsmen, has not been used to any extent remotely comparable to the use of ivory in the ivory countries.  The deduction here is that we feel equal to the materials that yield but evade the challenge of materials that resist.  Third: that having mastered a material, craft or product, we tend to rut in it and don't move on to a next phase, a larger development, based on what we have learned.  In fact, we instantly lay down even what mastery we already possess when confronted by a challenge from outside of something more masterly, instead of being provoked to develop by the threat of competition.  Faced by the challenge of Chinese porcelain, the native art of pottery simply declined, though porcelain should have been the next phase for our pottery makers.  There was apparently no effort to steal and master the arts of the Chinese.  The excuse that we did not have the materials for porcelain making -- unites in glum brotherhood yesterday's pottery makers and today's would be industrialists.  Our pottery buried by Chinese porcelain as our tobacco is buried by the blue seal.

Our cultural history, rather than a cumulative development, seems mostly a series of dead ends.  One reason is a fear of moving on to a more complex phase; another reason is a fear of tools.  Native pottery, for instance, somehow never got far enough to grasp the principle of the wheel. Neither did native agriculture ever reach the point of discovering the plow for itself, or even the idea of the draft animal, though the carabao was handy.  Wheel and plow had to come from Spain because we always stopped short of technology.  This stoppage at a certain level is the recurring fate of our arts and crafts.

The santo everybody's collecting now are charming as legacies, depressing as indices, for the art of the santero was a small art, in a not very demanding medium: wood.  Having achieved perfection in it, the santero was faced by the challenge of proving he could achieve equal perfection on a larger scale and in more difficult materials: hardstone, marble, bronze.  The challenge was not met.  Like the pagan potter before him, the santero stuck to his tiny rut, repeating his little perfections over and over.  The iron law of life is:  Develop or decay.  The art of the santero did not advance; so it declined.  Instead of moving onto a harder material, it retreated to a material even easier than wool: plaster which has wrought the death of relax art.

One could go on and on with this litany.  Philippine movies started 50 years ago and, during the '30s, reached a certain level of proficiency, where it stopped and has rutted ever since looking more and more primitive as the rest of the cinema world speeds by on the way to new frontiers.  We have to be realistic, say local movie producers we're in this business not to make art but money.  But even from the business viewpoint, they're not "realistic" at all.  The true businessman ever seeks to increase his market and therefore ever tries to improve his product.  Business dies when it resigns itself, as local movies have done, to a limited market.

After more than half a century of writing in English, Philippine Literature in that medium is still identified with the short story.  That small literary form is apparently as much as we feel equal to.  But by limiting ourselves less and less capable even of the small thing -- as the fate of the pagan potter and the Christian santero should have warned us.  It's no longer as obvious today that the Filipino writer has mastered the short story form.  It's two decades since the war but what were mere makeshift in postwar days have petrified into institutions like the jeepney, which we all know to be uncomfortable and inadequate, yet cannot get rid of, because that would mean to tackle the problem of modernizing our systems of transportation – a problem we think so huge we hide from it in the comforting smallness of the jeepney.  A small solution to a huge problem -- do we deceive ourselves into thinking that possible?   The jeepney hints that we do, for the jeepney carrier is about as adequate as a spoon to empty a river with.  With the population welling, and land values rising, there should be in our cities, an upward thrust in architecture, but we continue to build small, in our timid two-story fashion.  Oh, we have excuses.  The land is soft: earthquakes are frequent.  But Mexico City, for instance, is on far swampier land and Mexico City is not a two-story town.  San Francisco and Tokyo are in worse earthquake belts, but San Francisco and Tokyo reach up for the skies.  Isn't our architecture another expression of our smallness spirit?  To build big would pose problems too big for us.  The water pressure, for example, would have to be improved -- and it's hard enough to get water on the ground floor flat and frail, our cities indicate our disinclination to make any but the smallest effort possible.

It wouldn't be so bad if our aversion for bigness and our clinging to the small denoted a preference for quality over bulk; but the little things we take forever to do too often turn out to be worse than the mass-produced article.  Our couturiers, for instance, grow even limper of wrist when, after waiting months and months for a pin -- a weaver to produce a yard or two of the fabric, they find they have to discard most of the stuff because it's so sloppily done.  Foreigners who think of pushing Philippine fabric in the world market give up in despair after experiencing our inability to deliver in quantity.  Our proud apologia is that mass production would ruin the "quality" of our products.  But Philippine crafts might be roused from the doldrums if forced to come up to mass-production standards.  It's easy enough to quote the West against itself, to cite all those Western artists and writers who rail against the cult of bigness and mass production and the "bitch goddess success"; but the arguments against technological progress, like the arguments against nationalism, are possible only to those who have already gone through that stage so successfully they can now afford to revile it.  The rest of us can only crave to be big enough to be able to deplore bigness.

For the present all we seen to be able to do is ignore

pagan evidence and blame our inability to sustain the big effort of our colonizers: they crushed our will and spirit, our initiative and originality.  But colonialism is not uniquely our ordeal but rather a universal experience.  Other nations went under the heel of the conqueror but have not spent the rest of their lives whining.  What people were more trod under than the Jews?  But each have been a thoroughly crushed nation get up and conquered new worlds instead.  The Norman conquest of England was followed by a subjugation very similar to our experience, but what issued from that subjugation were the will to empire and the verve of a new language.

If it be true that we were enervated by the loss of our primordial freedom, culture and institutions, then the native tribes that were never under Spain and didn't lose what we did should be showing a stronger will and spirit, more initiative and originality, a richer culture and greater progress, than the Christian Filipino.  Do they?  And this favorite apologia of ours gets further blasted when we consider a people who, alongside us, suffered a far greater trampling yet never lost their enterprising spirit.  On the contrary, despite centuries of ghettos and programs and repressive measures and racial scorn, the Chinese in the Philippines clambered to the top of economic heap and are still right up there when it comes to the big deal.  Shouldn't they have long come to the conclusion (as we say we did) that there's no point in hustling and laboring and amassing wealth only to see it wrested away and oneself punished for rising?

An honest reading of our history should rather force us to admit that it was the colonial years that pushed us toward the larger effort.  There was actually an advance in freedom, for the unification of the land, the organization of towns and provinces, and the influx of new ideas, started our liberation from the rule of the petty, whether of clan, locality or custom.  Are we not vexed at the hinterlander still bound by primordial terrors and taboos?  Do we not say we have to set him "free" through education?  Freedom, after all is more than a political condition; and the colonial lowlander -- especially a person like, say, Rizal -- was surely more of a freeman than the unconquered tribesman up in the hills.  As wheel and plow set us free from a bondage to nature, so town and province liberated us from the bounds of the barangay.

The liberation can be seen just by comparing our pagan with our Christian statuary.  What was static and stolid in the one becomes, in the other, dynamic motion and expression.  It can be read in the rear of architecture.  Now, at last, the Filipino attempts the massive -- the stone bridge that unites, the irrigation dam that gives increase, the adobe church that identified.  If we have a "heritage of greatness" it's in these labors and in three epic acts of the colonial period; first, the defense of the land during two centuries of siege; second, the Propaganda Movement; and the third, the Revolution.  The first, a heroic age that profoundly shaped us, began 1600 with the 50-year war with the Dutch and may be said to have drawn to a close with the British invasion of 1762.  The War with the Dutch is the most under-rated event in our history, for it was the Great War in our history. It had to be pointed out that the Philippines, a small colony practically abandoned to itself, yet held at bay for half a century the mightiest naval power in the world at the time, though the Dutch sent armada after armada, year after year, to conquer the colony, or by cutting off the galleons that were its links with America, starve the colony to its knees.  We rose so gloriously to the challenge of the Dutch war, that the impetus of spirit sent us spilling down to Borneo and the Moluccas and Indo-China, and it seemed for a moment we might create an empire.  But the tremendous effort did create an elite vital to our history: the Creole-Tagalog-Pampango principalia -- and ruled it together during  these centuries of siege, and which was the nation in embryo, which defended the land, climaxed its military career with the war of resistance against the British in the 1660's.

By then, this elite already deeply felt itself a nation that the government it set up in Bacolor actually defined the captive government in Manila as illegitimate.  From her flows the heritage that would flower in Malolos, for centuries of heroic effort had bred, in Tagalog and the Pampango, a habit of leadership, a lordliness of spirit.  They had proved themselves capable of the great and sustained enterprise, destiny was theirs.  An analyst of our history notes that the sun on our flag has eight rays, each of which stands for a Tagalog or Pampango province, and the Tagalogs and Pampangos at Biak-na-Bato" assumed the representation of the entire country and, therefore, became in fact the Philippines.

From the field of battle this elite would, after the British war, shift to the field of politics, a significant move; and the Propaganda, which began as a Creole campaign against the Peninsulars, would turn into the nationalist movement of Rizal and Del Pilar.  This second epic act in our history seemed a further annulment of the timidity.  A man like Rizal was a deliberate rebel against the cult of the small; he was so various a magus because he was set on proving that the Filipino could tackle the big thing, the complex job.  His novels have epic intentions; his poems sustain the long line and go against Garcia Villa's more characteristically Philippine dictum that poetry is the small intense line.  With the Revolution, our culture is in dichotomy.  This epic of 1896 is indeed a great effort -- but by a small minority.  The Tagalog and Pampango had taken it upon themselves to protest the grievances of the entire archipelago.  Moreover, within the movement was a clash between the two strains in our culture -- between the propensity for the small activity and the will to something more ambitious.  Bonifacio's Katipunan was large in number but small in scope; it was a rattling of bolos; and its post fiasco efforts are little more than amok raids in the manner the Filipino is said to excel in.

An observation about us in the last war was that we fight best not as an army, but in small informal guerrilla outfits; not in pitched battle, but in rapid hit-and-run raids.  On the other hand, there was, in Cavite, an army with officers, engineers, trenches, plans of battle and a complex organization – a Revolution unlike all the little uprisings or mere raids of the past because it had risen above tribe and saw itself as the national destiny.  This was the highest we have reached in nationalistic effort.  But here again, having reached a certain level of achievement, we stopped.  The Revolution is, as we say today, "unfinished."

The trend since the turn of the century, and especially since the war, seems to be back to the tradition of timidity, the heritage of smallness.  We seem to be making less and less effort, thinking ever smaller, doing even smaller.  The air droops with a feeling of inadequacy.  We can't cope; we don't respond; we are not rising to challenges.  So tiny a land as ours shouldn't be too hard to connect with transportation -- but we get crushed on small jeepneys, get killed on small trains, get drowned in small boats.  Larger and more populous cities abroad find it no problem to keep themselves clean -- but the simple matter of garbage can create a "crisis" in the small city of Manila.  One American remarked that, after seeing Manila's chaos of traffic, he began to appreciate how his city of Los Angeles handles its far, far greater volume of traffic.  Is building a road that won't break down when it rains no longer within our ability to accomplish?

One writer, as he surveyed the landscape of shortages -- no rice, no water, no garbage collectors, no peace, no order -- gloomily mumbled that disintegration seems to be creeping upon us and groped for Yeat's terrifying lines:

*Things fall apart; the center cannot hold:*
*Mere anarchy is loosed...*

Have our capacities been so diminished by the small efforts we are becoming incapable even to the small things?  Our present problems are surely not what might be called colossal or insurmountable -- yet we stand helpless before them.  As the population swells, those problems will expand and multiply.  If they daunt us now, will they crush us then?  The prospect is terrifying.  We may do well to ponder the Parable of the Servants and the Talents.  The enterprising servants who increase talents entrusted to them were rewarded by their Lord; but the timid servant who made no effort to double the one talent given to him was deprived of that talent and cast into the outer darkness, where there was weeping and gnashing of teeth: "For to him who has, more shall be given; but from him who has not, even the little he has shall be taken away."

**The end of Joaquin's essay**

This is Larry Henares making your day with my own comments on our heritage of smallness.  My mother a pioneer in the field of Nutrition in the 1920s, once told me that we Filipinos are well-fed but undernourished.  We eat too much rice, but not enough viands.  We eat too much carbohydrates, not enough protein, and that is why we are a small people, compared to the Caucasians, even those of Chinese or Japanese descent.  My father added that we think small because our assholes are too close to our brains.  And no better proof of our heritage of smallness can be offered than the proposal for federalism in our new Constitution.  With a country much smaller than the size of an American State or a Chinese Province, we choose to divide it further by opting to be a nation of federated states, each state smaller than Los Angeles County.  I am afraid we shall forever be small.

*December 12-20, 2005*


ooooo

# PERSONALITIES

## CHAPTER ONE:
## Tom del Castillo

**Part 1: To die of cancer is to have an orgasm**

Tom del Castillo, senior partner of Ortega, Del Castillo, Bacorro, Odulio, Calma & Carbonnel law office, died October 18, 2006 at the age of 65.  A graduate of the University of the Philippines, he was one of the best 500 lawyers in the country in one list, and one of the best of 10 in another, and had been classed alongside such greats as Enrique Belo, Felipe Gozon and Roberto Lucila.  He died of brain cancer, his body slowly wasting away in excruciating pain.  I cried at his funeral because he was one of my best friends, my lawyer who won all the court cases brought against me, and rarest of all, he was like me a Sinatra Fan and a reader of books, my books in particular, of which he has a complete collection of all 24 books.

He laughed at all my jokes and had many of his own. Once he gently chided me for calling Dick Romulo Small Dick with an asymmetrical aberration for a face, Christian Monsod a nigger, Cesar Buenaventura a Villainous Convexity of a Face, and Bernardo Villegas an Alopecic Misogamic Gynander, saying "As if *naman*, Larry, you are so handsome."  Tom del Castillo was a highly intelligent man with a gargantuan sense of humor that I often wonder how he coped with the excruciating pain of cancer, its randomness, and the inevitability of its final closure.

Then I read a small piece by one of my favorite writers, Nick Pichay who at the age of 45, underwent, double whammy, a triple heart bypass and a diagnosis for colon cancer. It is entitled "Sunflower, Stigma, Stigmata," a masterpiece, probably the best ever written on death by cancer. Knowing Tom del Castillo, I know for sure that he felt the same way Nick Pichay does, that to die of cancer is to have an orgasm. I am sure Nick does not mind my quoting and paraphrasing his wonderful words.

Nick Pichay wrote: *"Twice confronted by death's proximity, I woke up to a world transformed into an inimitable, precious, and fragile place — what poet Rolando Tinio aptly described as a 'crystal universe' — where everything takes on the nature of a very shiny, rainbow gilded, fragile, breakable soap bubble. Colors are brighter, hugs are warmer. Each day burns itself into vivid, sensoramic technicolor memories. I become ecstatic one moment and then sad the next. You might have once been familiar with this feeling — the first time you fell in love. Could this be the reason why the French refer to an orgasm as petite mort, a small death?"*

Dying by cancer is Orgasm indeed. *"The knowledge of a possible impending death — unlike the suddenness of an accident or the vulgar directness of a coronary thrombosis — brings with it a haze, a presence, an unavoidable grandiloquence about it. Rare is the man or woman who receives a cancer diagnosis in calm aplomb. As soon as my soul realized the situation, my mind zoomed in all directions like an Independence Day firecracker exploding and careening into a kaleidoscope of fear, anger, hope, and then surprisingly, celebration.*

*"At first, I noticed a heightened, paranoiac observation of the ordinary. It is no longer a meal, but maybe 'my last meal,' – ever so luscious, ever so sweet. Every word I speak suddenly becomes my "famous last words" – ever so eloquent, ever so wise. Just waving goodbye to a friend suddenly acquires spine-tingling nuances as the Last Farewell, ever so poignant, ever so sad. But surprisingly, other than the morbid, I discovered that intimacy with death has another emotional but familiar effect.*

*"Having cancer is an art form, a performance art, like a horror movie or your favorite telenovela, full of expectations on what the definitive narratives must contain."*

**Part 2: What is normal sex?  Cancer, a stigma or stigmata?**

Having cancer is an art form, a performance art, like a horror movie or your favorite *telenovela*, full of expectations on what the definitive narratives must contain.  And Tom del Castillo and his family, as well as Nick Pichay and his family, must have been familiar with it by now.  We movie-goers have seen it again and again.

For example, no Cancer story is complete without the scene where the doctor, with the CT scan plates in front of him, break the news to a stone-faced patient and his family.  This is followed by the breakdown scene – why me, oh God, why me?  And is there a cancer story not populated with prayerful friends, doting relatives, or the incompetent resident who is unable to properly insert an intravenous needle?  My favorite, of course, is the timely appearance of the mysterious generous donors who come to the rescue in the nick of time to contribute for the payment of the medical bills.  *"All these have become the stock characters of the cancer drama.  I am pleased to have made their acquaintance, mannerisms and all."*

Nick Pichay, traveling the road that Tom del Castillo has traveled before him, writes:  *"Although mortified by manifestations of decay, I've observed that people, after knowing that I'm on chemotherapy, generally seem to develop an interest in the changes in my body.  Am I losing my hair?  Do I experience nausea and fatigue?  They examine my darkening extremities, look closely at the pallor of my face more keenly than my oncologist.  The brave even trace their fingers through the snaking scar on my chest and abdomen as if figuring the escape route on a map.  Friends who are bolder delicately inquire about the blisters in my penis.  They wonder politely if I can have normal sex again after it heals. And I reply, 'What is normal sex?'"*

But their interest, I suspect, goes beyond the clinical.  We can trace our awe and wonder of pain from the initiation rites in our tribal roots – the pain of birth, of circumcision, of fraternity initiations, of first love, of the loss of virginity, of the loss of loved ones, even the martyrdom of heroes  – all awesome wonderful pain.  How much is man's capacity to bear?  Instinctively, we reserve a place of honor for those who can stand up to hardship and pain.  A long suffering mother, a wronged mistress, a boxer in the ring, survivors of catastrophic events, and others who have similarly passed a test of physical and emotional endurance -- all share various levels of admiration and respect. Suffering, when made public, seems to serve as a magnet for sympathy and esteem.

But the personal battle to survive cancer has a special niche.  The arbitrariness of the disease marks it differently.  More so when there is no reason to be sick, no logic in the attack.  HIV AIDS is caused by promiscuous sex, Tuberculosis by exposure to germs and the elements, Heart Attacks by eating fat and cholesterol and by living a life full of stresses.  BUT Cancer?  *"In my life of moderation, I never smoked; regularly ate my vegetables; and engaged in dutiful exercise.  And yet I've been stricken with not one, but two deadly diseases." Under the circumstances, the manifestation of cancer becomes a holy mystery, a misterio—a stigma or a stigmata?  Depending on the perception, cancer is seen either as a reward for a life of blessedness or a punishment for a life of excess.  Cancer leads the sufferer to a road to sainthood or the front gates of derision."*

But if cancer is a prize for holiness, why do cardinals and popes live so long?  And if cancer is punishment for sins, why don't politicians and crooks die excruciatingly of it?  God Almighty, why does cancer wreak havoc on the lives of powerless innocents??  And what does this say of heavenly justice??


**Part 3: My own sweet dance with death…. the chance to write my dying scene**

My lawyer and good friend Tom del Castillo died of brain cancer in excruciating pain.  In a masterpiece entitled, "Sunflower, Stigma, Stigmata," my favorite writer Nick Pichay writes of that pain as part of an orgasm, like a maiden's loss of virginity, like a martyr's crucifixion, awesome and wonderful, as he struggles to cope with the double whammy of a triple heart bypass and colon cancer.  Death by cancer may indeed be likened to an orgasm – heightened senses, a toboggan rush of time, a sharp clarity in the halo of a haze, an explosive climax, followed by restful sleep.  We quote and paraphrase Pichay as he travels the same road that Tom del Castillo just traveled.

*"Thoughts cross my mind as I lay sideways on a cold metal table while the doctor, with the help of a thin tube, inserts a micro-camera up my ass.  Groggily, I look at the monitor and see the inside of my colon.  I am amazed by the technology and, under the influence of drugs, find myself on a strange trip. 'Look,' I say to an imaginary friend, 'What a beautiful sight!  The intestines are like some creature from inner space.'  I think other thoughts to distract me from the slow bloating inside.  If cancer is the physical manifestation of the wrath of the giant Om, why are dirty politicians and crooks still alive and well and living in palaces?*

*"Under heavy sedation, I am transformed into St. Sebastian, captured in that characteristic pose — half-naked, arms raised and tied to a post, with arrows sticking out of his white torso and leg — and despite the pain caused by the giant acupuncture needles, still looking sensuously beatific, eyes heavenward, standing contra-posto.  Bravery is the virtue I am supposed to uphold as I fight this cancer into remission.  Although I know, I am no saint, not even close to being a martyr, I look at my agony, not as a chance for heroism, but as my own sweet dance with death — a many-splendored-thing.*

*"How else can one describe being alone on the operating table?  Aware of the sharps and the clang of metal medical equipment that will be used on me, there is no escape.  I welcome fear with a hug I reserve only for intimate friends.  I anticipate the care I will receive from relatives.  I bask in their love.  With friends, I will celebrate each day with the joy of knowing that hope is a bridge being built everyday.  And with God, I hold up my right hand, two fingers forming a V: Peace!  But the best thing about being treated for cancer is the blessing that there, in the interruption of normal life, one is forewarned, one is given advance notice.  Most of all, having received a notice of possible eviction from this life, having cancer gives one the chance to write the dying scene."*

If I were dying of cancer, as Tom del Castillo was, as Nick Pichay is, and having been given a chance to write my dying scene, I will do so thus:

I shall die, not in the ICU of the hospital, but in my own home, on my bed surrounded by pictures of my wife, and the presence of friends and loved ones. It will be my farewell party, and I shall have the UP Madrigal Singers in attendance singing old familiar songs. I shall weep and so will my loved ones, but not because of my departing, but because the songs we sing are part of our shared lives, part of remembrances of the first stirrings of the heart, of school and friendships, of love and marriage and children, and common experiences, sad, joyful, and bittersweet. We shall weep for our lost youth, our forgotten dreams, and all the things that might have been – and for our loved ones departed, sadly missed and long remembered, like Tom del Castillo.

Then I shall volunteer to be a messenger of God, asking everyone to whisper into my ear, a message for some dear departed, which I shall deliver in person when I get to heaven... or to hell.

Thus having my last Orgasm, I shall sleep the sleep of peace for all eternity, in the arms of my beloved Cecilia.

ooooo

# CHAPTER TWO:
# Rosemary "Baby" Arenas

### Part 1. Baby Takes a Bow, Bringing Up Baby

Baby Arenas is probably the most controversial Filipino woman in this century, in her defiance of conventions even more controversial than Imelda Marcos. Nowhere except in France in the era of the French Revolution has there been such a woman -- Madame Pompadour and Madame DuBarry of King Louis XV, Marie Antoinette of Louis XVI, Desiree and Marie Walewski of Napoleon Bonaparte. Well, perhaps Cleopatra at the time of Julius Caesar and Mark Antony.

She reminds us of two famous movies: *Baby Takes a Bow*, the first starrer of Shirley Temple as Miss Fix-it, the role Baby played in the elections of 1992; and *Bringing up Baby*, a classic screwball comedy starring Katherine Hepburn and Cary

Grant, in which Baby is a leopard who sets her sights on Cary Grant and makes shambles of his life.

Born Rose Marie Magdalena Bosch Jimenez, of Catalan-born opera singer Remedios Bosch and Alfredo Jimenez of San Pedro Makati, Baby lived a sheltered life, trained in voice culture, piano and ballet, in a world "of class, breeding and culture," spoiled and protected by parents and relatives. She studied in a convent school, Maryknoll (now Miriam) College, then to University of Sto. Tomas and the University of the East, graduating in accountancy.

She married  Ramon Arenas, the son of a sister of Vice President Fernando Lopez, with whom she has four children, one girl and three boys.  She was separated from him since 1986, "So I call my husband ex, although we get neither a divorce or annulment, I was supposed to get an annulment before the last presidential elections but my friends in the judiciary advised against it.  I did not want to hurt my mother-in - law.  Anyway, when Mr. Right comes along, it won't matter if I am divorced, or annulled, or whatever.  What alone should matter is that I'll know he is Mr. Right."

Baby has another son, 15-year-old Roberto "Bing" Arenas, rumored to be a son of Mr. Right.  Of him with whom gossip links her, she readily admits he is the Mr. Right of her life, "the soldier she admires most," whom she first took interest in when she was one of the Blue Ladies of Imelda, and he was a neglected official of the Marcos regime.  One of her more enjoyable memories was that of Juan Enrile and Jose Aspiras putting on women's dresses on a dare.  She left the Blue Ladies when the Marcoses split up with the Lopezes who were related to her husband.

At Edsa, she claims to have prepared 6,000 lunchboxes in 2 hours, and brought forth the priests, the nuns, the holy images.  During the 1992 presidential elections, people say she was the Big Difference, "meaning the two million votes that might have gone to two or three other candidates.  As Imelda remarked -- and Teddy Benigno was listening --'You'd better realize that your candidate won because of that lady over there' -- referring to me."

As for Mr. Right, Baby Arenas says, "In my life I made only one big mistake.  I fell in love with someone I should not have loved.  But that is not the unforgivable sin nor am I the first to commit it.  There are worse sins, like stealing the people's money, which seems to me the greatest crime of all.  The mistake I made was a sin against God -- and only God can say if he forgives or not."

### Part 2.   Baby Arenas, Present Tense, Subjunctive Mood

Probably there has never been a woman like Rose Marie Arenas, socialite, philanthropist, the woman behind the throne, aspiring politician who lost twice and always managed to land on her feet, a dangerous opponent, a good friend, a prime mover, a major player and sheer survivor in the dangerous shoals of politics and business.  Known as Bravo Alpha, Kabuki, and Baby Arina during the heady days of the Ramos Administration, she was rumored to have played a major role in the appointments and happenings of the times.  Today we explore the truth and the consequences of Bringing up Baby Arenas, with the same madcap screwball humor as the original movie Bringing Up Baby starring Gary Grant, Katherine Hepburn and a pet leopard who made a shamble of their lives.

First, Baby in the present tense and subjunctive mood.  For the information of you guys who flunked your English grammar, subjunctive mood is indicated when the statement is of one of doubt or condition.  So what's Baby now?  Having lost a senatorial bid and a congressional bid in rapid succession, she still seems to be in good spirits, despite her conviction that she was cheated.  She is still engaged in her charities, and still nursing some grudges regarding what she feels are slights experienced during the last administration.  After she sold three houses to finance the Ramos campaign in 1992, she finds it extremely irritating to have been given a pittance and no party support during her two incursions into political life.  She is above all, mad at General Jose Almonte and his cohorts, Tony Carpio and Tony Abaya for having botched the 1998 campaign with their Charter change, and choice of Jose de Venecia as the party candidate.

Second, I remember that Baby was a good friend of vice president Erap Estrada when few people were giving him any importance.  Some of her personal staff is already working in

Malacañang, and she is always asking people to support Erap as ex-President Ramos has suggested. So it is safe to assume that Baby is indeed on the good side of President Erap Ejercito Estrada.

**Part 3. Baby Arenas, past tense, indicative mood**

Now let us take up Baby in the past tense and in indicative mood. Indicative mood, as your English teacher will remind you, is indicated when the statement is presented as a fact. This part of the story we get from Pastor Boy Saycon, who earned a terrible reputation as a backroom manipulator whom Security Adviser Jose Almonte accused of planning the assassination of Baby Arenas. My erstwhile publisher Jarius Bondoc once wrote a series of articles depicting him as a sleazy operator with no visible means of support, manipulating our political leaders for his personal benefit. Baby Arenas says all these are not true. So says my good friend Teddy Benigno whose opinions I respect.

Teddy tells me that his relationship with Boy Saycon is a long and interesting one, Saycon having initiated him into the inner circle of the Ramos campaign to get elected. "Sometime in one's life, one meets a man like Boy Saycon," says Teddy Benigno, "Then your life assumes a larger dimension and great possibilities come into being. For Saycon is the Ultimate Insider. He is independently wealthy, knows everyone worth knowing, and never takes advantage of his position. The insiders of the Ramos Administration which included myself, and Baby Arenas, swore from the very start that should Ramos win, we will never accept a government position under him. Of all of us, only Joe Almonte repudiated this pledge."

**Here, the articles on Baby Arenas abruptly ended. All we have left is a series of questions we wanted to ask her in order to carry on the series. Witness the following :**

What is occupying you nowadays? I remember you were a good friend of Erap Estrada when few people gave him importance. How are your relations now? How about your Wednesday Club – General Joe Almonte, Tony Carpio, Tony Abaya, what are they doing now and are you still keeping up relations with them. I understand you were also close to Boy Saycon who was in the inner circle in the Ramos Administration until he somehow ran afoul of General Almonte. I wish you could give us an assessment of the character of each player and the roles they all played in the Ramos Administration. We shall have your answer in the next segment after these words from our sponsor.

How did it all begin, your connection with the Ramos Administration? And you, Boy Saycon, how did you get involved with President Ramos. How did the two of you meet? What roles did the two of you play in the crucial election of President Ramos? What roles did Almonte, Carpio and Abaya play in the 1992 elections? How did you get the Cardinal to endorse Ramos?

**Part 4.    Baby in the pluperfect tense, imperative mood.**

What were the members of your Wednesday Club and what were their activities?

What caused your fallout with General Almonte and the administration? What role did Almonte in the Cha-cha and House Resolution #40, and the decision to support Jose de Venecia in the presidential elections? How did you fare in the last elections? Why and how did you lose?

**Part 5. Baby in the future tense, transitive and copulative.**

What are your plans in the future? What role do you think Ramos should play in the future? What will your role be?

If we are to believe Baby and Boy, without Joe Almonte and his cohorts, there would have been no Pirma, no Chacha, no September 21st confrontation with the forces of Edsa, no presidential endorsement of Speaker Jose de Venecia. Ramos played by the rules and being a true champion of democracy, he deferred to the will of the people who overwhelmingly elected Joseph Ejercito Estrada to the Presidency.

Indeed, Baby Arenas has in her own small but special way, left her indelible mark in our history. She made a difference in the life of one president, and without her, things might not have been the same for Ramos, and history might have been different. As they say, you can love her, hate her, but you cannot ignore Baby Arenas. She won't let you.

*February 4-6, 1999*

ooooo

# CHAPTER THREE:
# Earl Hornbostel

**Part 1. Filipinos helped liberate Indonesians from the Dutch**

Indonesian friendship has always come to our rescue whenever white bastards threaten our interests. Indonesians threatened to retaliate when the British and the Australians planned a preemptive strike in the wake of our Sabah claim. Indonesians put a lid on the British and Malaysian support of our Muslim separatists. They gave us rice and oil on concessional terms white the British and American oil companies were ripping us off, as they are still doing now.

The Indonesians always regarded us as bloodbrothers ever since 1928 when thy launched their independence movement, and sought our advice and help during the time of Quezon and my grandfather. After World War II, in 1948 the Indonesians began their war of liberation with arms taken from the Japanese, against the asshole Dutch colonizers. They came to us for equipment. And we did not fail them.

The company Radio Electronic Headquarters Company (REHCO), headed by Teodoro Kalaw Jr. and the American-Filipino Earl Hornbostel was involved in supplying field radio equipment to the Indonesia freedom fighters. Earl is an American who became a Filipino citizen, as distinguished from a Filipino American, a Filipino who became an American citizen. There is a world of difference between the two, you know.

REHCO at that time, among other things, were supplying communications equipment to the Philippine Army Signal Corps and to the lesser extent, to the Philippine Constabulary. The Indonesians were trying to drive the Dutch out of what was then called Netherlands East Indies. This was a naturally very difficult for them and communications were badly needed.

At that time the Chief Signal Officer was Colonel Licuanan and the vice-president of REHCO was Teodoro Kalaw Jr. Both asked Earl Hornbostel to supply certain specific kinds of field-radio equipment for the Indonesians who had an unofficial mission in Manila procuring supplies and equipment. Of course, Col. Licuanan's request were naturally not known to the public because the Americans were as usual on the side of their white cousins. And this transaction was completely separate from the normal procurement in what was then Camp Murphy, now Camp Aguinaldo.

REHCO put together a number of field radios and when necessary, auxiliary equipment to go with it, such as generator motors, antennas, telegraph keys, microphones, handcrank generators, etc. This is possible was in 1947, REHCO had been able to purchase the contents of a signal corps depot in Parañaque in the Tamaraw Club grounds from Engineer Pongos who was my father's protégé and Earl's schoolmate in UP when he studied Electrical Engineering in UP and a radio ham as was Earl. Earl had all kinds of signal corps equipment but not necessarily always complete sets so he had to get materials from other sources as well. The Indonesians sent up 3 or 4 men whom RHECO taught how to use the equipment. Unfortunately, Earl did not record their names so he has forgotten who they were. The Indonesians spoke little English, only one has spoken up for us to do a reasonably good job to teach them to use and function of the equipment.

**Part 2. Why an American helped the Indonesians in their war**

There must have been other kinds of help given to the Indonesians by Filipino entities or government agencies at that time but since these matters were not openly discussed at that time, I did not know of other activities but I did receive hints of what was going on, through my senator grandfather and friends.

It might be appropriate to tell you why Earl Hornbostel, an American by blood, was willing to help this Indonesian effort. In 1933, his uncle, his mother's brother, who was an agronomist working with the Pampanga Sugar Mills, was sent to Indonesia by the Philippine Sugar Association. His mission was to determine why it was possible for the Dutch in Indonesia to turn out sugar at much lower prices than the Philippines could. Earl's uncle spent six months there and he came back with the conclusion that there was no way we could really compete with Indonesia the way things were ran down there. The reason was simple. The Dutch sugar milling firms that ran the sugar industry there had complete control over the entire acreage that supply their mills.

As you know, one of the earliest laws passed during the American period in the country was to limit any corporation from controlling more than 1,800 hectares so the sugar industry here developed mainly through haciendas limited to that acreage and controlled by families of the elite. A sugar central to be economically run must have a milling season as long as possible in order that the milling capacity should be used over the longest part of the year as possible. Furthermore as terrain soil and other conditions vary from place to place, the choice of cane varieties, the proper time of planting in sequence, the correct fertilizer, and all the other aspects that went into crop planting were too much in the hands of the hacienderos and the better farmers in the Philippines.

In Indonesia, it was against the law for the well-to-do to purchase large hectarage, but there was no restriction on leasing so the Dutch simply would make 99 year lease contracts with the landowners, who are usually poor farmer families who had been on the land for generations. The lump sum payments for 99 years would naturally be quite substantial. The Indonesian farmer, like the Filipino farmer who is uneducated and unskilled in finance, quickly spent his money and then found out later that in order to live, he had to work for the sugar central. This way, the sugar central operator could use the most scientific methods to assure a long milling season, proper cane selection, proper timing of planting, proper fertilizers, etc.

Earl Hornbostel's uncle came back from Indonesia with the news for the Phillipine Sugar Association that there is no way for us to compete with Indonesia. Furthermore, with the way the Dutch were running Indonesia, Earl's uncle developed a great liking for the people of the Philippines, married a Filipina and had four children with her. A gifted linguist he could speak over 10 dialects.

Earl had known Col. Licuanan in pre-war time when he was a lieutenant in the signal corps under the chief signal officer at the time, Col. Tanco. Colonel Licuanan had been assigned as the signal officer for the off-shore patrol whose vessel required radio communication equipment. In 1940, when the off-shore patrol was set up, Earl supplied the radio receivers and transmitters. As we recall, this offshore patrol served gallantly in 1942. Based in Corregidor during the war, this offshore patrol was able to bring out people like Quezon and Osmena to the Del Monte in Mindanao, from where they were flown to Australia. Also of course, MacArthur left the Philippines in the same way.

### Part 3. Philippines, Puerto Rico were not the only US colonies

Earl Hornbostel, my friend and my father's, is an American who chose to a Filipino citizen. He was born in Guam, in the same house where Apolinario Mabini lived during his exile after Aguinaldo lost the Philippine American War. He spent 70 years in the Philippines, married a Filipina, carries on an export business, and considers himself a real Filipino.

His maternal uncle who went to Indonesia to study the sugar industry there, told him about the conditions in prewar Indonesia as the Dutch ruled it, and compared to conditions here in the Philippines, and struck a deep sympathy for the Indonesian people. Earl Hornbostel made at least four trips to Indonesia between 1965 to 1979, to learn more about our Indonesia bloodbrothers, and came to the conclusion that Indonesians differed little from the Filipinos, whom he has come to love and respect.

There are many differences, of course. The Dutch did very little for the education of the Indonesians, in contrast with American policy to establish an excellent public school system in the Philippines. This fact reported by his uncle impressed Earl Horbostel at the time he enrolled in the University of the Philippines, especially when he learned that Sukarno who started the war of liberation against the Dutch was only one of the 27 Indonesians with an engineering degree. For a country had three times the population of the Philippines, that is a remarkable and scandalous difference. This is one reason why Hornbostel decided to help the Indonesians liberate themselves from the Dutch, by supplying them with war-surplus field radio equipment in 1948.

In the 1920s there was another difference between Indonesians and Filipinos, owing to the Prohibition Era in the United States and its territories.  The passage of the Volstead Act and the amendment of the American constitution banned the sale, purchase and consumption of alcoholic beverages containing more that 3.2 percent alcohol.  Here in the Philippines, liquor was forbidden in the naval base.  Believe it or not, this is true, although the police in the Philippines did not enforce the Volstead Act in the same way it was enforced in the United States, with the result that official corruption and gangsterism took over in many American cities.

Earl Hornbostel, American Filipino, watched my television show Make My Day on the Indonesian, economic and political crisis, with Indonesian Ambassador Harbono in attendance.  He was supportive and laudatory, but takes exception to my statement that in prewar days, only the Philippines and Puerto Rico were American colonies.  In the Caribbean area in 1917, the USA took over the Virgin Island from Denmark and it still is an American colony today. The first colony of the United States in the Pacific was Bonin Island, an uninhabited island which Americans settled; it was lost to the Japanese during the American Civil War.  In 1897, the kingdom of Samoa was in political turmoil; and the Americans, Germans and the British each sent warships ostensibly to protect their nationals in that group of islands.  In reality, they wanted to annex the islands.  A typhoon badly damaged the German flotillas and forced them to withdraw.  When the political crisis deteriorated, the British and the Americans swiftly took over. They agreed that the Americans take over the largest island Samoa which together with Guam is today still an American territory.  Western Samoa which the British took over, has since become an independent nation.

It is interesting that the people of Guam the Chamoros are presently going through a period of questioning their status in this world.  They want a bigger say in their government, even a few are speaking of independence and I can understand this. As a boy in Guam Earl lived under the most autocratic government ever operated under the American flag up until WWII.  The governor of Guam is always a retired navy captain and the whole island was classified as naval base, so the people were governed almost as if they were military personnel.  An extreme example of this is when a Guam governor whose palace was situated in Agana had been complained to by his wife that the crowing of cocks at dawn always woke her up which she didn't like.  Therefore, the governor put out an order to the effect that the cocks must not crow at dawn.  Believe it or not but this is true.  Another thing that bothered the people was the ban on liquor.  This was doubly so because it was at the 20's, the time of the Volstead act and the prohibition amendment in the U S constitution and secondly because it was a naval base where in any event hard liquor were not allowed, so the farmers who want to make their own version of lumbanog which they call agua diente were constantly being harassed by police.

Again, my article was cut short at this point.  Shortly after, my good friend Earl Horbostel died suddenly.
*July 27-29, 1998, for ISYU*


ooooo


# CHAPTER FOUR:
# Jaime Cardinal Sin


**Part 1. Jaime Cardinal Sin, the greatest Filipino of this century!**

He is the 8$^{th}$ Cardinal Sin, the first 7 being Pride, Wrath, Envy, Lust, Gluttony, Avarice and Sloth.  He is a Mortal Sin, since he is not immortal.  He is a prince of the Church, who played a major role in the election of the present Pope John Paul II.  He is the Archbishop of archdiocese of Manila, the biggest and most influential in the country.  He played the instigator and catalyst of the great Edsa Revolution that toppled the Marcos Dictatorship without bloodshed and riveted the attention of the world to a people-power revolution that served as a model to topple the American-supported military dictators of Asia, Latin American and Africa, and topple as well the monolith Soviet Communist world.  If he succeeds in toppling the Erap Presidency as well for lack of moral ascendancy, he may conceivably be the greatest Filipino in the 20$^{th}$ century (the next millennium does not officially begin till the year 2001) – greater than any of our presidents, and comparable to Rizal, Bonifacio and Aguinaldo of the 19th century.

Cardinal Sin, Pastor, Patriot, Sinner or Saint?   Many priests of Metro Manila, especially those who do not belong to the so-called "Ilonggo Mafia" of the Catholic Church, question the abilities of Cardinal Sin as a good Pastor of the Church.  He is criticized by hypocritical priests like Opus Dei's Spanish overlord, Father Jose Cremades, as more of a politician than a prince of the Church.  This is because Opus priests like Cremades whose minions Mario Camacho, Rex Drilon, Lito Sandejas, and Tony Ozaeta manned the corporations of Kokoy Romualdez, and the Number 3 Opus Dei Dodo Mandanas was the right hand man of Imelda Marcos in her Human Settlements Department – and Cremades resented Sin's involvement as the spiritual father of the EDSA revolution that deprived him of power and wealth in the Marcos Administration.

The critics of Cardinal Sin say that he throughout his quarter of a century reign as Archbishop of Manila, he has given the best parochial posts as Parish Priest or Parochial Vicar to his favorites, most of them priests from the island of Panay or of Negros, as long as they can speak Ilonggo.

Sin himself is from Washington, Aklan, from a big, big family of 9 where he was the youngest.  As such, Cardinal Sin, like the Opus Dei (and this is where he is criticized by the Jesuits' Opus Dei's chief rival for hegemony in the Catholic Church today) is against any form of birth control and would only tolerate natural rhythm method as acceptable alternative to family planning or artificial contraception.

He almost did not make it to the priesthood.  As a seminarian, he was very sickly due to asthmatic attacks.  So, he asked the Blessed Virgin Mary for a sign.  He wrote her a letter asking for a miraculous cure and hid this letter inside a hole at the base of the statue of Our Lady of the Miraculous Medal (Virgen Milagrosa) which was in the seminary chapel in Iloilo where he was studying.  Mother Mary granted his wish and he was cured and was eventually ordained.  Years later, when he was already Cardinal of Manila, some seminarians in Iloilo found this letter, and brought him this statue (a gift of the Archbishop of Iloilo) with the handwritten letter.  This statue is now enshrined in one of the side altars of the EDSA Shrine Chapel in EDSA corner Ortigas Avenue.

### Part 2. Cardinal Sin prefers to die first before giving up the fight

As a patriot, Jaime Cardinal Sin has established his credentials as the main protagonist of Marcos during the 4-day Edsa revolution during which he marshaled the Filipino people to march to Edsa to support the beleaguered forces of General Fidel Ramos and Defense Secretary Juan Ponce Enrile. The millions who responded to his call turned the tide of battle and installed Cory Aquino as President of the Philippines before the astonished eyes of the entire world. He hopes to do the same against Erap whom he accuses of losing the moral ascendancy to rule.

As a saint or sinner, let me recount two personal anecdotes he narrated during an exclusive live interview in Make My Day! Once, as a seminarian, while helping the parish priest of his hometown Washington, Aklan, during their summer practicums, he was almost seduced by a beauty queen, but he resisted because he told her that if he succumbed to the pleasures of the flesh then, he would probably never be ordained as a celibate priest unless he joins the Eastern Rite of the Church which allows married priests. A joke of course, because a baptized Catholic is forbidden to transfer to the Eastern Rite. Many years later, he met this lady at a social function, and jokingly she told the Cardinal that if something had happened then, she wouldn't be the wife of a general and he wouldn't be the Cardinal Archbishop of Manila.

Another incident like this happened in the US where a pretty US born Pinay tried to seduce him when he was already a priest and was then accompanying Iloilo Archbishop Cuenco after they had attended sessions of the Second Vatican Council and on their way home from Rome through the USA. He also resisted her charms.

The Opus Dei, specially their Spanish lord and master, Father Jose Cremades, keep saying that Cardinal Sin does not have the necessary spirituality to be a good Bishop. They think he does not pray enough. They think he does not practice enough mortification or bodily punishment in atonement for sins of the flesh.  Former priest Esteban Latorre, released from his vows by Pope John Paul II himself, once the No. Six man in the Opus Dei hierarchy, says emphatically that that Cardinal Sin probably spends more time in prayer on his knees than all of Opus Dei combined who just doze off in their hour-long afternoon meditations in their fully air-conditioned oratories or chapels.  He said these hypocrites prohibit their poor members (jobless Supernumeraries who can't even afford a decent electric fan in their homes) from taking siestas because it is against the spirit of the Work of God whose members are supposed to be always working and of course making money for the organization.

Right now, undergoing almost daily dialysis to make up for his dysfunctional kidneys, Cardinal Sin practices more physical moritication than Cremades, Villegas, Estanislao, and Cuisia combined, with their high living life style.  The Cardinal offers God this very painful medical procedure when he could have very easily retired and have the Pope appoint an Archbishop *cum iure successione* like Cardinal Vidal who succeeded Cardinal Rosales when he retired.  But Sin is a real saint!  He prefers to die first before he gives up the fight for social justice, for morality and honesty and integrity in government.

*December 11-12, 2000.*

ooooo

# CHAPTER FIVE:
## Gloria Macapagal Arroyo

**Part 1.  Now it can be told: how Gloria became veep candidate**

Now it can be told, the travail that led Gloria Macapagal Arroyo from the top to second place in the presidential race. She was always on top of the heap, rivaling the popularity of Erap Estrada as a presidentiable.  She was the only viable and credible challenge to the candidacy of Erap Estrada, yet amazingly she decided to humble herself as the vice presidential running mate of Lakas' candidate Jose de Venecia, still among the lowest in the survey ratings.

She was offered the same deal by Erap Estrada months before, and with him might have formed a team that would have been unbeatable.  She was offered P200 million to reimburse her for her expenses, a large campaign kitty of her own, and half of the cabinet positions.  It was tempting but she refused.  Asked why, she answered, "Well, I became a presidential candidate because my supporters felt that Erap should not become the president.  It would have been a betrayal on my part, it would have reflected on my credibility and sincerity."

So why and how did she wind up in the vice presidential slot?  She entered the presidential sweepstakes on the strength of her showing in the polls of 1995, garnering more votes than anyone in the whole history of the Philippines, her record in the senate, and her expertise and participation in the economic recovery of the nation.  She was sponsored by Teddy Benigno, columnist and kingmaker, as well as political strategist Boy Saycon, and former Speaker Peping Cojuangco.

Her travails started when a group headed by lawyers Pancho Villaraza and Tony Carpio gave her a considerable campaign contribution.  According to Teddy Benigno, this group formerly connected with Malacañang, together with Gloria's husband Mike Arroyo, began to question the strategies employed by Teddy and company, to go out on their own without informing him, and started to undermine the relationship between Gloria and her supporters.  According to Gloria, Teddy and Boy resented her touching base with a group they considered rascals with dubious loyalty.  Eventually, Teddy and Boy left Gloria Macapagal Arroyo's political entourage, "with a broken heart."

According to one of ISYU's columnists, Villaraza and Carpio then stopped their flow of campaign contributions, leaving Gloria high and dry, as per the design of Joe Almonte, to force Gloria into an alliance with Speaker Joe de Venecia.  This is of course pure speculation, and according to Gloria, black propaganda.  But she did admit that without Teddy and Boy, she was left without any political organization.

It was then that I passed on to her colleague Senator Alberto Romulo a suggestion by columnist Nelson Navarro that if she runs out of funds, she joins Joe de Venecia. Most likely, according to Half-Nelson, Erap will win and so will she, and that puts her in the same career path as her father Diosdado Macapagal, who won as opposition vice-president and became the titular head of the Liberal Party and the next president of the republic. Half-Nelson reasoned out that if Gloria loses the presidency in 1998, that is the end of her ambitions. But if she is vice-president, she is within reach of the presidency, by a heartbeat or by the next election time.

**Part 2. Beset by Lakas, Third Force and Kampi, Gloria consults God**

To continue with the story of how Gloria slid to the vice-presidential slot. I remember in a meeting at the Ayala Alabang residence of a common friend, Gloria agreed to join the Third Force of General Rene de Villa and Mayor Alfredo Lim, without any preconditions, with every intention to slide down to the vice presidency or out of the race if need be to support a common candidate. Unfortunately this was not to be. They met on December 25, 26 and scheduled one for December 28 for the other candidates that may join. Rene deVil who called for the meeting postponed it, because Lim wanted to be the candidate no matter what, having already gotten the support of Cardinal Sin, Cory Aquino, Teddy Benigno and Boy Saycon. Time was running out as an agreement between the Third Force candidates seemed unattainable.

In the meantime, a group of loyal supporters of Gloria urged her to join Joe de Venecia on the outside chance that before the January 23 Lakas Congress to ratify the party candidates, something close to a miracle might happen. In the event that Joe de V does not improve his survey ratings, they reasoned, the Lakas party members, fearful of losing their jobs and their perks, may demand that the President anoint a more winnable candidate. The president exercising the prerogative previously granted him by the party members, would then ask Joe and Gloria to switch positions, with Gloria as the presidential candidate. If Joe balks he may be asked to head the Senate slate and eventually become the Senate President. In such case, the President may exercise his constitutional right to run again, this time as Vice-President, senior statesman and backstop to President Gloria Macapagal Arroyo.

Gloria quickly dismissed this scenario with a curt "If I join Joe de Venecia, it will be to support him to the end. I will never never turn my back on him, even if the President asked me to, which he won't."

Her friends and financial supporters were already telling her that with the votes scattered among many candidates, Erap Estrada might just win as minority president. Jaime Cardinal Sin told her that she is not yet ready for the presidency and should just like her own father Diosdado Macapagal, seek first the vice-presidency before running for the highest post of the land.

During the birthday of Jose de Venecia on December 25, Gloria met with Joe's wife Gina and fellow schoolmates from Assumption College, among them Nona Ricafort. In the course of the conversation, the subject of joining Joe de V came up, and the newspapers began to take notice of it. On December 29, Peping Cojuangco called her up and asked her what is going on. And she reported that she was being offered a deal by Joe de V and since then his emissaries are getting more aggressive. Peping said, "Do not believe any proposal that does not come from the President himself." Then on January 5, a definite offer was made by President Ramos for Gloria to be Joe's running mate.

So Gloria was beset on all sides: by the Lakas offer, by the Third Force advocates, and by Kampi colleagues who wanted her to continue pursuing her presidential ambitions. Gloria decided right then and there to enter a religious retreat and consult... God.

### Part 3.  Clinton is Gloria's classmate and pen-pal

Asking for the guidance of God on a matter of great importance to the nation, Gloria Macapagal Arroyo went on a religious "discernment retreat," with the retreat master and close friends and schoolmates attending and participating in frank and soul-baring discussions. When a definite offer came from President Fidel Ramos on January 5, Gloria knew it was God's will that she should run as the vice presidential running mate of Jose de Venecia. "We offer an economic team to usher the Philippines into the 21st century," Gloria said, as she stressed the need to restore confidence to the peso, by reducing interest rates to a level more conducive to good business, and by urging our people to buy Filipino goods made by Filipino workers.

Born the eldest child and only daughter of President Diosdado Macapagal and his wife Eva, Gloria grew up in an austere and disciplined environment, where her mother insisted that she live an "ordinary life" outside the glare of public attention.  I remember her quite well as I came to the Palace regularly as a member of Macapagal's official cabinet, and became one of her favorite lecturers at the Assumption College where she was chairwoman of the Economics department.  She calls me Uncle Larry.

Gloria went to school at the Assumption College, unattended by bodyguards or *alalays*, and went on to graduate school in the Georgetown University where she found herself the classmate of Bill Clinton.  She recalls that Clinton was in the honor roll as she was, was the most popular student in the campus being president of the Student Council, and escort to the most beautiful girls in school.  He used to walk beside her, this six foot of a man, alongside a cutie barely five feet tall, and teased her loudly, "Shrimp!" with a laugh, and would not acknowledge any show of displeasure on her part.  They were good friends, and he used to write to his own grandmother about her.  She wrote congratulating him when he got elected governor of Arkansas and again when he won the US presidency.

When Gloria got elected topnotcher in the senatorial race, he was already president of the United States, and he remembered to write her a congratulatory message.  When she went to the United States with President Ramos, no one in the entourage knew she was the classmate of Bill Clinton, until President Clinton greeted her with delight, "Gloria, is it really you?  Why you have not aged in all these years!"  He wrote a personal note again offering his condolences when her father died.  She wrote back thanking him, and he wrote again acknowledging her letter.  After APEC he wrote her once more, thanking her and congratulating her for her participation.

What role will she play in the next administration, that is, if her running mate Joe de Venecia becomes president?  She believes she can best serve the country as Secretary of Finance, in which capacity she wants to prove that we can raise revenues

without raising taxes, with a scheme once proposed by Washington Sycip; that the government may be prevented from borrowing from the capital market and contributing to high interest rates that is killing business; and that one can work and pray and dream only when his stomach is satisfied.
*January 19-21, 1998, ISYU*

### Part 4.  An evil spirit rules our lives

As we wind up our National elections of 1998, and it has become pretty obvious that Joseph Erap Estrada Ejercito will be our next president, we wish we could do our act all over again, avoid all our mistakes, and do better for the nation.

There is a group of do-gooders led by a relative of mine who saw everything coming since 1994, foreseeing the inevitability of having a movie star as our next president.  They bombarded President Ramos with memos, telling him it was a mistake to appoint Erap Estrada as Crime Czar.  They pointed out that as such, if Erap succeeds, he will have a launching pad for the presidency.  And if he fails, he can always blame the president for not giving him needed support.  It was, according to my relative, a lose-lose situation.

This group of do-gooders shifted their attention to the choice of a candidate to beat Erap for the presidency.  They promoted the cause of Gloria Macapagal Arroyo, No. 2 in the 1995 elections with more people voting for her than anyone in the history of Philippine politics.  She is a doctor of economics and an honest and dedicated public servant like her dad, ex-President Diosdado Macapagal, one of our best presidents.  She had a name that is easily recognizable, and a face like movie superstar Nora Aunor.  For a long time she vied with Erap Estrada for top position in political surveys.

My relative says there is an evil spirit that rules our lives, and he meant General Joe Almonte, whom he blames rightly or wrongly for the twists and turns that has led us down the road to disaster.  Almonte, he says, was behind the Pirma signature campaign and House Resolution 40 that decreed a Charter Change to allow the President to extend his term or run for re-election.  This in turn triggered the September 21st Luneta rally that denounced the president for trying to hold on to power.  That deeply hurt the president who had absolutely nothing to do with Pirma and Cha-Cha. The subsequent alienation of the forces of Edsa gave rise to the two politicians who were not there, Erap and Joe de V.

The Luneta rally which he felt was an unconscionable attempt to demonize him, left President Ramos resentful, and alienated him from his favored successor Secretary Rene de Villa who was now ensnared in the clutches of moneybags Boy Blue del Rosario and Peter Garrucho of the Makati Business Club, arrogant ingrates who dared wag their fingers at the President.

In the meantime, my relative blamed Almonte for advising the President to encourage a lot of presidential wannabees to seek the presidential anointment, a step that only promoted rivalry and disunity among his party-mates. The do-gooders advised Gloria not to participate, and to wait for them to convince the president to reach outside the party for his ultimate choice, with the Quezonian injunction, "My loyalty to my party ends where my loyalty to my country begins."

The do-gooders, led by my relative, now focused on the possibility of Gloria Macapagal for President and Fidel Ramos for Vice President. They pointed out that the continuity and stability of the government and the economy demanded the participation of Ramos as a senior adviser like Lee Kwan Yew. Ramos as vice president would be free to travel abroad as our ambassador plenipotentiary, at government expense and greeted by a 19-gun salute. Stung by the September 21st rally and accusations that he is trying to hold on to power beyond his term, President Ramos refused to discuss this possibility.

Jaime Cardinal Sin loved the idea and saw no conflict with the constitution. A group of businessmen led by Jose Pardo was delighted at the idea of the President as a common running mate for all presidential candidates. The cardinal and the businessmen were just about to start a movement to draft the president when the kidnapping and murder of Gokongwei's son in law caused a temporary delay in the issuance of their manifesto. At that point the president flabbergasted the nation by choosing as his successor, Speaker Jose de Venecia. Still the group wanted Ramos to run as vice president, anticipating a Gloria-Ramos ticket to prevail: Domingo de Ramos and Sabado de Gloria.

In the meantime, Almonte's boy, Atty. Pancho Villaraza contributed to the campaign kitty of Gloria M, and alienated her from her original support group of Jose Cojuangco, Boy Saycon, and Teodoro Benigno, who left Gloria with "a broken heart." Left to the tender mercies of Almonte and Villaraza, according to my relative, with no money and machinery, Gloria M, even while still enjoying a popularity rating equal to Erap, was forced down to the vice-presidential slot of Jose de Venecia, and both were enrolled in the ticket of President Ramos. Frustration. Regrets. And Anger at the evil spirit who rules our lives.

*May 5, 1998, ISYU*

### Part 5.  Edsa Forces at first refused to support Gloria against Erap

I am a friend of Gloria Macapagal Arroyo.  She calls me Uncle Larry.  She is the daughter of my President Diosdado Macapagal, the Mr. Big in my life, who recruited me to serve in his cabinet as his economic Czar.  I'd like to think that Gloria Macapagal became an economist because she was inspired by her father's example and by me.  For a while I was a frequent guest lecturer in the Assumption College where Gloria was head of the Economics Department.  She was not only of the academe, she was a capable technocrat as Undersecretary of Trade in the Cory cabinet, and a popular senator elected with the highest number of votes in 1995.  In 1998 she decided to run for the Presidency of the Republic.

It was then that I began to play a role in her campaign.  She was neck to neck with Erap Estrada in the opinion polls, outstripping all the rest of the candidates.  My cousin Tony Oppen and I were determined to have her run under a coalition of Edsa Forces led by Cory Aquino, Jaime Cardinal Sin and President Fidel Ramos.  As such she would have beaten Erap Estrada handily.

Unfortunately, personal feelings and prejudices stood in the way.  Ex-president Cory Aquino dismissed her outright and won't even deign to mention her name: "That woman would do anything to be president!" she said in an uncharacteristic display of spite.  A friend explained, "Cory has developed a Queen Bee syndrome, she probably thinks no other woman should rival her."

Jaime Cardinal Sin was more specific. "Gloria is not yet ready to assume the presidency. She is too young and lacks maturity. She will cry at the first crisis." No amount of argument that Gloria is of the same age as Clinton and Kennedy when they became US presidents, could sway the Cardinal. "Tell her to run for vice president and go the way of her own father."

As the childhood friend and Consultant on National Affairs of President Fidel Ramos, I advised him to endorse the presidential bid of Gloria Macapagal as the only candidate who has a chance to beat Erap Estrada. And to make sure she wins, my cousin Tony Oppen and I urged Ramos to run as her vice president. As such he could, with Gloria's consent, be the unofficial co-president who takes over when she is out of the country (instead of the Executive Secretary). I told Ramos that he is too young to retire and the trajectory of his career should lead to being the secretary-general of the United Nations. He may be in line for this if he were the vice-president, foreign affairs secretary and elder statesman. Unfortunately he probably listened to the advice of his Rasputin, General Jose Almonte and his gang, a very naughty man who manipulates people. Eventually Ramos chose as his candidate Speaker Jose de Venecia who had less than a Chinaman's chance of being elected. What a waste!

Cory's brother Peping Cojuangco and his Kampi Party (together with newsman Teddy Benigno and Pastor "Boy" Saycon decided to support Gloria Macapagal, and supply her with funds and an organization. At last Gloria was on her way to the presidency competing with so many other candidates: Erap Estrada, Miriam Defensor Santiago, Jose de Venecia, Renato de Villa, Alfredo Lim, Santi Dumlao, and Imelda Marcos.

## Part 6. Gloria earns the right to lead the fight

At the outset, Gloria Macapagal Arroyo was refused the support of the Edsa Forces (Cory, Cardinal Sin and Eddie Ramos) and was one of the seven candidates for the presidency in 1998. She was adopted by the Kampi party under Peping Cojuangco, Teddy Benigno and Boy Saycon. Later a wild card was introduced into the picture.

Among General Jose Almonte's intimates is Attorney Tony Carpio who was appointed Legal Officer of Malacañang, in charge of looking over government contracts, drafting executive orders and such. Tony Carpio had a law partner Pancho Villaraza, an Opus Dei whose law firm became lucrative and very popular among those seeking presidential favors. It was Attorney Pancho Villaraza who entered the picture as one of the contributors to Gloria's campaign, and was soon one of her advisers. This bothered Teddy Benigno and Boy Saycon who felt that Gloria should not seek help from anyone connected with General Almonte. After a series of confrontations, Teddy and Boy left in a huff. Somehow, what they feared would happen, really happened. Left without an organization and little funds, Gloria Macapagal consented to be the vice presidential running mate of presidential candidate Speaker Jose de Venecia, the patron of Jose Almonte, Tony Carpio and presumably the Opus Dei supernumerary Pancho Villaraza.

Without a presidential candidate to support, I drifted into the camp of Cardinal Sin and Cory Aquino who convinced my cousin Tony Oppen and our group to support the candidacy of General Alfredo Lim. And during Lim's campaign, I finally came to meet Boy Saycon together with Teddy Benigno, my childhood friend.

History repeats itself. Gloria was elected vice president like her father Diosdado was, and like her father is now in the direct line of presidential succession. In view of the overwhelming victory of Erap Estrada and herself, she felt there was a mandate to have her cooperate with Erap and serve the people. When Erap offered her a seat in his cabinet, she dutifully accepted as Secretary of Social Welfare and Development. When the jueteng-gate scandal exploded, Gloria felt compelled to resign and join her partymates at the Lakas Party.

"Above the din of battle," Gloria was overheard to have said over the radio, "there must be one who remains calm and sober, to plan ahead and solve our economic problems. I intend to be that one leader and I will lead the united opposition. But I cannot call for Erap's resignation because I am a direct beneficiary, and it would be self-serving."

In the Internet and among the street parliamentarians, there appeared messages and placards that said "Erap, resign, but no glory to Gloria!  No guts, no glory, no Gloria!"  Gloria was advised by her friends, "Eighteen months of silence and cooperation with Erap has already eroded your credibility.  You cannot hold yourself above the fray, you must speak out strongly and dare Erap to fight like a man, as Cory did against Marcos.  We need a leader, and you are the logical one.  This fight will not be fully resolved legally, constitutionally, or politically – among politicians who have their own conflicting private agenda.  This fight will be won by street parliamentarians who will drive Erap to the breaking point.  You must earn the right to lead them.  Hope and anger and hunger will fuel the flames, not calm sobriety."  And Gloria to her credit, spoke out "Resign Erap!" prompting her followers to cry out "This little girl has the guts to lead us!"

**Part 7.   At last the Edsa Forces coalesce around Gloria**

Gloria Macapagal Arroyo must be doing something right, because she was able to unite the opposition against Erap Estrada.   Senator Raul Roco advocated a snap elections because he wants to run against Erap and Gloria in a three-way race that can only increase the chances of Erap for a new mandate.   Senator Serge Osmeña is one who wants to be independent because he reportedly feels that Gloria is not fit to lead the opposition or assume the presidency.   The street parliamentarians feel that Gloria after having cooperated with Erap for so long, has not yet earned the right to lead them and enjoy the fruits of their sacrifices.   There are so many politicians with their own ambitions and private agenda.

Yet within a week after she declared war on Erap Estrada, she was able to make them realize that as vice president she is the logical leader to unite and lead them all.  Joined   by Senator Raul Roco, and by erstwhile Erap partymates, Senate President Frank Drilon, Senator Biazon and House Speaker  Manny Villar, she appeared in the rally of the parliament of the streets organized by Boy Saycon, Teddy Benigno and the COPA (Council of Philippine Affairs) under the sponsorship of the Edsa Forces – Cardinal Sin and ex-President

# *Heaven and Hell*

Cory Aquino who proclaimed Gloria as the soon-to-be president of the republic.  And joining them is the third leg of the Edsa Troika, ex-President Fidel V. Ramos.  Before that, she was able to convene the Kompil 2 coalition of NGOs in the Ateneo Grade School Covered Court, and got the opposition politicians together in Cebu in a brilliant show of force.  "The little girl has the balls to stand up to the big bully!" cried her followers, as they did when Cory Aquino stood up to challenge the dictator Marcos.

Watching Gloria on the television screen, you get the first impression she is just a little girl (less than 5 feet tall) who should be playing with her dolls.  She smiles and she is as pretty as Shirley Temple.  She speaks and she is as intelligent as Madame Curie.  With every word she gains in stature, and she becomes in succession each and all of our female heroes: Joan of Arc, Indira Gandhi, Golde Meir, Cory Aquino, and Wonder Woman.

The union at last of Edsa forces (Cory, Cardinal Sin, Eddie Ramos) and the opposition Lakas Party with Gloria Macapagal Arroyo, with a rainbow coalition of street parliamentarians from extreme right and extreme left, to militant NGOs, women's liberation, the professions, the managers, the Makati Business Club, Chamber of Commerce and Industry, the students, the academe, bureaucrats, labor and politicians joining the bandwagon – constitute a critical mass with enough fusion power to blast the present administration off its perch.

All the dirt that her opponents throw at her – unexplained wealth in the USA which is found to be her brother-in-law's, the reported P30 million payoff to her husband by the Pepsi Cola which is found to be only a nasty rumor with no one in the Erap Administration to even give it a semblance of truth, her connection with jueteng lord Bong Pineda which is neither collaborated by hard evidence nor by allegations by the administration's minions – could not tar her image of honesty and integrity.

Leaving everything to Providence, Gloria finds herself showered with divine blessings. We wish her the best.
*November 22-24, 2000*


ooooo

# CHAPTER SIX:
# Jose Mari Gonzalez

**Part 1. Jose Mari: ham actor, radio ham, smoked ham**
The first time I ever met Jose Mari Gonzalez was when I joined the Philippine Amateur Radio Association. I was taking my examination to get my license for ham radio, and there was brash handsome young man beside me teaching me, an MIT engineering graduate, about the principles of electronics, in plain view of the examiners. Of course I knew more than he did, but I humored him anyway, because he looked like the kind of a guy who would swat me if I did not write what he said. I am glad I humored him because when it came to the Morse Code Test, he knew more than I did, and I am the kind of a guy who would swat him if he did not give me the correct answers.

Who dat? I asked. Watsa matta wid you? He is Jose Mari, the movie superstar of the late late show, movie sweetheart of Susan Roces in the 1960s. He couldn't act his way out of a paper bag, but he became a teenage idol before Erap and Ronnie Poe became one. Jose Mari, the ham actor, was now a radio ham, and years later he would lose three elections in San Juan and become a smoked ham. Well, Jose Mari is electronic and communications engineer, one of the very first to be licensed. He is also a certified pilot, the first ever to fly backwards like a floo-floo bird with an old propeller plane, as he encountered strong headwinds and saw Mount Arayat overtaking and leaving him far behind.

He was born with a silver spoon in his mouth, the first born of the owner of the country's biggest electrical contractor Romago, Inc. He owned and operated the country's best recording company, Cinema Audio which he sold to Ronnie Poe as he built up a newer, better electronic and digital TV and audio recording company, The Digital One, together with his son Michael.

Once I built a 100-foot free-standing antenna tower in my house lot in Dasmariñas Village. I could not climb a flight of stairs without suffering cardiac arrest, so Jose Mari with another ham Marble Tinio volunteered to climb the tower and install a gigantic rotating antenna on top of it.  He made it a fetish to install and climb antenna towers even in the midst of typhoons, to establish communications for the government even as the army and local government radio facilities failed to function.  He became the president of PARA and I served as his executive vice president and editor of its magazine QTC.  As such he graced our activities and festivities with his movie star friends and recording talents; Helen Gamboa, Pilita Corrales, Lorna Tolentino, and an up and coming singer named Sharon Cuneta.  He also brought along his magnificent hi-fidelity audio equipment the likes of which I have not even seen and experienced even in MIT (the Boston branch of Mapua), the best engineering school in the world.  And he led DX-expeditions, in which radio amateurs go camping on mountains and isolated islands to test the efficacy of their equipment.  And he was there with the most sophisticated transceivers ever manufactured.

Jose Mari (as Bouncer) and I (as Aries) helped found the Rainbow Communications group, members of which were allowed to keep high powered guns and roam the streets during curfew time with fast cars, escorting police officers to trouble spots in emergency situations.  In this pulis-pulisan, as citizens police, we networked with the Armed Forced Civil Affairs office under Col. Noe Andaya and Col. Honesto Isleta, our link to the Philippine Constabulary under General Fidel V. Ramos.  As such Jose Mari was actively involved in the radio communications of the Edsa Revolution.

### Part 2.  Jose Mari shows off his *je ne se qua*

To continue our story on Jose Mari Gonzalez.  He is not only a movie star, a radio amateur and DXer, outdoorsman, a licensed electronic engineer, a hifi fi buff and businessman, an airplane pilot, and a "citizens police" with a yen for guns and fast cars who manned the communications for the Edsa revolution, he is also a scuba diver, a fist-fighter, a great lover, a spoiled brat, an exhibitionist who just wants to show off his *je ne je qua.* His wife Chayong who believes she has an exclusive right to it, had his picture stricken from the pages of the QSL magazine which I edited.  All in all, he is a hell of an egomaniac.

During the trial of those who assassinated Ninoy Aquino, in defiance of Marcos himself, Jose Mari presented a frame-by-frame analysis of the assassination tapes to prove that it was the military who killed Ninoy and that the CIA knew about it. He was appointed director of the Bureau of Radio Communications during Cory's time and Chairman and President of RPN-9 television station during the times of Ramos. In this capacity he initiated me into television as a Talk Show host.

Once he and Ronnie Poe traveled together through the Texas route in the USA. Mistakenly identified as Mexican by white-trash red-necks, and refused a table in a roadside restaurant, Ronnie and Jose Mari proceeded to beat up all-comers and wreck the entire restaurant. Jose Mari is always ready with his fists to protect a friend, or to defend his honor, as when he was suspected by American airport authorities as an Arab terrorist. Once I was arguing heated with someone, and Jose Mari came up and slapped him without warning. He specially dislikes the Anglo-Saxons, and that made him specially equipped to deal with rowdy and drunken Australians during our citizen police days.

Once, the First Lady Ming Ramos, whispered to me as she squinted at Jose Mari Gonzalez, "Larry, I think that is the man who bloodied and broke the nose of my boss at the International School." Quickly, I said "Oh no. Ming, that was his brother who did it!" Actually I fibbed, Jose Mari did it in the face of American arrogance and contempt for the Filipino.

Jose Mari was the first to initiate the Original Pilipino Music (OPM) movement. He urged the radio stations to allocate a portion of broadcast time to Filipino artists and compositions. And it was his recording of Freddie Aguilar's "Anak" that was the first Filipino hit in the international scene, translated into and sung in Japanese, Chinese, and English.

Jose Mari as we noted, was a ham actor, a radio ham and a smoked ham in the political scene. In 1987 he ran for congress in San Juan/Mandaluyong against the Ronnie Zamora, and lost by a small margin. In 1989 he ran for mayor against the incumbent Ben Abalos and again lost by a small margin. In 1992 he ran for congress against Ronnie Zamora, won and was congratulated by Vice President Erap Estrada, but alas, he lost in the counting. This time in 1998, he asked his family if he can run again and lose another fortune. His son Michael said, "It did not matter anymore. We were so used to losing, and so my mom said okay." He ran for congress against the young Ben-Hur Abalos (named after the most famous cochero in the world). And as luck would have it, running with presidential candidate Erap Estrada, Jose Mari Gonzalez won! He is now our congressman representing the lone district of San Juan. Can you beat it? No longer a smoked ham, he is transformed into a cured and candied political ham, a dish fit for the gods.

**Part 3. Not embalmed or cremated but stuffed by a taxidermist**

Jose Mari Gonzalez is one rare movie superstar who stuck to one wife, Charito "Chayong" Malarkey, who is so beautiful even now that she is sometimes mistaken for Jose Mari's sister, or a movie star herself. Above all, Jose Mari is, well, the father of Cristina "Kring-Kring" Gonzalez, a beautiful movie star who just retired from the screen to marry Congressman Albert Romualdez, son of Bejo and nephew of Imelda. In my TV program, I had the whole family of Jose Mari in the show, including wife Chayong, children Ana Christina, Michael, and Jose Mari Jr. Sick and absent was the oldest Jose Luis, and Kring Kring who was in Cebu, preparing for her coming marriage. We called her up during the show, and teased her about her husband Congressman Alfred Romualdez who might be known as Mr. Kring Kring Gonzalez, in the same way that Congressman Ralph Recto is known and registered in the Comelec as Mr. Vilma Santos. I reminded her that she was the classmate of my daughter Rosanna at the Assumption College, and of all her schoolmates, she may not be the brightest, but she is certainly the most successful. She wanted to make a clarification. All this talk about her owning a mansion in Forbes Park is not true, she said, simply not true. And her father interjected, "Otherwise the whole family would have already moved to Forbes Park."

Jose Mari's other daughter is Anna Cristina, a spit image of Kring Kring, a movie star in her own right, who quit the movie business to go to London and study Interior Design. How wonderful, this most beautiful girl who could have made it as a great star in the movie firmament like her father and sister, chooses instead to create beauty within our living spaces.

The other son Michael helps his father run his new company Digital One, a Recording and Mastering company, all completely digital, bringing a new cutting edge to services.  Half his customers are foreigners, earning the country much needed foreign our Science and Technology, luring Asian artists to our shores for the best in recording exchange.

The Gonzalezes are so handsome, so beautiful, that if they ever resign from the human race, they should be best mounted and stuffed by a taxidermist, rather than be embalmed or cremated.  And so we thus salute Jose Mari Gonzalez, movie hero off and on the silver screen – who for years generously donated his time, talents and resources to the service of his fellow men for one continuous gigantic ego trip, as the leading man in a true-to-life motion picture.

Taking the role of a Prince giving largesse to the multitudes, he lavished cash, the use of his magnificent equipment and performances of his movie star friends on many projects for many purposes.  He shows off the best amateur radio gear, the best hi-fi system and the best looking wife.  And like the movie hero that he is, he goes to the limit to prove that he can drink the greatest amount of beer, collect the most number of QSL cards, drive the fastest, dive the deepest, climb the highest and make love to the most beautiful woman.

He is used to winning, and if defeat comes once in a while, as it comes to all mortals, he gets into a terrible tantrum, and tries and tries again.  Eventually he wins anyway.  And what goes with Jose Mari, goes with the rest of his family, his wife Chayong, his daughters Kring Kring and Anna, his sons Michael, Jose Luis and Jose Marie Jr.

For bringing Technicolor, Cinemascope and Stereophonic Sound into our lives, Jose Mari deserves a plaque in lieu of an Oscar.

*July 30, August 3-4, 1998, ISYU*


ooooo

# CHAPTER SEVEN:
# Pastor "Boy" Saycon

### Part 1. Happy Birthday, Boy!

Pastor Boy Saycon was born July 8, 1951 to an illustrious family, that of Honorio Saycon of Negros Oriental and Leticia Tinio of Nueva Ecija, a descendant of Martin Tinio, revolutionary hero.  Most of his friends suspect that he was not born at all, that he was ushered in to this world as a full-fledged adult like Adam of Eve.  He had a bad reputation as a backroom manipulator and an influence peddler among those who do not know him.  But one renowned columnist describes meeting him in the following words: "When one meets Boy for the first time, his perspectives heighten, his horizons widen, because he realizes he is in the presence of a unique individual, Boy Saycon, the Ultimate Insider who knows everything that's going on, all the important persons doing it and most especially, the unimportant people to whom he gives so much importance."

His name, Pastor Boy Saycon, is not even appropriate, because he is neither a pastor nor a boy nor a psycho. And he does not fit into any category of those who move the nation.  He is neither an Atenean nor a lawyer nor a red-hot lover.  He studied in St. Theresa's where women normally go and in Letran College, where failed Ateneans are exiled.  He is not a lawyer, he is an Interior Decorator and he is not even a faggot, but a real macho.  A lover he is but not red-hot.  He is cool and collected even when he makes love.  He was a student agitator and a political prisoner during Martial Law.

President Erap once referred to him as the "the great destabilizer," which he was to Erap as Erap was to the nation.  But aside from the fact that Erap and Boy are both destabilizers and look alike in build and in manner of walking, there is nothing in common between them.  Boy walks like Erap for a very different reason.  He contracted polio at the age of 9 months, and was nursed back to health by a loving mother who dotes on him as the firstborn son and surrogate father to the rest of the family, three elder sisters and one younger brother.

Because unlike Forrest Gump he could not run as an athlete, he concentrated instead on developing his entrepreneurial and management skills. He started his business career by financing ice-drop vendors with a total capital of P25.00 and wound up managing Davao Sugar Central for Manny Pangilinan while serving as his business consultant as well. He helped manage the Toyota Comets basketball team and exposed the point-shaving racket of the national sport; managed the political strategies of Fidel V. Ramos and in part those of Gloria Macapagal-Arroyo and Alfredo Lim --- with an uncanny ability of raising campaign funds in millions of pesos. But his passion for athletics found expression in Rallye competition where he achieved national recognition as a good driver and the best navigator; a novice champion 1967 to 69, national champion from 1982 to 85, having driven in partnership with the best of them, Dante Silverio, Rad Ocampo, Robert Aventajado, Arthur Tuason, Antonio Mapa, both locally and internationally, competing in Indonesia, Australia and other parts of the globe.

Boy Saycon is the secretary general of the Council of Philippine Affairs, COPA, the organization that unified the diverse forces from right to left, from civilian to military, to fight a common cause: EDSA 2, in which he played his greatest role as protector of Chavit Singson, organizer of street demonstrations and liaison with army supporters.

The whole life of Boy Saycon is a response to the challenges of his trials and tribulations. From prison, he developed conviction and resolve. From polio, a zest for life and a determination to succeed. From Rallye driving, patience and the ability to make fast decisions. We have not heard the last of Boy Saycon. At the age of 50, he starts the next half a century of his life's journey. Fasten your seatbelts, the best and the worst of Boy Saycon are yet to come. Happy birthday, Boy Saycon!

*Boy's Response: Na-inggit lang kayo na mga Ateneans. The Dominicans of Letran and UST gave the Philippines six of its best presidents: Aguinaldo, Quezon, Laurel, Osmeña, Qurino and Macapagal, while all Ateneo contributed is its dropout Erap Estrada. Letran also gave us all the heroes of the 1896 revolution, much more than Ateneo did. That is because the students hated the Donimicans so much they lost their faith and became Free Masons, swearing to dedicate their lives to expel all the Dominicans from the Philippines. Erap did call me a great destabilizer in New York, in the presence of Danding Cojuangco and Larry Henares to whom he said, "Make My Day, and make my night!"*

**Part 2. Making a Difference** by Boy Saycon as told to Larry Henares

I was a rally driver and navigator defending our national title for the third time with my partner Robert Aventejado. We were preparing for a motor sports event to survey the north route through Dalton Pass, Nueva Vizcaya, on the way to Baguio City via Aritao and Ambuklao dam towards Baguio. At this point the news of the Edsa Revolution broke out. We made the decision to join the break away group. At the time we were working closely with the Rainbow Communications group – Bernie Niguidula, Johnny Angeles, Joey Mundo, who immediately called for all available units to monitor events happening around Malacañang, Camp Crame, Aguinaldo and Fort Bonifacio. We made contact directly with General Fidel Ramos through General Rene Cruz who was coordinating, through radio communications, the movements and activities of loyal and friendly troops.

On the day Marcos fled, I was stationed at Nagtahan when a report came that four Kadiwa buses together with an APC tank convoy has left the the summer residence used by Kokoy Romualdez in Malacanang Park. We were advised that these buses contained newly printed pesos left over from the snap elections, firearms and communications equipment. Since I was the closest to the group operating in Malacanang, I was asked to assist in shadowing the convoy while reporting to Camp Crame for guidance.

I intercepted the convoy in San Marcelino Street going towards Gil Puyat Avenue. There were three Kadiwa buses, two land cruisers and an APC tank escorting the convoy. As we radioed the positions of the convoy along South Superhighway, we were advised that a blocking force was being established on Buendia and Superhighway by General Escarcha. But apparently our radio communications were being monitored by the convoy because it immediately made a right turn at Vito Cruz. We were advised by the Rainbow Communications Center that the convoy might proceed to the old residence of Kokoy Romualdez in Menlo street. As we were approaching the Rizal Memorial Stadium, the Land cruiser made a sudden stop in front of me and a soldier jumped out pointing his machine pistol at me. I had no recourse except to retreat, driving backwards faster than I ever did in my life. Thus I lost the convoy.

I asked for guidance on how to proceed and trace the convoy. I was instructed to proceed to Central Bank area because a friendly force by a certain Col. Nicolas was trying to secure the Central Bank with forces under Secretary Enrile and General Ramos. I was to ask for assistance but they could not spare any mobile unit to assist. I learned at the time that there were already other units trying to assist me in the operation. One unit chanced upon the convoy inside Pistang Filipino at the Boulevard, and that began the long car chase from Manila to Quezon City. The Roxas Boulevard was filled with people celebrating the flight of the Marcoses. This made it difficult for us to follow the convoy. And as they turned into Ayala avenue towards Ayala bridge, we followed them slowly though the crowd. They were apparently proceeding toward Malacanang.

These guys we were following were wearing yellow headbands and pretending to be with the Yellow forces. The convoy was finally intercepted in Quezon City by forces under the command of General Alfred Lim, head of the Northern Police District. A certain Major de la Fuente provided the blocking force that finally seized two of the three trucks at 1 AM, and brought them to the Northern Police District office at Edsa. The contents of the buses which we were asked to identify, were only 5 Galill assault rifles and reloading machines and one 30-caliber machine gun, all brand new and still in the styroform containers. The marine officer earlier reported to Niguidula the contents of the Kadiwa buses, were 64 units of Galill rifles and three machine guns. Apparently there were those *who* helped themselves to the guns during the interception and only 5 rifles were declared. I complained: *"Tinapon na ang dictador, pero nag nagnanakaw pa rin."* We found out that we were the ones being investigated by Major de la Fuente for the missing guns, so we radioed General Rene Cruz to send someone to clear the matter for us.  At this time that General Lim arrived and asked Bernie Niguidula and myself who we were were.  Bernie answered, "I am One Ball (his Rainbow handle)."  This irritated General Lim.  This was followed by the timely arrival of then Captain Anicetes Katigbak (sent by General Ramos), followed by General Rene Cruz.  They identified us.

We found 64 by-pods in the truck, clear evidence that there were originally 64 firearms that were missing.  General Lim reprimanded Major de la Fuente and his policemen.  The baggage compartments of their patrol cars were searched and the missing rifles were restored.  The members of the northern police district were confronted with the evidence of the 64 by-pods, which go together with the rifles.  General Rene Cruz introduced to Lim the members of the tracking team including Katy Katigbak who was the aide camp of General Ramos.  General Cruz whispered to me to give all the credit for the intercepted rifles to General Lim.  I agreed.

Later in the first press conference of Ramos and Enrile in Camp Crame, the firearms were presented as evidence that these were being transported to Paoay, Ilocos Norte, and intercepted in Quezon City by General Lim.  As we found out later, the other truck containing the money was intercepted by General Escarcha, and contents also brought to Camp Crame.  The money bills were in crates, and as they were inventoried, Rene Cruz asked permission from General Ramos to have his picture taken lying down on all the money.

This is my first contact with General Fidel Ramos.  We went back to our normal activities, interrupted only by the Manila Hotel incident (1987) and the God Save the Queen attemped coup (1988), and the Channel Seven incident (November, 1988).

I gathered my business associates and personal friends for a brainstorming session on the prevailing political and peace-and-order situation which forced entrepreneurs to operate in a climate of uncertainty.  Our group consisted of Luis Morales (CEO of Philippine Advertising Counselors, later President of the Centennial Commission), Teodoro Benigno (Cory's Press Secretary), Amaury Gutierrez (chair of Caltex), David Arcenas (president of Inchrome Mining), Father Antonio Lambino SJ, Juan C. Raña (became director of PNB), Ray Hidalgo (Treasurer of Roxas y Cia).  We all had through a process to be admitted into Ramos' inner circle.  Rose Marie Arenas was requested by General Ramos to gauge the commitment and ideology of each member of the group.  The weekly meetings started the later Wednesday group of Baby Arenas in 1989.  The process consisted of feeling one another, and dissecting the total image of FVR on a freewheeling no-holds-barred discussions.  Teddy Benigno coined the word Horseman to identify Ramos in the formulation of plans and programs undertaken in the plot to make him president.

This process was interrupted by a crippling attempted coup in November 1989.  Everyone unanimously agreed that we will make the sacrifice of activity helping the nation, instead of just mouthing criticisms and complaints.  We decided that the times of military adventurism called for, not economists or social reformers, but a strong leader to stop the coup-d'etats.  Among all the leaders (Miriam Santiago, Jovito Salonga, Salvador Laurel, Erap Estrada, Danding Cojuangco), only General Fidel Ramos passed the test for the choice of a leader to succeed Cory Aquino.  So everybody in our group committed to give personal and executive time to establish the core group, serving as the think-tank of the Horseman.  At this point in time, Baby Arenas, on my recommendation, requested for a more structured meeting sessions with the other operators headed by Jose Almonte (EIIB director).  The formal marriage of the civilian and the military faction took place in the first quarter of 1990 at the Executive Office of Jose Almonte in Camp Aguinaldo.  The military group consisted of Colonel Noe Andaya (president of AFPSLAI), General Antonio Lucban (assistant secretary of DND), General Rene Cruz (Deputy Director-General PNP), Col. Pio Roda (president of PHIVIDEC), Colonel Carlos Tañega (CO, ISAFP).  The civilian counterpart was led by Rosemarie "Baby" Arenas, assisted by Josine Elizalde, Baby's daughter Rachel, and Francis Lee (who owns Diamond House in Hong Kong), and our group.

This started the weekly meeting at the Special Operations Group, at the back of the GHQ quarters in Camp Aguinaldo. The crafting of the vision and mission of the Horseman was a product of a deep understanding of Ramos' historical background.  Among the stories told by Ramos, is the incident that happened when he was in West Point while riding the bus.

The driver ordered him to sit at the back of the bus. This was at the height of the civil rights movement. But his classmates insisted that he sit with them in front. This apparently planted in Ramos' mind, a social awareness of the inequality in a nation that was teaching us democracy and social justice. The inner soul of Ramos was bared open to the group.

### The loose ball situation.

With the evident threat of the putschist right wing elements, came a formula the group had to adopt for Ramos' consideration. Father Antonio Lambino stated in one of our meetings that "It is the moral obligation of a leader to sieze the opportunity to seize power, as his legal right for reasons of national interest." The scenario simulated was for the putschists to achieve the near-success of taking over the control of government like the November attempt, and for President Cory Aquino to lose control and the confidence of the people. Ramos as Secretary of National Defense, with great influence on the better elements of the AFP-PNP forces, should seize control and establish a civilian military junta under a Plan B scenario. The composition of the junta was to be Corazon C. Aquino, chair, Jaime Cardinal Sin, Fidel Valdez Ramos, Cecilia Munoz Palma, and others to be considered: General Renato de Villa, Jose Diokno, Lorenzo Tanada, and Jose Concepcion. When some observed that there are only two military members of the junta, and that in all likelihood they will be outvoted at every turn, I said in jest: "He who has the gun, rules." Nobody laughed, they really took it seriously. Then Ramos banged the table, and cried, "Don't push me. You people think more military than I do. You do not know the consequences. Pulling the trigger is easy. But to stop it – how?" That Plan B was shelved and an alternative was crafted called Plan AB. Plan AB was concocted to bear the democratic process as the only viable way to get Malacañang, without prejudice to implementing the loose ball scenario during a time of clear and present danger under extraordinary conditions.

### Who is Bravo Alpha?

In 1988, a group of matrons led by Baby Rodriguez Almendras (daughter of Amang and widow of Gene Magsaysay) wanted me to meet with Baby Arenas, for which purpose she did not disclose. Alejandro "Leandring" Almendras once sold to the First Pacific of which I was partner, the Davao Sugar Central located in Hagonoy.

I met Baby Arenas (code name: Brava Alpha) through Baby Almendras in 1989, in the Via Mare Restaurant in the company of Bella Caedo, and Justa Tantoco. Initial meetings were very guarded, for Baby suspected that I was CIA agent. This is because beforehand I investigated the status of relationship between her and Ramos, even to the extent that I had her followed in Hong Kong, to determine where and from whom she bought her jewelry. She invariably went to the famous jewelry store known as Diamond House, owned by Francis Lee, located at Luk Hoi Tong Building in the Central area.

Gradually mutual confidence was established as we all proceeded in unity of purpose to have Ramos elected to the presidency. The Wednesday Club meetings were transferred to the Penthouse at the Mayfair Mansions on Perea St., Legaspi Village, on the 7$^{th}$ floor of which Bravo Alpha maintained her residence.

The purpose of these weekly discussions was to produce a crafted governance program based on the economic, social and political conditions., and called for the election of a strong leader that can command the respect and loyalty of the soldiers, and prevent attempted coups and other forms of military adventurism. Baby's access to Horseman was on a daily hour to hour basis, transmitting developments on the formation of our networks. Another person that Baby would have this daily collaboration was with General Jose Almonte who we believe was the central figure among the military constituency pushing for a Ramos presidency.

Providing the early funding requirements for the various multi-sectoral groups was the responsibility of Baby Arenas. In this instance Baby Arenas sold one of her residences to provide the needed funds. All in all in the course of the entire campaign she sold three houses in Dasmariñas and San Lorenzo Village.

At this point entered the Alabang Group, initially cleared and processed by Joe Almonte upon instructions of the Horseman for possible integration to the core group. This group is headed by Col. Cesar Pio Roda together with Antonio Abaya, his wife Annabelle, and Antonio Carpio.  Part of the processing is the acceptance of the core group members of the reality that Baby Arenas is part of the team; and that was the joint responsibility of mine and of Joe Almonte.  Of all the people involved in the campaign, Joe and I are the only ones who knew the exact relationship between Ramos and Arenas.  The most frequent question was always, *"Talagang malakas ba si Baby Arenas kay Ramos?"*  Whatever evasive reply I made, the true answer is that, *"Hindi malakas si Baby, kundi mahal iyan."*

In the course of my being by Ramos' side, his body language and reaction reveal real affection for Bing, her son, and Baby herself.  In the Philippine participation in soccer world championship for juniors (aged 10-15) with the Gothia Cup at stake, in Sweden, in which Bing was the goal-keeper (from San Agustin College), the Philippine team won the championship.  Receiving the news of this feat, Ramos, DND Secretary, was excited to the extent that when I showed him the pictures of Bing in action, his eyes teared and nodded his head in approval and pride.  This is where I slowly learned to observe Ramos who was not expressive or demonstrative in his feelings.  I learned to interpret his body language.

Another instance of his guarded show of emotions was when Baby was in London together with Bing, and in jest Ramos asked: "How are they?"  And followed this up, "Do you know how to contact them?" skirting his desire to talk to her.  I would proceed to get a clean line and contact her, and give him the opportunity to converse with her.  Sometimes when he wants to talk to Bing, Baby would sulk (make *tampo*) and refuse to have Bing talk to the Horseman.

There was an instance when we were having lunch at Mayfair Mansion, when Baby brought out a tape and played it.  The voice singing on the other line was unmistakably Horseman singing an Ilocano song.  Listening to the taped conversation wherein Bravo Alpha urging him to sing, *"Malongkot ako. Sige na Kantahan mo ako!"*  This sent fears into my spine for this the biggest breach of security we do not want our enemies to know.  Attempts to get possession of the tape was initiated, and concluded.

How did I accomplish this?  While the Horseman was

talking and singing *Pamulinawin* to Brave Alpha over the telephone at the Palace, I had a creepy feeling the song was being recorded. I got into my car and raced to the residence of Baby. I am a rally car driver and I made it in record time, and arrived while Baby was in the telephone in her bathroom still talking. I waited in the next room, till she got up from the tub and went into her bedroom. At that point, I rushed into the bathroom where I saw her tape recorder. After making sure the tape contained what I needed to have, I confiscated it and rush out of her house. I had the feeling someone was chasing me, yelling, "*Magnanakaw!*"

With this understanding of what Baby means to Ramos, we decided to host a dinner for those who were being recruited for the think tank. This was an opportunity for them to directly have a formal dialogue with the woman whom they had feared to be the negative factor in the campaign. Everybody was of the belief that Baby cannot make Ramos win, but definitely will contribute to his downfall if this is not handled properly.

Joe Almonte and I succeeded in handling this delicate situation, to the extent that Father Antonio Lambino together with Father Nico Bautista acted as friends and confidants to tolerate and understand this moral impediment. No less than the Manindigan members such as Rafael Alunan, Baby Lopez, Boy Blue del Rosario, who initially were unsupportive of Ramos because of the Arenas factor, eventually campaigned for him and ultimately became cabinet members. The need to expand a vehicle for all the support groups, to be identified as directly supportive of Ramos, caused the creation of the United People's Power Movement, launched in 1991 at the PICC.

Teodoro Benigno then known as Cicero, crafted this mission and vision statement of the Horseman, the first speech he delivered after resigning his post, making his intentions of running known to his constituency. The officers constituted to head the UPPM was RR de la Cruz, PR man, as chairman, Jose Alejandro, Leo de Guzman, Gloria Gonzalez (now married to Manny Lim, a widower), Ruben Valerio, Ted Javier (later BCDA director), Jun Arroyo – all of whom were against Baby Arenas, but except Gloria Gonzalez (whom Ramos offered the DSWD portfolio which she declined), the rest ultimately accepted her.

Other things I should talk to you about: (1) my open

discussion with Ming and Letty, reared like angels, who never to think ill of anyone.  They are both Methodist, mother disciplinarians.  Letty aspired to be in the Foreign service. (2) FVR always awaited orders, all the time till he became President.  (3) FVR reli on a Committee to take care of the process of what has to be done. Almonte took advantage, used Bravo Alpha to advance his ends. I kept my cards close to my chest.  I could not help.  We were wrong,  my brother is a weakling.  (4) Operation *Tres Marias.*  Al the trapos and Baby herself, I concluded, cannot contribute to the success, of the Ramos presidency,  only to its downfall.  I contacted the *Tres Marias* – Cory Aquino, Letty Shahani, and Ming -- to pressure the President to admit the affair is a thing of the past.  Meeting with the three was refused.  I will meet with them separately.

*In the Year 1998*

**Part 3.  A Requiem for Becky Saycon**

She was the prettiest of news editor Jose Bautista's grandchildren, prettier than Senator Loren Legarda by Loren's own admission.  In 1967, Becky at 17, fell in love with a skinny, long-haired hippie named Boy Saycon with a limp from a bout with polio, who was judged by the clan as unworthy of Becky. Loren only 8 years old at the time was given the task of chaperoning Becky when she went on dates with Boy Saycon. She recalls that Boy Saycon used to bribe her with candies to keep her distance out of earshot and her mouth shut.  "Even then Boy Saycon was a real operator," said Loren Legarda as she spoke of the man who would manipulate events to bring about the Edsa II revolt against Erap.  "Boy Saycon caused two great scandals in the family," Loren recalled, "First when he got caught kissing Becky, and second when he eloped with Becky using our house as his base of operations, and our gate as his escape hatch."

Becky was not only the prettiest in the family, she was the most loving and caring, "When I gave birth to my first child," recounts Loren, "I just did not know what to do.  But when I got home from the hospital, I found a nursery all set up for my child, complete with all kinds of garments, facilities and toys.  And it was done with loving care by my cousin Becky.  On my way to Edsa on the fateful morning of January 20, Becky called me up in my car on my celphone and asked me to join her in a prayer of thanksgiving along with the rest of the members of the clan. It was a moving prayer. I did not know it at the time but she was in the hospital and already dying. Nobody knew except Boy."

Becky Saycon was dying of a rare disease that affected her heart, and filled it with water. Medicines were available only from abroad and were hard to find. Soon she had to be taken off her medication because her medicines were no longer effective. She lingered briefly, fully awake and lucid to the very end.

Becky Saycon was only 49 when she passed away. In the funeral wake that followed, several friends stood up to bear witness for Becky Saycon who helped set up the religious organization Bethseda with plans for a Hospice for the Poor way down in Bukidnon, to retire there with the consent of husband and three children. One of these friends was Mrs. Patricia Aquino, the third wife and widow of Tony Aquino, eldest half brother of Ninoy Aquino, who testified, "We both got converted into the Charismatic Movement after a failed marriage. And we both loved to serve the poor in spirit. I will never forget how she came to the house bringing me food. She was always ready to listen to my frustrations and pains. She was the kind of daughter I wished I had. Some people leave footprints in your heart. Becky's loving nature walked all over me. When I am sad she would envelop me in one of her patented hugs. She was my patron saint for hugs." Boy Saycon in his turn called her his one and only love, and in a voice choked with emotion that left us in tears asked her forgiveness for all his shortcomings, and promised to dedicate the rest of his life to her concerns. One by one all her friends said that Becky's whole life was a testament to God.

What then if God does not really exist, as my friends, Hans Kasten, Joe Assad and JFK Nasser contend? If God does not exist, then the quest for Truth, Beauty, Goodness and Virtue will go unrewarded. Sacrifice, suffering, and the struggle against adversity will have no meaning. If God does not exist, then there will be no hope eternal, no everlasting love, no ultimate justice. If God does not exist, life would be intolerable, and Becky Saycon would have lived and died in vain.

*March 12, 2001*

***Heaven and Hell***

## END OF BOOK

www.ingramcontent.com/pod-product-compliance
Lightning Source LLC
Chambersburg PA
CBHW051739250726
48659CB00001B/154